D0712351

Big Crisis Data

Social Media in Disasters and Time-Critical Situations

Social media is an invaluable source of time-critical information during a crisis. However, emergency response and humanitarian relief organizations that would like to use this information struggle with an avalanche of social media messages that exceeds human capacity to process. Emergency managers, decision makers, and affected communities can make sense of social media through a combination of machine computation and human compassion-expressed by thousands of digital volunteers who publish, process, and summarize potentially life-saving information.

This book brings together computational methods from many disciplines: natural language processing, semantic technologies, data mining, machine learning, network analysis, human-computer interaction, and information visualization, focusing on methods that are commonly used for processing social media messages under time-critical constraints, and offering more than 500 references to in-depth information.

CARLOS CASTILLO is a researcher on social computing. He is a web miner with a background on information retrieval, and has been influential in the areas of web content quality and credibility. He has co-authored more than seventy publications in top-tier international conferences and journals, a monograph on adversarial web search, and a book on information and influence propagation.

Dedicated to the people who spend countless hours in front of digital devices helping others, sharing their time, energy, and skills.

Big Crisis Data
Social Media in Disasters and Time-Critical Situations

CARLOS CASTILLO

CAMBRIDGE
UNIVERSITY PRESS

CAMBRIDGE
UNIVERSITY PRESS

One Liberty Plaza, 20th Floor, New York, NY 10006, USA

Cambridge University Press is part of the University of Cambridge.

It furthers the University's mission by disseminating knowledge in the pursuit of education, learning, and research at the highest international levels of excellence.

www.cambridge.org
Information on this title: www.cambridge.org/9781107135765

© Carlos Castillo 2016

First published 2016

Printed in the United States of America by Sheridan Books, Inc.

A catalog record for this publication is available from the British Library.

ISBN 978-1-107-13576-5 Hardback

Contents

Preface

Social media is an invaluable source of time-critical information during a crisis. However, emergency response and humanitarian relief organizations that would like to use this information struggle with an avalanche of social media messages – often exceeding human capacity to process.

Emergency managers, decision makers, and affected communities can make sense of social media through a combination of machine computation and human compassion. Machine computation takes many forms, including natural language processing, semantic technologies, data mining, machine learning, network analysis, human-computer interaction, and information visualization. Human compassion is expressed by thousands of digital volunteers who publish, process, and summarize potentially life-saving information.

This book brings together computational methods from many disciplines, focusing on methods that are commonly used for processing social media messages under time-critical constraints, and offering over 500 references to in-depth information.

Researchers and computer science students can read this book as an extended survey of methods to be improved, extended, or built upon through research. It can also be used in an integrative, applied course or seminar on mining the real-time Web.

Developers and practitioners can read this book as an overview of composable state-of-the-art methods that can be used to architect solutions for handling time-critical social media data. The discussion uses examples from current social media platforms, which of course may merge, become abandoned, or disappear in the future, but every effort has been made to make the discussion platform-agnostic.

Emergency relief and humanitarian response are fascinating topics that should attract some of the best minds in the scientific and technical communities. This book is an invitation for computer scientists and technologists who want to apply their skills to help disaster-affected communities by providing information, a basic need during disaster response.

Check out the website at www.BigCrisisData.org

Acknowledgments

The Qatar Computing Research Institute (QCRI) supported me during most of the writing of this book. Sapienza University of Rome was also kind to host me during part of the writing.

Special thanks to Patrick Meier for introducing me to "Big Crisis Data" concepts, including digital humanitarianism, and for his contagious passion for social innovation.

My colleagues Marcelo Mendoza and Bárbara Poblete, coauthors in Mendoza et al. (2010) and Castillo et al. (2011, 2013), were the first to get me interested in information credibility during disasters, after their experience with the earthquake in 2010 in Chile. I want to thank Muhammad Imran, Sarah Vieweg, and Fernando Diaz for our work together and joint survey (Imran et al., 2015) which formed the starting point for Chapters 1, 2, 3, and 6.

I am very thankful to PhD students who codeveloped many of the ideas in this book, including Aditi Gupta, Alexandra Olteanu, Hemant Purohit, Jakob Rogstadious, Soudip Chowdhoury, and Irina Temnikova during her postdoc. Thanks to Leysia Palen for her advice and all her contributions to this topic over more than a decade, both directly and through her students. Thanks to Jaideep Srivastava for his support and guidance during my last year at QCRI, and for coining the "machine computation and human compassion" phrase.

I asked colleagues to review early drafts of this book: Ken Anderson, Fabricio Benevenuto, Luis Capelo, Fernando Diaz, Hamed Haddadi, Muhammad Imran, Ponnurangam Kumaraguru, Alexandra Olteanu, Leysia Palen, Jürgen Pfeffer, Robert Power, Hemant Purohit, Kate Starbird, and Ingmar Weber. I am very thankful for their expert advice and detailed feedback, and of course I am responsible for all errors and omissions in this book.

Cambridge University Press editor Lauren Cowles was patient and persistent, and her dedication was invaluable for this project.

Last but not least, I would like to thank my wife Fabiola for her unconditional support during the writing of this book and almost two decades of joint adventures.

1

Introduction

When faced with a sudden crisis, people quickly try to gather as much information as they can from the sources most immediately available to them: those in their immediate vicinity, friends and acquaintances via phone and texts, governments, nongovernment organizations, mass media such as radio and television, the Internet, and social media (Gao et al., 2014). Based on this information, they quickly take cover, flee, or act in a way that keeps them away from danger (Dynes, 1994).

Popular depictions of human response to crisis in movies and TV series tend to show widespread mayhem and panic. These scenes in "disaster movies" are plot devices, not very different from typical scenes in horror movies in which people irrationally run straight into danger (Mitchell et al., 2000). They are part of a long-standing myth that understands emergency management from a managerial perspective (Calhoun, 2004), and perpetuates the idea that disasters need to be policed because otherwise people will panic and riot.

As Palen (2014) emphasizes, an agenda of research about social media on disasters can uncover fascinating points if it avoids these misconceptions, and pays attention to the pro-social behavior of people during an emergency. Most people do not panic, but instead rapidly and effectively collect information, make decisions, and coordinate with others through a variety of channels. People affected by a disaster are the first to respond to it, often improvising complex rescue operations that save lives.

During a crisis, everybody involved – the public, the media, the government, emergency services, relief organizations, and others – try to quickly gain *situational awareness*. This is a complex process, which involves perceiving, comprehending, and being able to make predictions about the near future (Endsley, 1995; Vieweg, 2012). Gaining situational awareness is essentially a collective intelligence process that involves many actors interacting with a combination of various sources of information (Hutchins, 1995; Palen et al., 2010). Social media can contribute to situational awareness during a crisis, but handling its volume and complexity makes it impractical to be directly used by analysts.

This book is about how to use computing to help bridge this gap. This chapter explains what is the importance of social media for crisis management, exemplifying through recent crisis situations (§1.1). It provides some key concepts (§1.2) and describes information flows happening in social media during disasters (§1.3). Next, it summarizes the main problems when dealing with crisis-related social media (§1.4), as well as the expectations and needs of formal emergency response and humanitarian agencies (§1.5), and their organizational challenges with respect to social media (§1.6). This introduction also presents an overview of the remaining chapters (§1.7) and pointers to background readings on disaster research (§1.8).

1.1 "Sirens going off now!! Take cover ... be safe!"

In times of crisis and disaster, "people tend to gravitate towards the systems and networks that are more relevant to them" (Potts, 2013). Internet users, particularly those who rely and trust more on the Internet, are prone to go online when faced with a disaster (Lu et al., 2007).

The Internet and social media are now key information channels through which people collectively build awareness about a crisis situation. Compared to other types of media, the main advantages of the Internet as an information source is that it is distributed, far-reaching, and instantaneous. Before emergency services, fire fighters, police, and filming crews from TV stations arrive at the scene of a disaster – indeed, very often before they even leave their base – firsthand witnesses are already broadcasting status updates, photos, and videos through the Internet.

As with everything on the Internet, messages during a disaster are extremely varied. The specific class of messages that is often the focus of computing efforts are those that contribute to situation awareness, that is, the messages that can expand our understanding of the situation on the ground. Examples cited in recent work include:

- *"OMG! The fire seems out of control: It's running down the hills!"* (bush fire near Marseilles, France, in 2009, quoted from Twitter by de Longueville et al., 2009).
- *"Red River at East Grand Forks is* 48.70 *feet,* +20.7 *feet of flood stage,* −5.65 *feet of 1997 crest. #flood09"* (automatically generated tweet during Red River Valley floods in 2009, quoted from Twitter by Starbird et al., 2010).

- *"My moms backyard in Hatteras. That dock is usually about 3 feet above water [photo]"* (Hurricane Sandy 2013, quoted from Reddit by Leavitt and Clark, 2014)
- *"Sirens going off now!! Take cover ... be safe!"* (Moore Tornado 2013, quoted from Twitter by Blanford et al., 2014).
- *"There is shooting at Utøya, my little sister is there and just called home!"* (2011 attacks in Norway, quoted from Twitter by Perng et al., 2013).

Unlike these selected examples, most social media posts do not include new and useful information. Many repeat information that is already available through other channels. Many include personal impressions and/or messages that are only relevant for the user who posted them and perhaps a small circle of family and friends. However, some really interesting and important messages do get posted, sometimes providing information that is not available through other channels.

Social media information is often irreplaceable immediately after a sudden-onset emergency or disaster. It plays a role not only in the immediate aftermath of a disaster, but during its entire life cycle, for instance, to coordinate donations and volunteering, or to propagate messages of safety from authorities:

- *"Anyone know of volunteer opportunities for hurricane Sandy? Would like to try and help in any way possible"* (Hurricane Sandy 2013, quoted from Twitter by Purohit et al., 2014a).
- *"We have taken control of the ground floor and we urge you to be patient"* (police during the attack in Westgate Mall, Kenya in 2013, quoted from Twitter by Simon et al., 2014).

Many other types of information, including photos and videos, are posted in huge amounts during large-scale crises. They all contribute to get a more accurate picture of a developing situation.

1.2 What Is a Disaster?

Sociologists of disasters have been working toward a definition of disaster for decades. There is a broad consensus that *disasters are social phenomena*, characterized by a disruption of routine and of social structure, norms, and/or values (Perry, 2006). This definition implies that the severity of a disaster is more related to the extent of the disruption of social life (e.g., the extent of its disruption of processes and capacities of governments, business, and individuals), than to the measurable physical magnitude of the hazard that may

Table 1.1 *Hazard categories and sub-categories, adapted from Olteanu et al. (2015).*

Category	Subcategory	Examples
Natural	• Meteorological • Hydrological • Geophysical • Climatological • Biological	• tornado, hurricane • flood, landslide • earthquake, volcano • wildfire, heat/cold wave • epidemic, infestation
Anthropogenic (Human-Induced)	• Sociological (intentional) • Technological (accidental)	• shooting, bombing • derailment, building collapse

have triggered the disaster. The emphasis on disruption also implies that long-duration situations or conflicts that redefine what is "normal," may not match a strict version of this definition.

Not all crises are disasters: *a crisis is an unstable situation* that may or may not lead to a disaster. Not all emergencies are disasters: a serious situation, even a life-threatening one affecting a group of people, such as a traffic accident involving multiple vehicles, would be considered a disaster only to the extent to which it disrupts social routines and/or social order.

In this book, we focus on evolving, time-critical situations, which means that we can often adopt a broad definition of our subject of study. For instance, a police raid on a marginalized neighborhood may be met by violence that can escalate into riots. This would match the definition of disaster in the later stages where social order is disrupted, but not in the earlier stages. For our purposes, we would consider a possible response of social media to the police raid as a signal of a potential disaster precursor, even if it is not certain that it will become one.

Disasters have many characteristics; one of the most obvious ones is the *type of hazard*. Olteanu et al. (2015) consider two taxonomies used in Europe[1] and the United States,[2] as well as the traditional hazard categories listed by Fischer (1998). The resulting list is reproduced in Table 1.1. These are to some extent idealized categories (Calhoun, 2004); for instance, global warming implies that some meteorological phenomena can be traced back to human causes;

---

[1] EM-DAT, The International Disaster Database. http://www.emdat.be/classification.
[2] "Ready" campaign by U.S. Department of Homeland Security (DHS) and US Federal Emergency Management Agency (FEMA). http://www.ready.gov/be-informed.

similarly, some hydrological phenomena such as floods are sometimes the consequence of intentional deforestation.

Different hazard types affect human populations differently and are expressed differently on social media. To a large extent, the focus of research in social media during crises have been natural hazards. Floods are the more common type of disaster in the world (UN OCHA, 2014b), and, indeed, many case studies on social media usage during disasters are related to floods. In addition to natural hazards, research on social media during crises is sometimes about large-scale industrial accidents, and occasionally intentional violent acts such as shootings and bombings. "Complex emergencies" such as war present significant challenges because of issues such as accessing data, maintaining neutrality, and being responsible for the safety of all involved, which make them a much more difficult context to do research on.

Other categorizations for a disaster are possible, particularly in the dimensions of time and space. With respect to time, we considered that a disaster is *instantaneous* if it "does not allow pre-disaster mobilization of workers or pre-impact evacuation of those in danger," and, it is *progressive* if it is "preceded by a warning period" (Adams, 1970). With respect to space, a disaster is *focalized* when it affects and mobilizes response in a small area (e.g., a train accident) or *diffused* when it impacts a large geographic area and/or mobilizes national or international response (e.g., a large earthquake) (Adams, 1970; Prelog, 2010).

These categorizations are important because, among other reasons, the type of disaster influences the volume of the different classes of information that are shared in social media (Olteanu et al., 2015).

1.3 Information Flows in Social Media

Social media comprises a variety of social software platforms in which people can create, share, and exchange user-generated content. *Social software* are computer systems and applications that serve as an intermediary or a focus for social relationships (Schuler, 1994). *User-Generated Content* (UGC) is content published online in a publicly accessible manner or to a group of people, containing a certain amount of creative work, and created outside of professional routines and practices (Vickery and Wunsch-Vincent, 2007).

Social media is used intensely by people affected by a disaster for a variety of ends, including getting updates about the crisis, personal updates from family and friends, emergency contacts, and information about relief efforts (Vieweg, 2012; Olteanu et al., 2015). Disasters also bring a response in social media from people around the world, many without a direct connection with the incident, but that feel touched or somehow affected by a developing situation (Fraustino et al., 2012; Kogan et al., 2015).

Reuter et al. (2011, 2012) classify the different uses of social media during disaster according to their role with respect to organizations. From their perspective, social media information flows from citizen to citizen, citizen to organizations, organizations to citizens, and organizations to organizations. The last type of communication is not frequently observed at present, because organizations often have other ways of communicating and coordinating with each other (Sutton et al., 2012; Sarcevic et al., 2012). The remaining three are the basis of the prototypical flows we describe next.

Social media for interpersonal communications. From the perspective of many social media users, social media platforms are essentially tools for staying in touch with friends and family (Whiting and Williams, 2013). From this perspective, people use social media during a crisis to signal to those in their social circle that they are safe, or that they need help. This is the motivation behind Facebook's Safety Check[3] and similar systems. Social media, with its one-to-many capabilities, has advantages over voice calls or text messages for this type of activity. Indeed during the 2012 Sandy hurricane in the United States, the Federal Emergency Management Administration (FEMA) asked residents to use social media for personal status updates, to avoid overloading other channels (Ludwig et al., 2015b).

Interestingly, the fact that communications are interpersonal, but occur in a public space in certain types of social media (but not in all of them), presents an opportunity for learning from those communications. For instance, a message describing a relatively mundane situation, for example, a person posting that she is staying at home with fever, can be used in conjunction with similar messages to identify a global phenomenon, such as an emerging epidemic.

Social media for citizen sensing. Social media can be understood as a form of *distributed cognition*, a mechanism for understanding a situation using information spread across many minds (Hutchins, 1995). The interactions among people in social media are a form of collective intelligence, as they allow people to collectively make sense of a developing situation (Palen et al., 2009, 2010). Social media during a crisis generates a wealth of data conducive to better *situational awareness* (Farnham et al., 2006; Vieweg, 2012).

During a crisis, social media users can become "social sensors" or "citizen sensors" (Sheth, 2009; Nagarajan et al., 2011; Corley et al., 2013;

---

[3] Introducing Safety Check. *Facebook Newsroom*, October 2014. https://newsroom.fb.com/news/2014/10/introducing-safety-check/.

Hermida, 2014) – other terms are "participatory sensing," or "crowdsensors/crowdsensing" (Salfinger et al., 2015a) – whose postings are a response to the conditions they are experiencing as the crisis unfolds. For instance, information about areas where people are seeing or smelling smoke can be used as clues to locate a wildfire. An officer from the Los Angeles Fire Department explains this using an analogy with military operations: "The military has a model that every soldier is a sensor. Every soldier – we like to say that every citizen is a contributor" (Latonero and Shklovski, 2011).

Social media platforms may sometimes be sufficient to enable this form of cognition without any extra functionality or processing. Wilensky (2014) describes communications between stranded commuters after the Great East Japan Earthquake in 2011, where people used social media to determine how to get home or how to get shelter. However, social media platforms may not provide the functionality of summarizing information in a way that is useful for the public and for emergency response organizations (Vieweg et al., 2014). That is the task of computer scientists and other technologists working on this field (Palen et al., 2010).

Social media for official communications. Although some formal emergency response organizations do "listen" to the public through social media, the dominant view in many organizations remains that social media is essentially a one-way, "write-only" channel to push information to the public (Latonero and Shklovski, 2011; Díaz et al., 2014; Plotnick et al., 2015). These messages are written, among other reasons, for communicating risks, providing advice, countering rumors, or issuing calls to action, such as evacuation orders, alerts, and requests for donations or volunteers.

Social media users, however, are not entirely passive with respect to these messages. They filter and amplify them through the mechanisms already in place in these platforms, such as "liking," "favoriting," or "reposting" a message. They also have expectations of immediacy that need to be balanced with policies seeking to control the flow of information. Policies that are too strict may slow down public communications to a point where they are no longer useful by the public. Asking an incident commander to approve every social media message is impractical (Crowe, 2012). Instead, using social media for official communications effectively requires trust and "a more flexible organization within the command and control structure, with more autonomy for the public information team" (St. Denis et al., 2014).

In general, unidirectional communications in social media between the public and established organizations are problematic. The public can experience from disappointment to disempowerment when realizing that they are expected to listen but are not being listened at all, or that they are being solicited input, but not receiving any response (Crawford and Finn, 2014).

Over time, organizations go through several stages with respect to social media. They start with no social media presence or interactions at all. Then, many organizations enter an initial phase involving a limited presence and one-directional usage of social media (either only for sensing, or only to make announcements). Finally, some organizations reach a phase in which they are actually present in social media, and using it as an effective bidirectional communication channel in ways that positively impact their activities (Crowe, 2012, ch. 4).

1.4 The Data Deluge

Social media is a rich and chaotic environment in normal times as much as it is during crises. Many organizations tasked with emergency response are not prepared to deal with a "deluge" of unverified, sometimes incomplete reports arriving at a fast pace from a variety of previously unknown sources. The amount of unverified information arriving in real-time through social media channels can be overwhelming (Bressler et al., 2012). At the same time, people who work at these organizations cannot ignore the wealth of information present in social media, or avoid engaging with members of the public who are providing critical information to them through these channels (St. Denis et al., 2014).

Emergency managers and public information officers have expressed that most messages they see in social media do not contain new, useful information for them (see, e.g., Ludwig et al., 2015b; Vieweg et al., 2014). For instance, during a storm, most photos posted by Internet users may simply depict the storm, bringing nothing valuable that is not available through weather reports. In this scenario, many organizations indicate that they simply do not have enough people to monitor social media: "100 teenagers take loads of photos each, and five people are expected to assess them all" (Ludwig et al., 2015b).

Emergency managers often use the phrase "information overload" (Toffler, 1990) to describe this problem, as reported in interviews by Plotnick et al. (2015), among others. Indeed, during a disaster information overload affects both physical systems as well as people (Fritz and Mathewson, 1957). However, we need to be precise. If an organization receives more requests for help than what they can handle, it is their capacity to respond that has been exceeded, not necessarily their capacity to process information. By contrast, if an organization retrieves from a data source more data than what they can handle, it might be more appropriate to say that this is *filter failure*.[4] Filter failure can occur due to many causes, for instance because the information need is not expressed correctly (something that might be very difficult to do at the onset of a disaster), or because the methods used to retrieve and process the data are too naive or simplistic. For instance, trying to find critical actionable information by simply following a real-time feed of social media messages containing a given hashtag can be a frustrating experience, because the tool used (the standard interface of a social media site) is not appropriate for the task.

Incidentally, people who contribute content in social media during a disaster face similar difficulties with the standard interfaces of social media. "Familiar sites for sharing photos of weddings become locations for sharing breaking news … collaborative writing tools become locations to transcribe hospital faxes to confirm the injured. Participants are using social web tools in ways the designers of such systems have neither anticipated nor considered" (Potts, 2013).

1.5 Requirements: "Big Picture" Versus "Actionable Insights"

The users of the systems we describe in this book are an heterogeneous group of people that includes all those who have a stake in a developing crisis, particularly the people directly and indirectly affected, and the people tasked with response and relief operations. Software tools do not exist in isolation, nor operate on an empty informational context (Potts, 2013, ch. 6). Instead, social media is one of many information sources available. The information needs of users are almost never answered by social media alone, but only in combination ("triangulation") with information gathered from other sources. Indeed, social media and other types of "big data" can be used for augmenting and complementing existing informational products in which organizations already rely on, instead of for creating new informational products.[5]

Understanding user requirements is not merely asking "what data do you need?" Humanitarian organizations often request data but do not actually use it into their operations or decision making. Avoiding this situation requires to

---

[4] "It's not information overload. It's filter failure." Clay Shirky, keynote at *Web 2.0 Expo* in New York, USA, 2008. http://blip.tv/web2expo/web-2-0-expo-ny-clay-shirky-shirky-com-it-s-not-information-overload-it-s-filter-failure-1283699.

[5] "Guidance for incorporating big data into humanitarian operations." Blog post announcing Whipkey and Verity (2015) by Andrej Verity, September 2015. http://blog.veritythink .com/post/130055206939/guidance-for-incorporating-big-data-into.

clearly identify what is the problem or gap that social media data will be used to address (Whipkey and Verity, 2015).

User needs may not be fully defined at the onset of a crisis, and they may change as a crisis evolve. At the onset of a crisis the priority might be understanding the context and scope of the event, then it might shift to assessing affected populations and damage, determining specific goods and services that need to be provided, identifying which other organizations are operating on the ground, and so on, as the situation develops (Tapia and Moore, 2014).

The very set of people that we define as "users" may change as a crisis progresses and new people are affected or the scope of the response changes. Even within a single emergency response organization, different people may have different information needs. Mittelstadt et al. (2015) note that the needs of a first responder (e.g., a police or fire fighter) differ from the needs of a site commander (who handles a set of missions in a specific area), which in turn differ from the needs of a crisis manager (who oversees the response to a crisis).

Some users may have very concrete information needs, such as identifying resources on the ground, targeting humanitarian efforts, or identifying specific groups of volunteers or victims, while others may have more generic information needs, such as gaining better situational awareness or detecting events of interest (Morrow et al., 2011; McCreadie et al., 2015b). Indeed, we can sketch broadly two prototypical categories of information needs during a crisis. These are not necessarily comprehensive nor mutually exclusive.

Strategic information: capturing the "big picture." This is the prototypical need of a large humanitarian organization, or a government branch doing resource allocation and mobilization at the onset of a disaster. Preliminary assessment and resource allocation is often done based on incomplete and often contradicting pieces of evidence. Background knowledge, such as census data or historical data from similar situations in the past, usually forms the basis for this preliminary assessment.

A data gathering exercise aimed at understanding the "big picture" uses social media messages as a basis to create high-level summaries that speak about the situation as a whole, and not about specific requests for help or other individual messages. What is needed in this case is a way of seeing beyond individual messages, which are like the proverbial trees, that prevent us from seeing the forest.

Typical "big picture" questions include estimations of the area in which the effects of a disaster are felt, estimations of the number of people affected by a disaster, injured, dead, or displaced, and estimations of the damage to infrastructure, both public and private. Notions of representativeness, generality, and accuracy are important for the answers obtained for these questions through social media to be valid (more about this in Chapter 9).

Tactical information: capturing "actionable insights." This is the prototypical need of an emergency response organization, and corresponds to detecting that something of interest has happened at a given time, in a given location, and having certain characteristics. For instance, determining the location of impassable or debris-covered roads is an actionable insight that might be gleaned from social media messages referring to the aftermath of a severe storm. In general, actionable insights include specific urgent needs reported through social media. Notions of credibility, relevance and timeliness are important in this case (more about this in Chapter 8).

1.6 Organizational Challenges

Gathering and disseminating information has always been part of emergency recovery, but only in recent years has "information" been recognized as a basic need of affected populations (UN OCHA, 2012). Information needs are comparable, in due proportion, to other needs such as shelter or sanitation.

Many organizations, however, are slow to adopt new technologies, and some are used to make decisions with data that is two to three years old.[6] Fundamentally, these organizations value reliability over innovation, they are hard to change and slow moving, they are difficult to connect and communicate with, they restrict access to data, they have too many rules, and they may not fully understand their own needs and goals, or what technology can do for them (Waldman et al., 2013).

Additionally, despite perceiving its potential and utility as an information source, large organizations have expressed a number of reservations regarding the use of social media. These objections are usually related to: (i) capacity, (ii) data quality, (iii) operations, and (iv) policy.

Capacity. The first challenge includes concerns about lack of personnel time and staff that can be dedicated to monitor social media. This is perceived as an intense activity that requires the full-time dedication of at least one skilled person to deal with the expected amount of information (Morrow et al., 2011; Díaz et al., 2014; Hiltz et al., 2014; Plotnick et al., 2015).

---

[6] "Analysis: Potential, pitfalls of 'big data' for humanitarians." Dana MacLean, *IRIN News*, May 2013. http://www.irinnews.org/report/98104/analysis-potential-pitfalls-of-big-data-for-humanitarians.

Data quality. The next common objection pertains to data quality, representativeness, and veracity, and is usually expressed as concerns about whether social media information can be trusted or not (Morrow et al., 2011; Díaz et al., 2014; Hiltz et al., 2014; Hughes et al., 2014b; Vieweg et al., 2014). The data provided by social media, with its dynamic nature, may also not fit the rigid information requirements of an organization (Morrow et al., 2011), or it may require additional processing to be useful for decision making (Palen et al., 2010).

Operations. Organizations also have reservations about how social media monitoring affects their operations (Tapia et al., 2013). Part of their concern is related to technological barriers, including old software, hardware, or limited bandwidth while on the field (Morrow et al., 2011). Another serious operational concern are the commitments that emerge if organizations choose to embrace social media, as the expectations of the public with respect to governments and responders have increased (UN OCHA, 2012). A survey in the United States by the American Red Cross found that a large group of respondents expected help within three hours of posting a request on social media (American Red Cross, 2012).

Members of the public are already relaying critical information to authorities through social media. For instance, on May 1, 2015, a Twitter user sent a message to *@GarlandPD*, the official account of the police department of Garland, Texas, in the United States. The message alerted the police about an account affiliated with an extremist group, which had posted about an upcoming attack on May 3. After the attack effectively happened on the announced date, the police claimed they did not see the message, although they also claim they monitor their account in social media.[7] Monitoring social media, indeed, creates new responsibilities for organizations.

Policies, guidelines, and procedures. Individuals within an organization may be aware of the advantages of using social media years before their organizations recognize these advantages and incorporate them into their standard processes (Hiltz et al., 2014; Hughes et al., 2014b).

Especially in large organizations, individual initiative using a tool that is not prescribed by policies, may not be positively valued at an institutional level. "Everything we do must have a legal basis" indicated one fire department officer interviewed by Reuter et al. (2013). More worryingly, social media as an information source may be actually proscribed by policy instead of prescribed.

---

[7] "Anonymous activist warned Garland police days before ISIS attack" Kevin Collier, *Daily Dot*, May 2015. http://www.dailydot.com/politics/anonymous-warned-garland-police-department-isis-was-coming/.

In a survey of more than two hundred county-level emergency management organizations in the United States, Plotnick et al. (2015) uncovered that from the minority of counties that had social media policies (which mostly cover how to disseminate information, not how to gather it), in about one quarter of them the policy restricted or forbade the usage of social media. In general, the policies used in emergency management about social media tend to be more comprehensive with respect to how information should be communicated to the public, than with respect to how information should be collected and used.

Good policies and organizational support can make a big difference. The Queensland Police in Australia reports that the main factors of success in their social media engagement during the 2011 Queensland floods were the level of support among high-rank officers in the organization. An additional factor was that a trial of social media started several months before the disaster, allowing enough time for the team to become comfortable with social media and embed it in their daily processes (Charlton, 2012).

Changes in policy happen through changes in practice. Hughes et al. (2014a) present a very interesting example in which the Fire Department of New York City (*@fdny* on Twitter) asks people to call 911 instead of tweeting if they need help (as a consequence of the 2012 Hurricane Sandy), but actually dispatches emergency services based on reports sent by Twitter – a quick policy reversal that happens within less than one hour and during the disaster.

Crowe (2012, ch. 4) presents a framework for implementing a social media policy, including elements of employee access, account management, acceptable use, employee conduct, content, security, legal issues, and citizen conduct. Whipkey and Verity (2015) offer a series of questions to consider and a checklist of risks when dealing with big data in general, which also applies to the development of a social media policy.

1.7 Scope and Organization of This Book

There are a number of areas in which computer and information sciences can support crisis response. Computer systems can be used for modeling, simulation, forecasting, risk assessment, and a number of other tasks. All of these tasks, including the social-media related ones, may be considered *crisis informatics* (or crisis computing) activities. Palen (2014) defines crisis informatics as "The study of information and communication technologies in relation to actual or potential mass emergencies, with a particular focus on the role of social computing in such situations."

Crisis informatics is related to the broader research agenda of *computing for good*. It intersects other humanitarian areas including Information and Communication Technologies for Development (ICT4D), and other social computing topics such as Computational Journalism and Health Informatics.

As the Social Media for Emergency Management (SMEM) community coalesces and consolidates, it is clear that several computational disciplines can contribute useful algorithms and methods. Researchers from diverse areas including databases, natural language processing, information retrieval, data mining, machine learning, network analysis, and human-computer interaction have converged on this application domain. The "humanitarian data scientist" role requires a number of skills in data management, programming, statistics, humanitarian response, and social sciences.[8]

Social media includes a variety of formats including blogs, question answering sites, social bookmarking sites, and opinion/review sites. The focus of this book is the analysis of *microtext* (Rosa and Ellen, 2009), which corresponds to brief messages posted in online social networking, microblogging, and media sharing sites.

The initial steps in this area have focused on extracting and categorizing messages, however, this is not enough to produce insights or actionable knowledge (MacEachren et al., 2011). The end goal is to create systems that can provide these answers along with high-level analysis, that support decisions, instead of just providing data and information (Waldman et al., 2013).

As depicted in Figure 1.1, there are two parts in this book. The first part (Chapters 2 through 6) focuses on the technical aspects of data processing, and follows computing disciplines of databases, natural language processing, machine learning, network analysis, and online algorithms. The second part (Chapters 7 through 11) focuses on the context in which data processing occurs, and is more oriented to studies of information sciences and human factors, including crowdsourcing, human-computer interaction, computer-supported collaborative work, and information visualization. The names of the chapters extend the "3 Vs" mnemonic for big data coined by Laney (2001), originally volume, velocity, and variety.

Chapter 2, "volume," explains how to deal with the scale of the data. It covers methods to acquire, store, index, and search crisis-related social media messages.

Chapter 3, "vagueness," outlines how to use natural language processing to prepare the messages for analysis. After an overview of general and

---

[8] "Humanitarian Data Scientist – who and how?" Andrej Verity and Hildemar Cruz, December 2014. http://blog.veritythink.com/post/105715607274/humanitarian-data-scientist-who-and-how.

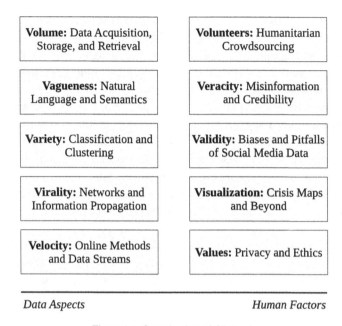

Volume: Data Acquisition, Storage, and Retrieval	Volunteers: Humanitarian Crowdsourcing
Vagueness: Natural Language and Semantics	Veracity: Misinformation and Credibility
Variety: Classification and Clustering	Validity: Biases and Pitfalls of Social Media Data
Virality: Networks and Information Propagation	Visualization: Crisis Maps and Beyond
Velocity: Online Methods and Data Streams	Values: Privacy and Ethics
Data Aspects	*Human Factors*

Figure 1.1 Organization of this book.

increasingly-complex processes from tokenization to dependency parsing, it goes into more detail on how to extract meaning from unstructured text.

Chapter 4, "variety," shows how to group data into several categories, describes information typologies, and presents supervised and unsupervised methods for classification and clustering.

Chapter 5, "virality," considers connections between messages and people, which are studied using network analysis techniques. Two main areas are covered: first, how to deal with static graphs representing connections between entities, and second, how to deal with information propagation histories, or information cascades.

Chapter 6, "velocity," adds a temporal dimension and online algorithms, offering an in-depth look at online event detection methods.

Chapter 7, "volunteers," recognizes that digital volunteers are an important player in social media during disasters, describes the emergence of digital volunteer groups, and describes volunteering efforts through the frameworks of crowdsourcing and human computation methods.

Chapter 8, "veracity," addresses misinformation and disinformation in social media. It includes human-based verification practices, as well as computer-based methods to automatically identify credible and/or reliable information.

Chapter 9, "validity," examines the social and technical biases that affect social media data and that might distort the results obtained when processing it. It deals with questions of time and space, including to what extent are alerts triggered from social media valid, and to what extent the geography of crisis events is reflected in geotagged social media.

Chapter 10, "visualization," presents visualizations paradigms, starting with the most popular one, crisis mapping, as well as other elements such as news/multimedia feeds, time series, distribution charts, tag clouds, and networks. It also briefly discussed issues of interactive visualization.

Chapter 11, "values," highlights some of the ethical issues regarding the treatment of crisis data, starting with the protection of the privacy of individuals, and also including the safety of response operations and the protection of digital volunteers.

Each chapter presents open research problems that could be addressed in future work, and includes pointers to related materials for further reading. The concluding chapter summarizes some of these issues and presents an outlook for the field.

1.8 Further Reading and Online Appendix

The literature on disaster research is vast; sociologists of disaster have been studying disaster phenomena for decades. One of the pioneers was the Disaster Research Center (DRC) in the United States. The trajectory of the DRC, outlined in Quarantelli (2002), provides a good overview of the historical development of this field. For a generic overview of disaster research, "Disasters by Design" edited by Mileti (1999) summarizes the state of the art of disaster research for a general audience. A more extensive survey is the "Handbook of Disaster Research" edited by Rodriguez, Quarantelli, and Dynes (2006), which is a detailed review of many aspects of disaster research.

The book by Crowe (2012) is a guide to social media written for emergency managers. It assumes a background on emergency management and it does not discuss computational methods, but it provides an interesting perspective for the computing practitioner about the way emergency managers interact with new technologies, particularly social media.

Online Appendix

This book's website, http://BigCrisisData.org/, includes numerous pointers to online materials:

- Software for natural language processing and machine learning.
- Datasets of crisis-related social media messages.
- Data repositories of humanitarian and emergency response information.
- Videos of talks and seminars on social media during crises by various researchers.
- Related conferences, workshops, and journals.

These resources are organized in a user-editable "wiki" to which you can contribute content.

2

Volume: Data Acquisition, Storage, and Retrieval

The 2010 earthquake in Haiti represented, in more than one sense, a collision between traditional crisis information processing practices and new information dynamics. Emergency relief organizations were not prepared to deal with high-volume data flows coming from two new sources. First, mobile-enabled communication technologies were being used to send a large number of messages by affected populations, who expected an answer from relief organizations. Second, vast quantities of data were being produced by volunteers in technical communities (Harvard Humanitarian Initiative, 2011, p. 19). In general, the amount of data generated during a crisis is overwhelming. Processing crisis-relevant social media messages requires careful attention to scalability issues, particularly because the production and consumption of data often surges unpredictably by several orders of magnitude.

This chapter focuses on the data volume, and presents scalable methods to acquire, store, index, and retrieve social media messages, with an emphasis on their textual content. We describe the data sizes that are typical of social media during disasters (§2.1), and methods to acquire (§2.2) and filter (§2.3) data. We then present methods for data representation (§2.4) as well as data indexing and storage (§2.5).

2.1 Social Media Data Sizes

Any characterization of social media risks becoming outdated quickly. The Internet Live Stats project[1] maintains a dizzying display of visual statistics depicting how much content is generated every day by social media users.

---

[1] Internet Live Stats: http://www.internetlivestats.com/.

Social media platforms usually report the number of users they have in terms of monthly active users, defined as people who interact with the platform at least once during a month. For the large platforms, this figure is usually measured in the order of hundreds of millions. Every day, the number of messages posted in large social media platforms such as Twitter, Facebook and Instagram is in the order of tens of millions to hundreds of millions of messages,[2] and hundreds of thousands of hours of video are uploaded to YouTube.[3]

In the case of microtext, while each message is short (e.g., currently a maximum of 140 characters in Twitter, and 420 characters in Facebook status updates), meta-data attached to messages causes a blowup in data sizes. A data record for a Twitter message, typically serialized as a string in JSON,[4] is around 4 KB when all the formatting and metadata attached to each message are included. Given that millions of messages are generated in large crises, several gigabytes of space are required to store them. Naturally, multimedia objects such as images and videos significantly increase the storage space requirements.

Social Media During Disasters

Just as mobile phone calls increase significantly during a disaster (Bagrow et al., 2011), the usage of Internet and social media also explodes. For instance, Internet usage increased by over 114% on the East Coast of the United States, in anticipation of Hurricane Sandy in 2012 (Whittaker, 2012). This increase was driven by increases in content demand (people looking for information) as well as content supply (people and weather/physical sensors posting information).

During large disasters, the increase in content demand affects many types of information sources, particularly those that are more familiar to users, including the websites and apps they use every day (Lu et al., 2007; Potts, 2013). Online searches of disaster-related terms increase (Guo et al., 2013a). People seek information from mainstream news sources, which tend to cover disasters extensively (Kwak and An, 2014a), and visit specialized sites providing emergency-related information. For instance, visits to websites offering seismological information increase substantially (sometimes by 800%) during an earthquake (Bossu et al., 2008).

Historically, online forums where the first place on the Web where disaster-related messages were posted (Palen et al., 2007). Today, disasters

---

[2] About Twitter: https://about.twitter.com/company. Facebook Company Info: https://newsroom.fb.com/company-info/. Instagram Press Page: https://instagram.com/press/.
[3] YouTube statistics: https://www.youtube.com/yt/press/statistics.html.
[4] ECMA-404, the JSON Data Interchange Standard: http://json.org/.

create significant surges in social media traffic, with people both providing information about their status and what they are experiencing, as well as asking questions to take the right decisions. These increases are not limited to Twitter nor to the developed world.

For instance, in Thailand social media usage increased by 20% when the 2010 floods started (Robinson and Wall, 2012). During the 2011 earthquake in Japan, Twitter usage referring to the earthquake reached 1,200 tweets per second (TPS) (Crowe, 2012). During 2012's Hurricane Sandy, Twitter traffic related to the storm reached about 250 TPS.[5] In 2013 following the Boston Marathon bombings, Twitter traffic related to the attack surpassed 700 TPS.[6]

Although these numbers are large, until now they have not reached the amounts observed during big entertainment, sports, and political events. For instance, when a new Catholic Pope was elected in March 2013, a month before the Boston bombings, traffic about the announcement passed the 2,000 TPS mark.[7] Later that year, a record 143,000 TPS was recorded in Japan, but not during an earthquake, but during the broadcast on television of "Castle in the Sky" (a 1986 movie by Studio Ghibli).[8] The World Cup final of Germany versus Argentina in 2014 attracted over 10,000 TPS,[9] while the Super Bowl XLIX recorded about 6,500 TPS in some moments.[10] Figure 2.1 depicts tweets per second observed for various recent events. We are using a logarithmic scale because, as in many other Internet phenomena, the distribution of user actions and attention is highly skewed.

Across different types of media, there are not many studies comparing traffic surges during a disaster. The 2011 Sendai earthquake is an exception, and Figure 2.2 depicts the content size dynamics in four text corpora: news, search queries, Twitter, and Wikipedia. The volume of content and searches grows very fast and sometimes by several orders of magnitude.

---

[5] "Social media a news source and tool during Superstorm Sandy." Chenda Ngak, *CBS News,* October 2012. http://www.cbsnews.com/news/social-media-a-news-source-and-tool-during-superstorm-sandy/.

[6] "Boston bombings led 2013 tweets." Darren Rovell, *ESPN,* December 2013. http://espn.go.com/boston/nba/story/_/id/10124297/boston-marathon-bombings-most-tweeted-sports-event-2013.

[7] "The New @Pontifex." Twitter report of 2013. https://2013.twitter.com/\#month-march

[8] "New Tweets per second record, and how!" Twitter Engineering Team, August 2013. https://blog.twitter.com/2013/new-tweets-per-second-record-and-how.

[9] "Insights into the #WorldCup conversation on Twitter." Simon Rogers, *Twitter Blog,* July 2014. https://blog.twitter.com/2014/insights-into-the-worldcup-conversation-on-twitter.

[10] "Super Bowl XLIX smashes Twitter records." Alexandra Gibbs, *CNBC,* February 2015. http://www.cnbc.com/2015/02/02/super-bowl-xlix-and-social-media-most-tweeted-nfl-game-ever.html.

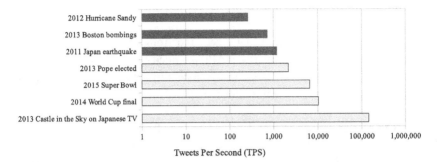

Figure 2.1 Comparison of the peak number of Tweets Per Second (TPS) in recent years during selected disasters (in dark gray) and nondisaster events (in light gray). Note that the scale is logarithmic. Data from various sources cited in Section 2.1.

Similar effects of changes in information seeking and information production behavior have been found after other events, such as the 2012 Sandy Hook shootings (Koutra et al., 2015). In particular, the activity of editors in Wikipedia has been observed to increase rapidly after all sorts of events, including disasters (Keegan et al., 2013).

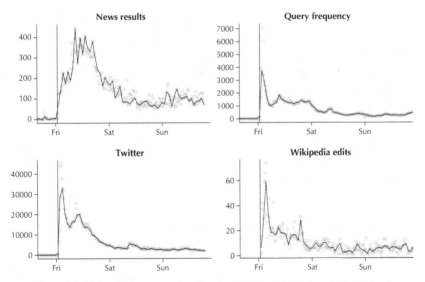

Figure 2.2 Volume of content related to the 2011 Sendai Earthquake for Yahoo! News (top left), Yahoo! Search queries (top right), Twitter (bottom left), and Wikipedia (bottom right). Figure from Guo et al. (2013a, extended version), reproduced with permission from the authors.

2.2 Data Acquisition

Social media messages are usually acquired from social media through an Application Programming Interface (API) provided by the social media service. These APIs enable researchers and developers to obtain a sample of all the messages posted to a platform, and/or a sample of messages posted to a platform and matching a given query.

This section contains a high-level discussion of general methods for acquiring social media data through APIs. The reader interested in specific query languages and technical descriptions of the APIs of Twitter, Facebook, LinkedIn, and other popular platforms can find them in Russell (2014).

Challenges

The main challenge when acquiring social media data is scale. Acquiring social media data involves receiving, processing, and potentially storing a large number of items arriving at a rapid pace. Data collection needs to be implemented using an architecture that is efficient and resilient to network and storage failures, which are common when dealing with large data volumes (Anderson and Schram, 2011).

Additional challenges arise due to API limitations. First, the type of interface offered is usually a "pull" instead of a "push" interface. Second, there are rate limitations and specific terms of service that may be too restrictive for some purposes. Third, query/filtering languages may have limited expressiveness for a particular application.

Commercial social media platforms do not want others profiting from their data and/or building competing systems. Through a series of technological restrictions on their APIs, they tend to forbid queries that simultaneously achieve timeliness, relevance, and volume, for instance, by allowing developers to either download a large volume of old items, or a small volume of recent items.

Pull APIs are more common than push APIs. *Pull* APIs, also known as *polling* APIs, enable a program to actively query a system, periodically fetching new data whenever such data has become available. In contrast, *push* APIs, also known as *subscription* or *live* APIs, enable programs to passively receive updates whenever the system has new data available, instead of actively asking for this data. Note that both pull and push APIs involve the same scalability challenges mentioned earlier, which depend on the volume and speed of data and not on the modality of the API.

For time-critical applications, the time between the moment a message is posted in a social media platform, and the moment it is captured by a computer system, should be ideally very short. The method of choice for achieving this are push APIs; however, they are currently not commonly offered by social media platforms. The fact that Twitter has offered a push API for several years may partially explain its dominance in the space of time-critical social media applications.

Some social media scenarios, however, may facilitate collection of data in a "push" manner. For instance, SMS messages are typically processed in this way, and an SMS gateway can push each received message through an API. In general, messaging platforms and citizen reporting applications are well-suited for this mechanism of data collection.

There are severe rate limitations. Commercial social media platforms in general are closed systems that carefully guard access to data, which is their main asset. When these APIs are provided to developers and researchers, they usually come with several limitations and restrictions. There are many ways in which these restrictions can be expressed, as surveyed by Reuter and Scholl (2014) for several popular platforms.

In all cases in which pull APIs are offered, the polling rate is limited. These rate limitations are expressed in one or two different time granularities. On a short-term time granularity (e.g., 1-, 5-, or 15-minute windows), they seek to restrict the peak rate at which data can be polled. On a long-term time granularity (e.g., a day), they seek to avoid others from collecting "too much" data through queries.

In cases in which push APIs are offered, there may be a fixed sampling rate (e.g., 1% of the data in the current public push API of Twitter), or a maximum sampling rate when using a broad query (e.g., even if a query matches more than 1% of tweets, Twitter currently returns up to 1% of tweets in response).

Query languages lack expressive power. The types of predicate that can be used to query or filter the messages are also usually limited to relatively simple conditions. At a high level, query languages offered through APIs allow programs to retrieve messages based on the presence of certain keywords, or by matching a certain condition on their metadata. Useful metadata conditions may include restrictions of language, time, and location. Restrictions of location can be expressed by location names, by geographical coordinates, or by a combination of both.

For efficiency reasons, expressing a generic boolean query may not be an option offered by some APIs. For instance, they may only allow a query that is a disjunction of terms, or only allow a query that is a conjunction of terms.

The combination of different types of predicate also may be restricted. For instance, as of January 2016 Twitter's filtering API does not allow queries for tweets within a geographical area *and* containing a certain number of terms (the disjunction, *or*, is allowed).

In any case, the expressiveness of a query language determines the kind of samples that can be obtained from the data. This can lead to different kinds of sampling bias. For instance, to obtain social media messages related to a crisis, keyword-based querying and geographical-based querying yield different sets of messages. Querying by keywords is often more precise than querying by geographical location, in the sense of retrieving less messages that are not related to a specific crisis – however, among the items that are related to a crisis, on aggregate both kinds of samples have similar proportions of different classes of messages (Olteanu et al., 2014).

Sampling methods are not transparent. The sampling methods applied by social media platforms when querying their APIs are typically not fully disclosed, and may change over time without notice. This introduces a series of biases in the data collection that are further discussed in Section 9.4.

Query Construction

Constructing the appropriate predicate for querying or subscribing to an API requires background knowledge about a developing crisis. This is usually obtained by collecting information from background documents (e.g., maps of the affected area), archived reports from similar situations in the same location in the past, news reports, and other sources. Naturally, it is also necessary to browse the social media platform for which the query is built to get a sense of the data that is being posted in the current crisis.

Geographical predicates depend on the specific phenomenon, and may be determined using hydrological, meteorological, or other physical models predicting the affected area by a disaster. This geographical area of interest may also change over time.

Keyword-based predicates are not trivial to construct. Their aim is to capture different ways in which people are referring to a crisis, including the different languages that people are using in social media during that crisis.

A typical keyword-based predicate is a combination of the name of the place and a word describing the situation, for example, *paris attacks*, *paris shootings*, *paris terrorism*, and so on. A good keyword-based predicate should be *discriminative*, that is, it should retrieve many messages related to a crisis, and few messages unrelated to it (Olteanu et al., 2014). For instance, if we are interested in physical landslides, a term such as "landslide" is not discriminative enough, given that it may refer to an election won by a landslide, for instance.

Hashtags can also be used in queries. As markers of crisis-relevant information, hashtags tend to be either (i) conventional, (ii) suggested by media or governments/organizations, or (iii) naturally emerging. An example of the first is *#wx*, a convention used to mark messages about weather updates, inherited from shorthands used in Morse code. An example of the second is *#PabloPH*, one of the first documented cases of a hashtag being suggested by a government (Philippines) during a disaster.[11]

Examples of the third type are *#earthquakechile* and *#chileearthquake*. We observe that in general, when markers emerge naturally, two or more competing hashtags can be proposed to annotate the same crisis. Over time, one of the proposed hashtags can become more popular than the others, and become the *de facto* standard for a crisis. Many messages related to a crisis do not have any keyword that one could have anticipated when starting a collection (Saleem et al., 2014), many do not use hashtags and may not even mention the name of the place but imply it, particularly for large-scale disasters in which people assume most of their social media contacts are aware of the developing situation. Also, different APIs may have different interpretations of how a keyword matches a hashtag. For example, "hurricane" may or may not also match "#hurricane," depending on the specification of the query language of each specific API.

Trade-off between precision and recall. A particularly difficult design choice when building a query is the compromise between *precision* and *recall*. In general, it is not possible to have 100% precision (i.e., that every message we acquire is related to a crisis) with 100% recall (i.e., that we acquire all messages related to a crisis) – we will discuss this in more detail in Section 4.2. The usage of a very specific keyword or hashtag for a crisis may increase precision, but may miss many messages that use other keywords. The usage of a broad geographical area may increase recall but may include many messages that are not crisis-relevant. Another source of irrelevant messages is the presence of ambiguous tags or keywords – such as the "landslide" example mentioned earlier – that can appear in both on-topic and off-topic messages (Qu et al., 2011).

---

[11] "Can standardised hashtags be effective in emergency responses?" Jessica MacLean, *European Interagency Security Forum,* March 2015. https://www.eisf.eu/news/can-standardised-hashtags-be-effective-in-emergency-responses/.

In general, the choice of a trade-off depends on a system's capabilities for postfiltering the data being collected. If the data will be postfiltered using automatic methods, having an emphasis on high recall would be appropriate. If the data will not be postfiltered, or will only be manually postfiltered, then the emphasis should be placed on having high precision.

Adaptive filtering. An effective choice of keywords should also have some flexibility to change over time. An analyst can monitor the messages being posted during a disaster and add/remove keywords to a query as the situation evolves; indeed, an experienced analyst may become quite skilled at this. However, to reduce the time and effort required by the analyst, and to increase his/her effectiveness, we may want to perform this adaptation automatically, or to provide automatically generated query suggestions for adapting a running query.

Automatically creating and modifying query keywords is related to a problem in Information Retrieval named *adaptive information filtering*, in which instead of crafting a query for a static collection, we create a dynamic query that is modified as new items of the corpus are discovered (Belkin and Croft, 1992; Lanquillon and Renz, 1999). This is also related to another classical problem in Web Information Retrieval, that of *focused crawling*, in which Web data about a particular topic must be collected, and a decision about whether to download a Web page or not must be done based on contextual information (Chakrabarti et al., 1999). Adaptive filtering is closely related to topic tracking (Allan, 2002), which we will discuss in Section 6.2.

With different variations, adaptive methods have been proposed to collect social media data about events (Wang et al., 2013) and crises (Li et al., 2012; Zielinski et al., 2013; Olteanu et al., 2014; Joseph et al., 2014). In general, these methods start with a set of keywords, and then refine that set, typically by adding new keywords that frequently co-occur with the current ones and/or that discriminate between crisis and noncrisis messages. This refinement process can be repeated iteratively, and it can be done in a fully automated manner, or using some level of human supervision. In both cases, the assumption is that the entire set of interesting and discriminative terms cannot be fully known in advance, but needs to be discovered as the situation evolves.

Enriching Data Context

The methods we have described are able to recover a collection of messages; however, these methods tend to lose some of the context of such messages. This process of decontextualization that affects disaster information in social media (Starbird, 2012a) happens to some extent by design, as many systems have a tendency to disaggregate knowledge into pieces of data (Brown and Duguid, 2002). Some data collection methods can aggravate this problem.

Connections. One aspect of context loss is that we have only a partial view of the online social network of users (which in turn is just a rough approximation of actual personal connections, as we will discuss in Section 5.1). We may know, for instance, only about connections between users that were visible during a disaster (e.g., through user mentions or repostings), but not about all user connections. Obtaining a better sample of online connections requires dedicated collection processes, for instance, by performing "snowball" sampling, in which the connections of each retrieved users are retrieved recursively (Mislove et al., 2007; Kwak et al., 2010), or by systematically retrieving data about a large set of users in a platform by scanning sequential user identifiers (Benevenuto et al., 2010; Cha et al., 2010).

Contextual streams. The set of messages posted by a user affected by a disaster may include some messages that are retrieved by using keywords or geographical queries, plus messages that are not retrieved but are still relevant for the disaster. These messages may form an individual timeline or a conversation with others, from which we only have an incomplete view. This in turn may affect negatively the conclusions that analysts can draw from looking at the message, as well as the output of automatic processing methods.

Obtaining a broader context may involve, for instance, an additional retrieval step in which we collect all the messages posted by a set of users during the period of time of the disaster, independently on whether they match a given query or not. This data capture method is recommended in Starbird et al. (2010), and referred to as a *contextual stream* by Palen (2014). Other ways of obtaining a contextual stream may also involve trying to reconstruct conversations, which can be done by applying clustering-based methods (Ritter et al., 2010) and/or heuristics that rely partially, but not entirely, on platform-specific elements such as "reply" buttons (Purohit et al., 2013).

Time. A narrow time frame may diminish context even further. As explained by Calhoun (2004), we tend to conceptualize all crises as "emergencies," which supposedly are clearly delimited in time – but this is not always the case. This affects the choice of a data collection strategy. Using a short time frame may hamper a deeper exploration of the context that contributes or causes the crisis, as a discussion on context and possible causes takes a longer time to develop than the discussion about immediate consequences and actions.

This problem may be exacerbated by the way in which people use social media during emergencies. Tufekci (2014) observed that during Turkey's Gezi Park protests in 2013, the volume of messages containing the hashtags used during the protest fell sharply after a few days, but the protest did not die nor did the demonstrators stop talking about it in social media. Discussion about the event continued very actively – but without using those hashtags.

2.3 Postfiltering and De-Duplication

Once messages are collected, they need to be postprocessed. This postprocessing includes the removal of items that can be identified, a priori, as irrelevant for a given application, and the identification of items that are either duplicates or near-duplicates of already-seen items.

Postfiltering. Since data collection processes that have near 100% of precision often have unacceptably low recall, most practical data acquisition methods collect a sizable fraction of irrelevant messages, up to 90% in some geo-based collections (Olteanu et al., 2014).

Automatic postfiltering can be done through keyword-based heuristics, but for large-scale systems it is best to do it through automatic classification methods, by applying a classifier that discriminates between messages that are relevant and messages that are irrelevant (more on this in Section 4.2).

Postfiltering of messages can be extended to postfiltering of users/accounts, for instance by automatically whitelisting accounts that post a sufficient number of messages of a given type. This, in turn, may lead to the capacity of filtering by type of author, such as eyewitnesses or "official" sources related to governments or established organizations.

Spam and bot removal. The attention that disaster-related topics generate in social media attracts unscrupulous parties, "spammers," seeking to exploit this attention for financial gain. They post messages offering products and services and including popular hashtags, independently of whether the products/services are related to the topics the hashtags represent. These messages are known as *social media spam* and there are well-studied methods that can remove a substantial portion of them (Benevenuto et al., 2010; Gupta and Kumaraguru, 2012; Uddin et al., 2014).

In some cases we might want to also remove messages posted by automatic agents or social media bots. Their identification is similar to that of spammers. However, bot removal may be harmful if we care about some specific bots; for instance, there are automated systems that automatically post meteorological or geophysical alerts in social media, which we may want to include in a data collection.

De-duplication. Repeated (reposted/retweeted) messages are common in time-sensitive social media, even encouraged, because in some platforms messages that gain notoriety are those that are simply repeated more. In social media, *redundancy is a form of relevance.* This means that redundant items cannot be simply eliminated. Instead, messages identified as duplicates or near-duplicates of other messages should be counted, and used as evidence to identify relevant messages (Rogstadius et al., 2013). Near-duplicate messages can be identified, for instance, using online clustering methods (which we will describe in Section 6.4).

2.4 Data Representation / Feature Extraction

Data representation is key for the text mining and search tasks that we describe in this book. Data representation maps the input data elements (in this case messages), to the input expected by a particular algorithm. Most of the data mining methods we describe in this book operate on vectors, which provide a convenient way of representing data. When representing a message as a vector, each of the positions of the vector corresponds to a measurable characteristic of the message.

Determining which characteristics should be included is a task known as *feature engineering,* and it is perhaps one of the most important steps to ensure effective mining and search. Feature engineering is informed by the observation of large volumes of messages, in order to discover which are the aspects of the messages of interest that might be captured computationally. Feature engineering can also take advantage of feature selection methods, which can determine if a given feature is discriminating of a particular class of messages (this will be discussed later in Section 4.2).

Textual Features

Textual features are derived from the text of a message.

Word features. One of the main paradigms for representing text is the *vector space model*, introduced by Salton et al. (1975). Within this paradigm, the presence of words in a text is signaled by nonzero positions on a vector.

If we use only *single-word features*, each position of the vector corresponds to a word. A natural extension are *multiword features*, which usually

correspond to sequences of words, known as *word n-grams* (sequences of letters are known as character n-grams). Word n-grams help reduce ambiguity in
texts. For instance, the presence of the bigram "rock fall" in a message has a
more strict interpretation that the independent presence of the words "rock" and
"fall." Words can be processed by Natural Language Processing (NLP) operations, such as the ones described in Section 3.2, before features are extracted.
This means, for instance, that we can discard stopwords (such as "the") before
word features are extracted. This also means that higher-level features using
parts of speech or named entities can be constructed (e.g., "number of verbs"
or "usage of first-person pronouns").

Word features can be binary variables, indicating the presence or absence
of a word or word sequence in a message, or they can be a number following a
particular weighting scheme. The Inverse Document Frequency (IDF) weighting scheme is frequently used in information retrieval, and gives more weight
to terms that are rare (Baeza-Yates and Ribeiro-Neto, 2011).

Nonword features. *Superficial text features* can be computed, such as the
length of the text in terms of number of words, or number of characters.
Nonalphanumeric characters may also be useful, including features indicating
whether question or exclamation marks are present in a message. Finally,
nonalphanumeric strings including *emojis* such as "☺" and *emoticons* such
as a smiley ":-)" or a frown ":-(" are commonly used to characterize text,
particularly with respect to the expression of emotions or sentiments.

It is important to note that textual features are either language-specific or
require some degree of adaptation to be used effectively across languages. In
particular, methods that are useful for dealing with messages in English need
to be refined when processing messages in other languages (Ciot et al., 2013).

Metadata features

In many applications, the *metadata* associated to a message is as important as
the message itself. The availability of different pieces of information depends
on the specific platform being used, and on whether the platform makes this
information available through a specific API. Typical metadata in social media
messages includes: (i) the author of a message; (ii) its publication timestamp;
(iii) categories, hashtags, or tags explicitly associated with it; (iv) user mentions, images or URLs embedded in the messages; and (v) the number of user
interactions it has received, such as views, comments, reposts, upvotes, or
downvotes.

Finally, in the case of multimedia elements, content-based features such as colors, textures, and shapes can be included – see Liu et al. (2007) for a survey of this type of feature.

2.5 Storage and Indexing

As we shall see in Section 6.1, storing all of the messages that are received is rarely a necessity in applications that perform live/online data analysis. In some cases, a bounded-size buffer of recent messages is sufficient. Data storage of entire datasets may be needed only for some types of analysis. Given the large data volumes involved and the ephemeral value of the data, many applications can fulfill their requirements without persistently storing data, or by keeping a minimal amount of data. However, data storage may still be necessary to enable retrospective analysis or to reproduce research results.

In cases in which data is stored, repeated data insertions can quickly become a bottleneck, and applications may need to be distributed across a number of computational nodes to keep up with computational demands. Data may also require to be updated, for instance, if counters of "upvotes" or "likes" need to be kept, or if we need to keep track of messages that might have been deleted by users.

Contemporary applications dealing with real-time updates usually do not rely entirely on Relational Database Management Systems (RDBMS), but instead use NoSQL systems ("Not only SQL") to store messages. Among other advantages, NoSQL databases are designed for performance and scalability, so that more data can be handled by adding more processing nodes. Social media has been a significant driving force behind the development of popular open-source NoSQL databases, such as MongoDB[12] and Apache Cassandra,[13] which was developed initially by Facebook.

Schram and Anderson (2012) describe the differences between using NoSQL and RDBMS for message storage, in the context of a system for collecting crisis-related social media messages. NoSQL databases are different from relational databases. Instead of predefining a schema to which each item must adhere, they organize data as a series of key-value pairs, in which the value is a semistructured record that, in some applications, may be completely opaque for the database management system. This and other differences with relational database systems may bring new challenges in terms of data modeling – see,

---

[12] MongoDB: https://www.mongodb.org/.
[13] Apache Cassandra: https://cassandra.apache.org/.

for example, Anderson et al. (2015) for an implementation in Cassandra of a data model for crisis-related social media messages.

Indexing. In the scenarios we describe in this book, searching means finding a set of messages satisfying a given criteria inside a collection, and sorting them according to some measure of importance. There are many algorithms for search, depending on the types of data being searched for. As collections grow large, the only methods that can continue to deliver fast search results, avoiding sequential scans over the entire dataset, are those that rely on an *index*, which is a particular data structure supporting a search operation. Modern databases used to store social media data in real-world applications, both RDBMS and NoSQL, typically support ordered indexes, spatial indexes, and textual indexes.

Ordered indexes maintain a logical view in which the data are sorted by a specific element, such as message-id, timestamp, or number of "likes." Ordered indexes allow for efficient *range queries,* for instance, to retrieve elements whose timestamp lies between two given dates. An ordered index also allows efficient insertions and retrievals of data items.

Spatial indexes are a specific type of index for 2-dimensional data describing points on a plane or over an sphere. It supports 2-dimensional range queries in a manner that is more efficient that what can be simulated using two separated ordered indexes (one for each coordinate). Spatial indexes are important to efficiently perform geographical queries and/or for representing data on a map.

Textual indexes, also known as *inverted indexes*, are used to index the content of a message. An inverted index has two parts: a vocabulary and a series of posting lists. The *vocabulary* is the union of all the word features extracted from all the documents. The *posting lists* contain all the documents that contain a given textual feature. To search all of the documents containing a set of key words or phrases, the vocabulary (which itself has an ordered index) is scanned to locate their corresponding posting lists. Then, the posting lists of each of the parts of the query are intersected, which is in general a fast operation if the posting lists are kept sorted. There are many optimizations that can be done when indexing: the area of Information Retrieval deals with many of the questions posed by text search. For an overview, see Baeza-Yates and Ribeiro-Neto (2011).

2.6 Research Problems

Performing intelligent and contextual data collection. Methods currently in use for collecting social media data have many shortcomings.

First, they tend to rely on *expert input*, which may or may not be available at a given moment. When a new crisis has been detected in some way, some degree of human intervention is required in order to define a data collection process. This may include, for instance, to define which particular search terms to use, or which geographical area to cover. Some exceptions include on-demand geographical-based collections triggered by natural phenomena detected through physical sensors, such as earthquakes.

Second, collections tend to be based on *static queries* which are not modified as time progresses. Disasters go through a life cycle (see, e.g., Fischer, 1998), which is also evident in disaster communications. There is a natural progression of different topics as a collection evolves: messages of caution and advice tend to appear first, while messages regarding donations or missing people tend to appear on days following a disaster (Olteanu et al., 2015).

Third, as we discussed previously, collections tend to capture *isolated messages* but fail to capture conversations. Human communication happens in context, and this context is often missing when using the typical data collection methods of keywords or geographical boundaries (Starbird et al., 2010; Palen, 2014).

Developing architectures for real-time analysis. A system built to support large-scale data collection and storage for batch analysis, may have architectural limitations that make it ineffective for real-time analysis (the difference between batch and online/real-time analysis is discussed in detail in Section 6.1). A system architect may have to choose between extending an existing system to support real-time analysis, for instance by modifying the way data is stored and indexing, or designing a new architecture for that purpose. In some cases, both types of systems may be used side by side. In general, the crisis computing literature includes more examples of batch analysis systems than of systems able to perform real-time analysis.

Reducing the overreliance on a single data source. Just as biologists intensively study certain organisms such as *Drosophila melanogaster* because of factors that include convenience (e.g., ease of manipulation and fast reproductive cycle), computational social scientists have also implicitly chosen Twitter as their "model organism" (Tufekci, 2014).

Twitter is used by researchers and developers due to the availability of its streaming API, and due to its popularity among the general public and among journalists: "While the vast majority of Haitians in Port au Prince, for example, are not Twitter users, the city's journalists overwhelmingly are and see it as an essential source of news and updates" (Robinson and Wall, 2012). However, there are many communities that rely on other social media platforms, and research is needed to understand to what extent the dynamics of interactions in those platforms resemble those that have been described for Twitter.

2.7 Further Reading

The "Humanitarian Big Data Wheel" is a simple framework that depicts how humanitarian organizations conceptualize the processing of big data within their organizations (Whipkey and Verity, 2015).

Russell (2014) describes the API of popular social media systems including Facebook, Twitter, and LinkedIn. It also includes programming recipes in Python to query those APIs.

Kumar et al. (2013a, ch. 1–3), describes how to use Java to access Twitter's API, download tweets, and store them in MongoDB.

Ramakrishnan and Gehrke (2002, part III), is an introduction to indexing in databases. Baeza-Yates and Ribeiro-Neto (2011, ch. 9) describes text indexing and search in information retrieval.

3

Vagueness: Natural Language and Semantics

During the 2015 Nepal earthquake, a 26-year-old Indian lawyer and activist posted the following on Twitter:[1]

Media must report about d alleged 20k RSS chaps off 2 #Nepal.here's a pic coz d 1 @ShainaNC shared isn't true.. ;)

Meaning: media must report about allegations that twenty thousand volunteers from India's *Rashtriya Swayamsevak Sangh* (RSS) had joined the relief efforts in Nepal, as falsely claimed on Twitter by Shaina NC (a member of the Bharatiya Janata Party, a political group close to the RSS). This message mixes shortened words ("d" for "the," "2" for "to," "coz" for "because," "pic" for "picture"), ambiguous abbreviations ("RSS," which may mean a number of things), British slang ("chaps"), platform-specific codes (such as the hashtag *#Nepal* and the user mention *@ShainaNC*), punctuation/capitalization issues (lack of spacing between *#Nepal* and *here*, usage of two dots instead of an ellipsis), and sarcasm expressed through a "wink" emoticon (";)").

In general, understanding a message in social media requires contextual information to compensate for fragmented, ambiguous – in other words, *vague* – text that is open to more than one interpretation.

This chapter is about Natural Language Processing (NLP), which encompasses computational methods created for dealing with human language. NLP methods incorporating statistical machine learning elements were developed in the 1980s and 1990s using mostly profesionally written texts, such as newspaper articles. Since the late 1990s and the 2000s, these methods have been extended to deal first with Web content, and in the late 2000s and early 2010s,

---

[1] https://twitter.com/Shehzad_Ind/status/592690719875342336

with social media messages and short text messages sent from mobile phones (SMS). Many modern NLP methods are based on machine learning.

The next section (§3.1) describes the text of social media messages. Then, we outline basic NLP methods such as tokenization, stemming, part-of-speech tagging, and dependency parsing (§3.2), as well as sentiment analysis/opinion mining (§3.3). Next, we describe how to locate references to entities such as people and organizations (§3.4), and, particularly, places (§3.5). Finally, we refer to methods for extracting structured data from unstructured text (§3.6), and for adding semantics to messages (§3.7).

3.1 Social Media Is Conversational

In general on the Internet "we find language that is fragmentary, laden with typographical errors, often bereft of punctuation, and sometimes downright incoherent" (Baron, 2003). At the very least, messages in social media tend to be brief and informal. Mobile devices, which are typically used for interacting with social media, offer slower text entry methods than desktop computers. Additionally, social media is often a form of speech, used to "chat" with others, which means many messages look more like the transcription of a conversation between two people than like a text written to be understood on its own. These conversations play an important role as enablers of coordination among users during disaster situations (Purohit et al., 2013).

Social media messages are highly *heterogeneous*, with multiple sources (e.g., traditional media sources, eyewitness accounts, etc.), varying levels of quality and grammatical correctness (Rosa and Ellen, 2009; Baldwin et al., 2013), and different languages present in the same corpus and sometimes in the same message – phenomena known as "borrowing" and "code switching" (Gardner-Chloros, 2009). In general, computational methods developed and optimized using corpora of professionally produced documents, usually require some level of adaptation to be effective when applied to social media content (Derczynski et al., 2015).

Brief messages in social media conversations, particularly those sent during a crisis, often assume a shared context from which only a minor part is explicit. The area of study in linguistics known as *pragmatics* focuses on "communication in context," and explains how people are able to infer the meaning of the communications because humans are very adept at understanding context – a reader can understand the intent of a message because she or he knows the context within which that message is being broadcast. Current computational methods to a large extent are not able to achieve this level of comprehension (Vieweg and Hodges, 2014).

3.2 Text Preprocessing

Natural Language Processing (NLP) is a large and well-established research area. This section overviews a few basic and commonplace text preprocessing operations that are done using NLP techniques. The main objective of these operations is to take an array of bytes representing text, and convert it into a structured representation consisting of annotated text segments (e.g., words, sentences, and paragraphs). The operations we include in this section are:

(i) character decoding
(ii) tokenization
(iii) normalization
(iv) stopword removal
(v) stemming/lemmatization
(vi) part of speech tagging
(vii) dependency parsing

Character decoding means converting an input array of bytes into an output array of characters. When a character encoding is explicitly declared in the input, this is straightforward process, in which bytes and sequences of bytes are looked up into a *character table* to determine the corresponding letter. When no character encoding is explicitly declared, a character encoding detection method is required.

The following example corresponds to a byte representation (in which each byte is written in hexadecimal) of the German word "Überflutung" (flood) in UTF-8, which is a widely used character encoding.[2] Notice that in some cases more than one byte is needed to represent a character.

Bytes	c3	9c	62	65	72	66	6c	75	74	75	6e	67
Characters	Ü		b	e	r	f	l	u	t	u	n	g

Tokenization consists on converting an array of characters into a list of words. For instance, the text "Attention: a tornado warning is in effect!" should produce

---

[2] Unicode 7.0.0 standard. June 2014. http://www.unicode.org/versions/Unicode7.0.0/.

a list of seven words ("Attention," "a," "tornado," "warning," "is," "in," and "effect"). Word separators include spaces plus punctuation symbols such as ":" and "!," as shown in this example. Tokenization in general is from trivial to easy in languages where spaces separate words (including Indo-European languages), but it can be challenging in other languages such as Chinese, which is written without spaces between words.

In this example, a warning in Chinese meaning "Beijing issued a flood alert" is separated into segments associated to different concepts:

Original	北京发出了洪水警报 (Beijing issued a flood alert)
Tokenized	北京 (Beijing) 发出了 (issued) 洪水 (flood) 警报 (alert)

Examples of tokenization and other preprocessing operations on crisis-related messages in Japanese are presented in Neubig et al. (2011).

Normalization consists on mapping words to a "normal" form, which is an application-dependent concept. This normalization can include a number of operations intended to remove differences deemed unimportant for a particular application. For instance, if for the purposes of filtering messages, "UN" and "U.N." are equivalent, then the normalization should convert all instances of these acronyms to one of the two variants. Another standard normalization operation is to reduce text to lowercase, so that "HELP" and "Help" can be found using the query "help". Normalization might also be used to convert slang terms to standard words or phrases, for instance, to convert "ikr" into "I know, right?" or "b/c" into "because."

In some languages, accents can be omitted in many cases without loss of interpretability, for instance, in Spanish the phrase "árboles caídos" (fallen trees), can be incorrectly spelled as "arboles caidos," which can be unambiguously interpreted as having the exact same meaning as the accented form. Misspellings due to accent removal are often done intentionally by people using a keyboard or a system that does not easily support them. Normalization, in this case, can map accented characters to their nonaccented forms.

In other languages, a technology-specific alphabet can be used, which must be converted into a standard alphabet. This is the case of the Arabic chat alphabet,[3] which is a mapping from the Arabic script to Latin letters and numbers. The Arabic chat alphabet is used by Arabic speakers in devices and/or situations where entering Arabic script is impossible or cumbersome.

---

[3] Arabic Chat Alphabet, Wikipedia. https://en.wikipedia.org/wiki/Arabic_chat_alphabet.

This example shows words in both Arabic chat alphabet and in the regular Arabic script:

English word	Arabic chat alphabet	Arabic script
heart	"8alb" or "qalb"	قلب
love	"al3ab"	أَلعب

Stopword removal consists on deleting from the input text words that are not useful for a particular application. For instance, for keyword-based matching in which no phrase-level matching is needed, function words can be removed. *Function words* have no unambiguous meaning by themselves, and instead are used to connect other elements on a sentence; they might include prepositions, articles, and conjunctions. The words that remain after stopword removal are the *content words*. The decision of which words to consider as stopwords is in general language- and application-dependent.

This example shows a sentence before and after stopword removal:

Original	To help those affected by the devastating earthquake, text DONATE to 5555
Without stopwords	help affected devastating earthquake text DONATE 5555

Stemming and lemmatization are methods to extract the "root" of a word. Stemming is a simple method based on applying a set of substitution rules on character sequences. In the case of English, it is implemented in the widely used Porter's stemmer (Porter, 1980), which does suffix substitution; stemmers for other languages are also available.[4] The result of stemming is not always an actual word, but stemming algorithms are simple and fast. Lemmatization is a more elaborate operation, and requires a sizable machine-readable corpus to be done: it converts each word into its morphological root.

Word	Stem (Porter's Stemmer)	Lemma
standing	stand	stand
destroyed	destroi	destroy
destroying	destroi	destroy

---

[4] Snowball Stemmers Overview: http://snowball.tartarus.org/texts/stemmersoverview.html.

Part of speech tagging (POS tagging), annotates each word with a part-of-speech tag, which indicates the class to which the word belongs. These classes are language-dependent and defined according to grammatical properties; in English some example classes are "verb," "adjective," and "noun." Part of speech tagging can be done automatically applying a structured machine learning paradigm, in which both the input and output are sequences (instead of single elements). The input is a sequence of words, represented by the words themselves and other features such as capitalization, and the output is a sequence of annotations (Brill, 2000).

This example shows two sentences ("They should fire him" and "There is a fire"), in which part-of-speech tags have been associated to each word:

Words	They	should	fire	him
Part of speech	*pronoun*	*adverb*	*verb*	*pronoun*

Words	There	is	a	fire
Part of speech	*pronoun*	*verb*	*preposition*	*noun*

In the first example, the word "fire" is a verb, while in the second example, the word "fire" is a noun. Part-of-speech tagging allows us to define more precisely a filter or a search query over a collection of messages, for instance, that we are interested only in occurrences of the noun "fire."

Dependency parsing is an analysis of the syntax of a text that finds dependencies among the different constituents of it. The output of a dependency parser is a a parse tree, which is graph representing the dependencies in the text (Jurafsky and Martin, 2008, part III). In this example, "The Met responded to an emergency call," the boldface word indicates the root of the tree.

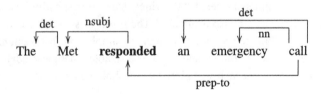

The arrows describe the relationship between the different elements as follows: "det" (links a noun to its determinant), "nsubj" (nominal subject, links a verb to a nominal phrase), "nn" (links noun to a noun premodifier), and "prep-to" (links using the preposition "to"). Dependency parsing is helpful to summarize multiple messages, by identifying important elements such as subject, main verb, and numerals related to these elements (Rudra et al., 2015).

3.3 Sentiment Analysis

Social media contains a great deal of subjective information; it is a mixture of messages containing facts, opinions, and a combination of facts and opinions (Ito et al., 2015).

Methods to analyze the subjective content of text are known as sentiment analysis or opinion mining. Essentially, they attempt to automatically infer authors' sentiments from their language expressions (Liu, 2010). The area has enjoyed a boom of activity in recent years, fueled by a demand from product marketers, political campaigners, and others who would like to know "what the world thinks about them" (Pang and Lee, 2008).

Sentiment analysis is relevant in the analysis of Web data in general, and of social media data in particular. Current methods for sentiment analysis are to a large extent based on the application of statistical machine learning methods, as well as on the exploitation of large and rich linguistic resources. In the case of social media, these methods include sophisticated analysis of the context in which messages are written, including past messages by the same user, as well as her explicitly declared social connections, when present.

Single dimension: polarity. In its most basic form, sentiment analysis attempts to figure out the *polarity* of a message, that is, to what extent it expresses a positive sentiment, or a negative one.

For instance, the following are two example messages posted during the September 2010, San Bruno, California (U.S.) gas explosion and resulting fires, quoted by Nagy and Stamberger (2012).

Negative	#SanBrunoFire What law are they using to keep the press away? Obviously it is not all a crime scene? #NannyState officials making up law.
Positive	Thank you to all the brave firefighters helping to save lives in the #SanBrunoFire and #BoulderFire

Multiple dimensions. Sentiment analysis can go beyond determining the polarity of a message, into determining different emotional states of the person who authors a message, together with the depth of that state. The well-known model of Plutchik (1991), usually depicted in "Plutchik's Wheel," includes eight dimensions plus intensity; for instance, "annoyance," "anger," and "rage" represent three different intensities along the same dimension.

In the domain of crisis-related social media, sentiment analysis might be helpful in answering questions that are relevant for emergency responders, such as "How bad is it out there?" (Caragea et al., 2014). A large amount of messages attached to negative sentiment clustered around the same geographical area, can be evidence of an ongoing crisis in that area. In general, changes in sentiment can be correlated with subevents related to an ongoing crisis (Sha et al., 2014).

For surveys on sentiment analysis, see the summary by Feldman (2013), the book by Liu (2010), and the survey by Pang and Lee (2008).

3.4 Named Entities

Named Entity Recognition (NER) finds *named entities* on a text, which are usually names of persons, organizations, or places. In this example, "PM Modi" (the fifteenth Prime Minister of India) is recognized as an entity of type "Person" and "Nepal" is recognized as an entity of type "Place."

<u>PM Modi</u> offered humanitarian assistance to victims in	<u>Nepal</u>
Person	*Place*

The lack of capitalization and the presence of typographic errors, are important contributing factors that reduce the effectiveness of traditional NER methods when applied to social media. This can be to some extent alleviated by preprocessing strategies that try to normalize text before entity recognition is attempted (Baldwin et al., 2013; Derczynski et al., 2015).

Named entity recognition identifies regions of interest in the text. The next step is to actually attach some semantics to those regions.

Named entity linking (also known as named entity disambiguation or resolution) connects an entity with a machine-readable reference in a specific knowledge base. There are many situations in which a named entity recognized in the text can have two or more different meanings, depending on the context. In some cases, the text of the message is sufficient to guess the intended meaning.

For instance, consider the entity "The Met" in the following two sentences:

(i) <u>The Met</u> is hosting an art exhibit.
(ii) <u>The Met</u> responded to an emergency call.

In the first case, "the Met" might be the Metropolitan Museum of Art in New York City, while in the second case it might be the Metropolitan Police Service in London. The more contextual information we have about a message, the more confident we can be when disambiguating. For instance, if the author of the first message declares in her user profile that she lives in New York City, we could be more certain about our guess that the Met refers to the museum in that city. In general, domain-specific approaches are useful to increase the accuracy of entity linking (Gruhl et al., 2009).

Entities are usually linked to knowledge bases through URLs (e.g., as described by Zhou et al., 2010). For open domain tasks, the knowledge base of choice against which entities are linked is Wikipedia,[5] or one of its machine-readable variants, such as DBPedia.[6] In the examples given earlier, these entities would be linked to http://dbpedia.org/page/Metropolitan_Museum_of_Art and http://dbpedia.org/page/Metropolitan_Police_Service, respectively. Domain-specific knowledge bases are useful for specialized domains, such as GeoNames[7] for geographical information. A good starting point for finding a knowledge base is the Linked Open Data Cloud.[8]

Faceted and semantic search. The result of named entity linking or disambiguation allows users to express very specific predicates over a set of messages, which can be much more powerful than simple keyword matching. We could, for instance, indicate that we want messages about the London police force, but not messages about the New York museum.

Going one step further, entity linking can use relationships between concepts (that we describe later in Section 3.7) to provide *faceted search*, a method to interactively navigate a complex information space. For instance, we can select "police" from a list of possible organization types, "United Kingdom" from a list of countries, and find messages that mention a police force in the United Kingdom (such as the Met), even if those messages do not include the specific word "police" or "United Kingdom."

Abel et al. (2011) describes and evaluates a faceted search system for Twitter, showing important advantages over traditional keyword search. In follow-up work (Abel et al., 2012a), they introduce *Twitcident*, a system to analyze Twitter during crises that supports semantic filtering, faceted search and summarization. A semantic-based approach is also used in *Twitris 2.0* (Jadhav et al., 2010) and *EDIT* (Traverso et al., 2014), which present event-related social media capturing semantics in terms of spatial, temporal, and thematic dimensions.

There are two special cases of named entity linking of particular interest in crisis scenarios: temporal and spatial references. Temporal references, such as "last night" or "next Saturday" can often be converted to time ranges given the timestamp of a message and the content of the temporal reference (Strötgen and Gertz, 2013). Spatial references correspond to the case when the entity is a location, and are studied in the next section.

---

[5] Wikipedia. https://www.wikipedia.org/.   [6] DBPedia. http://dbpedia.org/.
[7] GeoNames. http://www.geonames.org/.
[8] Linking open data cloud diagram. http://lod-cloud.net/.

3.5 Geotagging and Geocoding

Maps are used extensively by both the emergency response and the humanitarian relief communities to represent crisis-relevant information (we describe such maps in Chapter 10). Content that can be associated to a geographical location can be used for creating such maps, and also can provide location-based retrieval of content, that is, using queries that delimit a geographical region of interest.

Geotagged and nongeotagged content. We distinguish two classes of messages: geotagged and nongeotagged. *Geotagged* messages are explicitly associated with metadata about geographical locations. *Nongeotagged* messages do not have this explicit location information, but often contain implicit clues about locations.

Most social media platforms allow users to *geotag* the items they post (e.g., an image, video, or text). Hence, this information may be present in a social media message, in the form of metadata. In practice, whether content is geotagged or not depends on several factors, including: (i) that the user's device has the capacity to know its location (e.g., via Global Positioning System (GPS), or through other methods), (ii) that the specific client software being used has the capability to read this information from the device, and (iii) that the user has enabled this feature explicitly, that is, has accepted to disclose her location. These factors, in turn, depend on socioeconomic, demographic, and other variables (Malik et al., 2015).

Given these constraints, in practice a minority of messages include machine-readable location information; for instance Burton et al. (2012) indicate that this figure is about 2% for Twitter. Of course, as everything in the social media space, this can change quite rapidly in a short time.

Automatic Geotag Inference (Geocoding)

While explicit metadata about locations may be often absent, many messages posted on social media contain implicit references to names of places, for instance, "The Christchurch hospital is operational" (Gelernter and Mushegian, 2011). *Geocoding* refers to automatically geotagging content with inferred locations. In a disaster scenario, geocoding might be very useful to determine, for instance, where a certain emergency relief resource such as food or shelter is required (Bhatt et al., 2014).

User geocoding refers to automatically inferring the location of a user. A message can be posted by a user in one location, but refer to a different location.

This is not a rare occurrence: the response of social media to large disasters is often globally distributed, and does not necessarily follows a geographical proximity logic (Nagar et al., 2012; Kwak and An, 2014b; Kogan et al., 2015).

User geocoding can be done based on information on user profiles (Hecht and Gergle, 2010; Hecht et al., 2011), by aggregating information in their posting histories (Cheng et al., 2010), or by a combination of both methods. Knowing the location of users may be relevant for some applications, such as finding potential direct eyewitnesses of a situation (Starbird et al., 2012). The movement patterns of users, and even their behavior of switching from no geotagging to geotagging and vice versa, may also be indicative of the characteristics and situation of users (Palen, 2014).

Message geocoding. In many cases, the locations that messages refer to are more important than the location in which users are (Graham et al., 2014; Ikawa et al., 2013; Lingad et al., 2013). Message geocoding refers to automatically inferring location references on a text. This can be done in two steps, first by finding these geographical references in the text (a type of named entity recognition), and linking them to geographical coordinates (a type of named entity disambiguation).

For instance, MacEachren et al. (2011) use this approach, using named entity recognition to find potential candidates, and then comparing those candidates with a list of place names. This approach typically requires a comprehensive database of place names (Sultanik and Fink, 2012; Middleton et al., 2014). The GeoNames[9] database alone contains eight million entries as of early 2015, and OpenStreetMap (an open geographical database), 4.5×10^9 geographical points – but only a small fraction of these points has a name.[10] Interestingly, a database of geographic information can be enriched using data from social media itself, for instance, by exploiting messages containing both text and explicit geographic coordinates (Intagorn and Lerman, 2013).

In general, geocoding is not a mere dictionary lookup process, because many ambiguities can occur. These ambiguities are known as "*geo/nongeo*" and "*geo/geo.*" A geo/nongeo ambiguity occurs when a name might refer to a location, or to something else; an example is found in the sentence "Let's play Texas Hold 'em," that does not refer to the state of Texas in the United States but to a card game. A geo/geo ambiguity occurs when there are two or more locations with the same name. For instance, "shooting in Paris," could in principle refer to the capital of France, or to any of more than a dozen places on Earth sharing the same name.

---

[9] GeoNames: http://geonames.org/.
[10] OpenStreetMap Statistics: http://www.openstreetmap.org/stats/data_stats.html.

Ambiguities in geotagging are addressed using probabilistic methods (see, for instance, Cheng et al., 2010), often exploiting contextual clues. These clues may include the general location of a crisis, information about nearby places, previous messages posted by users, and location information disclosed by users in their profiles (Gelernter and Mushegian, 2011). The context of messages is also important when describing a series of locations when the focus of a disaster is moving. For instance, Sakaki et al. (2013) apply a *Kalman filter* over a set of coordinates of messages posted in social media, to determine the trajectory of a typhoon. A Kalman filter works by computing a weighted average between the current observation and a prediction issued by a model based on historical data.

An experimental comparison of geocoding methods for social media can be found in Jurgens et al. (2015).

3.6 Extracting Structured Information

At a high level, the end goal of the processes we have described in this section is the creation of a record with some structured data, from an input that has no structure. An officer from the UN Disaster Assessment and Coordination agency described this need exactly on those terms: "If you want to know where the biggest gap is, it's the extraction of structured data from unstructured inputs. And the unstructured inputs are situation reports, emails that go flying around, etc. And the structured data outputs would be points on a map with a few key values that matter for decision making" (Harvard Humanitarian Initiative, 2011, page 22).

This is a well-defined task known as *information extraction*, a topic whose development has been fueled in part by the requirement of converting semistructured Web pages, or completely unstructured text, into structured records; for a survey, see Chang et al. (2006). In general, information extraction is more difficult in open domains (general texts) than in closed domains (texts about a specific topic), and is more difficult when there is no structure (plain text) than when there is some structure (formatted text).

Crisis-related social media messages often have no structure, but they do belong to a specific domain. This can be exploited when performing information extraction. For instance, Imran et al. (2013b,c) first classify disaster-related messages into a set of crisis-relevant categories, thus narrowing even further the domain for the information extraction, and then extract category-dependent information from the messages. For instance, for messages reporting infrastructure damage, the element to be extracted is the name of the infrastructure reportedly damaged; for messages asking for donations, the element to be extracted is the specific item being requested. The specific approach used in this case is to build a Conditional Random Field (Lafferty et al., 2001), a probabilistic model for sequences, in this case, sequences of words.

Groups of related messages can be analyzed simultaneously to improve the accuracy of information extraction. For instance, Sellam and Alonso (2015) extract quantitative information (e.g., number of missing people) from social media by clustering similar message fragments. All other things equal, a piece of information present across many fragments is considered as more reliable than one having less support, similarly to the way in which modern knowledge bases are built from large unstructured corpora (Dong et al., 2014).

Information extraction can lead to applications beyond the retrieval of messages. In a crisis context, records created with information extraction methods can be used to match messages requesting donations of a specific item (e.g., clothing) with messages offering donations of that item (Purohit et al., 2014a,b), or to match messages expressing problems with messages offering solutions for those problems (Varga et al., 2013). Messages describing problems could also be mapped to explicit functional areas of emergency response, for example, a message about a damaged fuel pipe can be mapped to "operations support/fuel supply" (Link et al., 2015). Information extraction has also been used to perform event detection (Khurdiya et al., 2012), a topic that is discussed extensively in Section 6.6.

3.7 Ontologies for Explicit Semantics

The usage of semantic technologies becomes necessary once we start creating structured records with pieces of information extracted from messages.

Semantic technologies provide us a mean of abstracting concepts and knowledge. They enable automatic reasoning and inference, allowing us to automatically connect different pieces of information to reach a conclusion. On a very practical level, semantic technologies allow us to deal with a wide range of different ways used by people in social media to refer to the same concept. They also make it possible to integrate data from different sources, helping us deal with interoperability issues which are common in disaster response (Clark et al., 2015). Information management during a large crisis often involves interactions between software operated by different agencies, and/or provided by different developers or vendors.

An *ontology* is an explicit description of concepts within a domain and relationships among them. Machine-readable ontologies are key elements of semantic technologies; they are often expressed following a specific schema, such as the Ontology Web Language (OWL) or Resource Description Framework (RDF). For instance, the *Management of A Crisis* (MOAC)[11] ontology has 92 classes and 21 properties covering four areas: disaster (e.g., landslides, floods), damage (e.g., road blocks, collapsed structures), processes (e.g., rescue, search, evacuation), and resources (e.g., services, vehicles, tents). The objective is to describe different aspects of a crisis, including its consequences, the needs of those affected, and the response to the crisis.

Disaster-specific ontologies can also be used in conjunction with ontologies from other areas, including ontologies to describe people (such as FOAF[12]), ontologies to describe places (such as GeoNames' ontology[13]), or ontologies to describe elements specific to social media including follower-followee relationships (such as SIOC[14]). Liu et al. (2013) survey 26 ontologies related to different areas of disaster response. They note that most ontologies refer to a specific area.

A lightweight alternative, or a precursor to the usage of ontologies, is the usage of controlled vocabularies; for instance, Berlingerio et al. (2013) use the Integrated Public Sector Vocabulary (IPSV), which describes standardized terms for referring to matters affecting the public sector, such as "waste management" or "child health services." Another lightweight alternative is the hashtag-based Humanitarian Exchange Language (HXL), which is a standard that encourages humanitarian organizations to annotate columns on spreadsheets, using hashtags belonging to a controlled vocabulary.[15]

3.8 Research Problems

Develop new NLP methods for crisis-relevant social media. Social media applications have been an important force in the development of new NLP methods, by presenting a challenging problem to existing systems. Many of the elements needed for better understanding of social media messages during a crisis are not crisis-specific, such as locations or emotional states. Other elements might be crisis-specific, such as emergency relief resources (Purohit et al., 2014a,b). Arguably, domain-specific NLP research for other kinds of text, such as product reviews, has been much more intense and thus gone much

---

[11] Management of A Crisis (MOAC): http://observedchange.com/moac/ns/.
[12] Friend-of-A-Friend (FOAF) specification: http://xmlns.com/foaf/spec/.
[13] GeoNames documentation: http://www.geonames.org/ontology/documentation.html.
[14] Semantically-Interlinked Online Communities (SIOC): http://sioc-project.org/.
[15] Humanitarian Exchange Language (HXL): http://hxlstandard.org/.

deeper into identifying domain-specific elements, compared to developments in the crisis domain.

Applying and extending machine translation methods for crisis computing. Translation of messages from a language that is spoken by a small population, to a language spoken by a larger one, broadens the audience for those messages, potentially contributing to tasks such as fundraising or donation seeking after a disaster. Most translation efforts of social media content so far involve crowd-sourcing, but automatic Machine Translation (MT) might be a more scalable solution. A challenge is that the performance of MT systems depends heavily on the availability of linguistic resources (e.g., parallel corpora), which means that no MT systems exist for many languages spoken by relatively small populations in the world. Lewis et al. (2011) suggest a fast process to develop MT systems for low-resource languages, but more research is needed to evaluate these systems when applied to social media data during actual crises.

Encouraging the production of structured information. In principle, interpreting messages should be easier if they already have some structure. This is the idea of the early Tweak-the-Tweet proposal by Starbird and Stamberger (2010), in which specific hashtags are used to mark specific places of a tweet, such as *#loc* for locations. A more recent proposal, by UN OCHA, invites the public to use a vocabulary of specific hashtags to annotate their messages.[16] There might be obstacles to the wide adoption of these protocols – most people may be used to unstructured postings, and too many hashtags may make messages less readable (Temnikova et al., 2015) – but it is plausible that even if a small fraction of users adopt them, the extraction of relevant information from that subset of messages already can yield some benefits.

3.9 Further Reading

Bird et al. (2009) describes how to perform various Natural Language Processing operations using NLTK in Python. Ingersoll et al. (2013, ch. 5), describes how to perform named entity recognition using OpenNLP in Java.

Owoputi et al. (2013) describe the ArkNLP tool, which is a part-of-speech tagger trained on Twitter data. ArkNLP is able to recognize Internet idioms such as "lol" ("laughing out loud") and assign them the correct Part Of Speech (POS) tag (interjection, in this case).

---

[16] Hashtag Standards for Emergencies by UN OCHA, October 2014. http://reliefweb.int/report/world/hashtag-standards-emergencies.

Feldman (2013) is an overview of several aspects of sentiment analysis, while Liu (2015) presents an in-depth description of current methods for sentiment analysis for the Web.

Derczynski et al. (2015) studies the challenges of named entity recognition and linking in social media, comparing the performance of various state-of-the-art tools, and discussing how this performance can be improved.

Jurgens et al. (2015) is a critical survey of geocoding methods for social media messages, particularly on techniques that use the social network of users.

An AAAI symposium in 2015 explored the applicability of semantic technologies to disaster response, its proceedings are a good starting point for learning about this topic.[17]

The online appendix at http://BigCrisisData.org/ contains pointers to selected tools and libraries for NLP in various languages.

---

[17] AAAI Spring Symposium 2015: Structured Data for Humanitarian Technologies: Perfect Fit or Overkill? March 2015. http://www.knoesis.org/hemant/symposium/aaai2015.

4

Variety: Classification and Clustering

In 2005 the Inter-Agency Standing Committee (IASC), a permanent forum including agencies from the United Nations (UN) and agencies not belonging to the UN (such as the Red Cross), introduced a number of reforms designed to improve humanitarian response. A visible reform was the establishment of the *Cluster System*,[1] which organizes large-scale multiagency humanitarian response into eleven areas of action, each one with its own responsibilities: health, protection, food security, emergency telecommunication, early recovery, education, sanitation, water and hygiene, logistics, nutrition, emergency shelter, and camp management and coordination. The Cluster System is not without critics, but it serves to structure response and it is liked by national governments because it introduces a single focal point which is accountable for a specific response area.[2]

This chapter describes methods for automatic text categorization, which allow us to make sense of heterogeneous, *varied* messages by sorting them into categories. In the same way in which coordination among humanitarian agencies is facilitated by abstracting from specific response actions to response areas, coping with typical crisis collections from social media, involving millions of messages, is made easier by abstracting from the particular (a specific message) to the general (a class of messages).

There are two broad families of classification methods: supervised and unsupervised. In *supervised classification*, we first manually classify a set of items (messages in this case) into categories using human annotators, and then use these example items to automatically learn a model for classifying new, unseen items into the same categories. In *unsupervised classification* (or

---

[1] UN OCHA: "The Cluster System" http://www.unocha.org/what-we-do/coordination-tools/cluster-coordination.

[2] UN OCHA Annual Report 2006. http://www.unocha.org/annualreport/2006/html/part1 _humanitarian.html.

clustering), we do not provide any example item classified a priori, but instead allow a method to discover groups of related items based on their similarity.

We begin with a description of the main information categories found in social media and short text messages during crises (§4.1). Next, we introduce supervised (§4.2) and unsupervised classification methods (§4.3).

4.1 Content Categories

The first question when categorizing content is how to determine which information categories to use. There are many factors that drive the design of these categories. The first and most important are the *information needs* of the users for which the categorization is done, which may include emergency managers, humanitarian relief workers, policy makers, analysts, and/or the public. Different audiences may have different information needs.

When performing automatic classification, it is also important to take into account the *capabilities of the system* that will be used to categorize the messages. Even with a good data representation and with a state-of-the-art learning method, current computational methods for text classification are more accurate in distinguishing among information categories that have clearly distinct vocabularies, than in distinguishing those having many characteristic terms in common. Other tasks may be too hard for computers, such as determining if a message is sarcastic or funny, literal or metaphoric.

When performing manual classifications, the *capabilities of humans* constraint our choice of categories in the sense that we cannot deal with a number of categories that is too large. Using nonexpert annotators imposes another constrain: categories that are too fine-grained or involve subtle distinctions cannot be reliably annotated by nonexperts. Particularly in the case of volunteer annotations, it is best to have few, easily understandable categories (more on this in Chapter 7).

Another aspect that is relevant to consider for some applications is the *availability of information*, that is, what are the categories of information the public are actually sharing and discussing in social media. All other things equal, it might be more useful to use a typology that is more fine-grained in the information categories that are more abundant and more coarse-grained in the ones that are less abundant.

Existing typologies. A number of typologies have been proposed to categorize social media messages during crises. With the exception of systematic work in ontologies for crisis information, such as the ones presented in Section 3.7, most typologies are created based on observations from a small number of crisis situations. Existing typologies for crisis-related social media described in the literature cover many dimensions for categorizing content:

(i) By factual, subjective, or emotional content: to separate between messages conveying facts (or combinations of facts and opinions), and messages conveying opinions, or emotions, such as expressions of sympathy.

(ii) By information provided: to extract particular categories of information that are useful to experts or the public for various purposes.

(iii) By information source: to select messages posted by specific groups of users, for instance, messages by non-governmental organizations or messages from official government sources.

(iv) By credibility: to filter out messages that are unlikely to be considered credible, or whose authenticity can be questioned (more on this in Chapter 8).

(v) By time: to filter messages that refer to different stages of an event (in the sense of the natural progression of a disaster), when temporal boundaries for the event are unclear.

(vi) By location: for instance, to separate eyewitness accounts from messages posted by people away from the scene.

(vii) By embedded links: some messages may point to other material, including news articles, photos, videos, or live video feeds.

(viii) By high-level environment: a taxonomy by Mileti (1999) that divides information about a disaster into that pertaining the physical environment, the built environment, and the social environment.

Table 4.1 summarizes some of these dimensions and references previous work in which they have been mentioned or described.

Different types of crisis generate different types of messages in social media. In a transversal analysis involving 26 crisis situations, Olteanu et al. (2015) found that sometimes the information type that was the most prevalent in one disaster may be present only in very small amounts in another. This variability can be traced back to several factors, including whether the events are instantaneous or progressive, whether their effects are diffuse or focalized, and whether the causes are natural hazards or human action. We come back to these and other factors that affect content production in social media in Section 9.3.

The distribution of messages into information categories is also affected by time, as expected given the particular characteristics of different stages of a disaster (Petak, 1985; Fischer, 1998). For instance, in a meteorological emergency such as a tornado, the wind speed may be the initial focus of the conversation, while more detailed/useful information may arrive later (Smith et al., 2015).

Table 4.1 *Classification of various dimensions of content posted on social media during high-impact events, including their description and references to related work.*

By factual, subjective, or emotional content

Factual information	*(Examples under "By information provided")*
Opinions	opinions, criticism (e.g., criticism of government response)
Sympathy	condolences, sympathy (Kumar et al., 2013b); concerns and condolences (Acar and Muraki, 2011), support (Hughes et al., 2014a); thanks and gratitude, support (Bruns et al., 2012; Shaw et al., 2013); gratitude, prayers (Olteanu et al., 2014); emotional support (Taylor et al., 2012); emotion-related (Qu et al., 2011)
Antipathy	*schadenfreude*, animosity against victims (e.g., because of a long-standing conflict among countries) (Imran et al., 2015)
Jokes	jokes, trolling (Metaxas and Mustafaraj, 2013); humor (Leavitt and Clark, 2014); humor or irrelevant/spam (Sreenivasan et al., 2011)

By information provided

Caution and advice	caution and advice (Imran et al., 2013b); warnings (Acar and Muraki, 2011); advice, warnings, preparation (Olteanu et al., 2014); warning, advice, caution, preparation (Vieweg et al., 2010); tips (Leavitt and Clark, 2014); safety, preparation, status, protocol (Hughes et al., 2014a); preparedness (Wukich and Mergel, 2014); advice (Bruns, 2014); advice and instructions (Shaw et al., 2013); predicting or forecasting, instructions to handle certain situations (Sreenivasan et al., 2011); safety (St. Denis et al., 2014)
Affected people	medical emergency, people trapped, person news (Caragea et al., 2011); casualties, people missing, found or seen (Imran et al., 2013b); self reports (Acar and Muraki, 2011); fatality, injury, missing (Neubig et al., 2011; Vieweg, 2012); looking for missing people (Qu et al., 2011)
Infrastructure and utilities	infrastructure damage (Imran et al., 2013b); collapsed structure (Caragea et al., 2011); built environment (Vieweg, 2012); damage, closures and services (Hughes et al., 2014a); services (St. Denis et al., 2014); collapsed structure, water shortage/sanitation, hospital/clinic services (Caragea et al., 2011); road closures and traffic conditions (Truelove et al., 2014)

Table 4.1 (*cont.*)

Needs and donations	donation of money, goods, services (Imran et al., 2013b); food/water shortage/distribution (Caragea et al., 2011); donations or volunteering (Olteanu et al., 2014); help requests, relief coordination (Qu et al., 2011); relief, donations, resources (Hughes et al., 2014a); help and fund-raising (Bruns, 2014); volunteer information (Vieweg et al., 2010); help requests (Acar and Muraki, 2011; Neubig et al., 2011); requests and offers of donations (Purohit et al., 2014a,b)
Nonhuman animals	animal management (Vieweg et al., 2010), lost and found pets (White et al., 2014; Barrenechea et al., 2015a); animal evacuation (White and Palen, 2015)
Weather and status updates	weather updates (Vieweg, 2012); status (St. Denis et al., 2014); smoke, ash (Truelove et al., 2014)
Other useful information	hospital/clinic service, water sanitation (Caragea et al., 2011); reports about environment (Acar and Muraki, 2011); consequences (Olteanu et al., 2014)

By information source

Eyewitnesses and/or public	citizen reporters, members of the community (Metaxas and Mustafaraj, 2013); eyewitnesses (Bruns et al., 2012; Diakopoulos et al., 2012; Kumar et al., 2013b; Olteanu et al., 2014); local, personally connected (Starbird et al., 2010); local individuals (Starbird et al., 2012; Vieweg et al., 2010); local perspective, on the ground reports (Thomson et al., 2012); direct experience (personal narrative and eyewitness reports) (Shaw et al., 2013); direct observation, direct impact, relayed observation (Truelove et al., 2014); public (St. Denis et al., 2014)
Government	administration/government (Olteanu et al., 2014); police and fire services (Hughes et al., 2014a); government (Bruns, 2014); news organization and authorities (Metaxas and Mustafaraj, 2013); public institutions (Thomson et al., 2012); police (Denef et al., 2013); government (Bruns et al., 2012); public service agencies, flood specific agencies (Starbird et al., 2010)
NGOs	nongovernmental organizations (de Choudhury et al., 2012; Olteanu et al., 2014); nonprofit organizations (Thomson et al., 2012); faith-based organizations (Starbird et al., 2010)

(*cont.*)

Table 4.1 *(cont.)*

News media	news organizations and authorities, blogs (Metaxas and Mustafaraj, 2013), journalists, media, bloggers (de Choudhury et al., 2012); news organizations (Olteanu et al., 2014); professional news reports (Leavitt and Clark, 2014); media (Bruns, 2014); traditional media (print, television, radio), alternative media, freelance journalists (Thomson et al., 2012); blogs, newscrawler bots, local, national, and alternative media (Starbird et al., 2010); media sharing (news media updates, multimedia) (Shaw et al., 2013)

By credibility

Credible information	credibility (Castillo et al., 2013); credible topics (Canini et al., 2011); content credibility (Gupta and Kumaraguru, 2012); users and content credibility (Gupta et al., 2014); source credibility (Thomson et al., 2012); real images (Gupta et al., 2013)
Rumors	rumor (Hughes et al., 2014a; Castillo et al., 2013)
Corrections	rumor mitigation (St. Denis et al., 2014); rumor refutation (Castillo et al., 2013)

By time

Pre-phase/ preparedness	posted before an actual event occurs, helpful for the preparedness phase of emergency management: pre-disaster, early information (Iyengar et al., 2011; Chowdhury et al., 2013)
Impact-phase/ response	posted during the impact phase of an event, helpful for the response phase of emergency management: during-disaster (Iyengar et al., 2011; Chowdhury et al., 2013)
Post-phase/ recovery	posted after the impact of an event, helpful during the recovery phase: postdisaster information (Chowdhury et al., 2013; Iyengar et al., 2011)

By location

Ground Zero	information from Ground Zero (victims reports, bystanders) (de Longueville et al., 2009; Ao et al., 2014)
Near-by areas	information originating close to the affected areas (de Longueville et al., 2009)
Outsiders	information coming from other parts of world, sympathizers (Kumar et al., 2013b); distant witness (in the sense of Carvin, 2013); location inference (Ikawa et al., 2012); remote crowd (Starbird et al., 2012); nonlocals (Starbird et al., 2010; Thomson et al., 2012)

Olteanu et al. (2015) observed a general pattern of progression of information in disasters, with messages of caution and advice arriving first, followed by sympathy and support, followed at the end of the first day or on the second day by messages describing infrastructure damage and affected individuals, followed by useful messages covering various topics, followed from about the third day onward by messages regarding donations and volunteering. Parsons et al. (2015) also observed a general progression of themes following known stages in disaster life cycles.

4.2 Supervised Classification

There are three main scenarios for classification: binary, multiclass, and multi-label. *Binary classification* refers to a categorization into two disjoint classes: for instance, a message can be related to a certain crisis situation, or not. *Multiclass classification* refers to categorization into a series of disjoint classes: for instance a message during a tornado can be about providing advice, soliciting donations, reporting the weather conditions, or other categories. *Multilabel classification* refers to categorization into classes that do not need to be disjoint: for instance, a message can be simultaneously about donations of food and clothes – performing automatic multilabel classification is also referred to as *tagging*, in the understanding that a message can have more than one tag.

There are many ways of performing automatic classification of messages. A straightforward, but ineffective approach, is to use keyword-based rules to separate messages into categories. For instance, a message containing the word "shelter" or "camp" can be associated to the category "emergency shelter." This may work for certain information categories that have a small, well-defined, unambiguous set of terms that are highly discriminative, but in general they are ineffective for categories that lack those terms (Melville et al., 2013).

A more robust approach is to use statistical methods such as supervised classification (described on this section) or unsupervised classification (discussed on the next section). We present a high-level overview of these methods to explain them in their application to social media during emergencies, the interested reader can consult the material suggested in Section 4.5 for an in-depth exposition.

A supervised classification system is based on a *supervised learning* method, which is a statistical method that creates a general statistical description of a class of items, and/or learns statistical properties that discriminate among different classes of items. The process by which these statistical descriptions or models are created automatically is known as statistical *machine learning*.

Four main elements can be identified in a supervised classification system:

(i) the labeled examples from which the statistical model is created, known as training examples;

(ii) the method used to select the dimensions used for representing the elements, known as feature selection;

(iii) the algorithm used for creating the statistical model, known as the learning scheme; and

(iv) the evaluation metrics used to evaluate and report the performance of the system.

Training examples. Supervised learning methods require messages for which the label, that is, the specific information category, is already known. These messages are usually labeled by experts or volunteers. This manual labeling is orders of magnitude slower than what the automatic classification system can achieve, but it may also be considered more precise.

The number of labeled messages required to train a system depends on many factors, including the number of categories into which messages have to be classified, the distribution of messages into those categories, and the variability of messages inside each category. Situations with many categories, with skewed distributions of messages (e.g., categories having very few examples), and with broad categories containing many different kinds of messages, need a relatively larger number of training examples.

In practice, learning a model that can accurately place short messages into one category, requires hundreds or thousands of examples for that category, depending on the desired level of accuracy. More examples yield better results in general, with diminishing results after a certain point (see, e.g., Matykiewicz and Pestian, 2012). Training set sizes reported in the literature for training supervised classifiers on social media or text messages in crises range from hundreds (Yin et al., 2012) to thousands (Imran et al., 2014a) or tens of thousands (Melville et al., 2013) of elements.

As important as the number of training examples, is that they are sampled from the same distribution as the messages that we want to classify. This is a key assumption for many statistical machine learning methods, and indeed it has been observed that the accuracy of models created using training data from one crisis decreases when applied to a different crisis, or when applied to the same crisis but at a different point in time (Imran et al., 2014b). However, given the cost of creating large training sets, there are a series of methods that perform *domain adaptation* or *domain transfer*, which adapt a model created from one dataset to make it useful in another (Dai et al., 2007).

Feature selection. As we described on Section 2.4, messages are converted to a format suitable for algorithms (including machine learning algorithms) by means of feature extraction. Even if messages are brief, and even if aggressive stopword removal, normalization and stemming/lemmatization operations are applied, the feature space in which they can be represented is typically high dimensional. For instance, it could have one dimension for every word plus one dimension for every possible sequence of two words, which for collections of text messages of moderate to large size, quickly yields tens of thousands of dimensions. This may not only increase the amount of computational resources required for the data analysis, but it also increases the chances of overfitting the training data. Conversely, feature selection often yields faster and better classifiers.

Feature selection methods aim at finding a subset of the input features that, for a given purpose, represents the data as well as the entire set of features. Feature selection methods tend to discard features or groups of features that are redundant (e.g., highly correlated with other features) or irrelevant (i.e., not related to the target label).

A simple example of a feature selection criteria is *pointwise mutual information*, in which each single feature is evaluated in isolation in terms of its mutual information with respect to a class.[3] Using this criteria, if a word appears with the same frequency in elements of the training set irrespective of their label, then its mutual information with respect to the label is zero, the word is considered irrelevant and its respective feature discarded.

Feature selection based on analyzing the utility of one feature at a time, and then greedily picking a set made of those features with the largest utility, are not guaranteed to find an optimal subset of features, because of statistical dependencies among features (e.g., two features in isolation may each one be irrelevant, but combined might be relevant). For feature selection methods see, e.g., Guyon and Elisseeff (2003) and references therein.

Learning algorithms. After features have been extracted and selected from the training examples, a machine learning algorithm can be applied. Machine

---

[3] The pointwise mutual information between a term t and a category c is $\mathrm{pmi}(t, c) = \log(p(t, c)/p(t)p(c))$ where $p(t, c)$ is the probability of a message belonging to the category and containing the term, $p(t)$ is the probability of a message containing the term, and $p(c)$ is the probability of a message belonging to a category.

learning algorithms have two modes of operation: learning (or training) and labeling (or testing). The first mode is usually more time-consuming and complex than the second one, which is expected to be fast, given that it will be applied to a large set of data.

There are many supervised classification algorithms that have been used for text classification. They include, among others, naïve Bayes, Support Vector Machines (SVM), logistic regression, decision trees, and random forests; for a survey, see Sebastiani (2002).

The choice of a specific method is to a large extent dependent on the specific problem setting. In most cases, researchers in the literature tend to test two or three different algorithms, and then decide which one is better for their problem setting given their evaluation metrics. The choice of an algorithm may also depend on practicalities such as the availability of an efficient and robust implementation in a given programming language or a given platform. For instance, *ESA* (Yin et al., 2012; Cameron et al., 2012) uses naïve Bayes and SVM; *EMERSE* (Caragea et al., 2011) and Neubig et al. (2011) use SVM; *AIDR* (Imran et al., 2014a) uses random forests; *Tweedr* (Ashktorab et al., 2014) uses logistic regression. While in most cases algorithms are used to predict a single label for each element, adaptations of these algorithms for the multilabel case are sometimes employed (e.g., Caragea et al., 2011).

Supervised learning methods typically produce parametrized models, in which the only difference between two models is a vector of parameters, coefficients, or weights. In general, learning algorithms are often used as "black boxes" in which those parameters do not need to be inspected. However, there are cases in which we seek to understand how specific aspects of the input are related to the output label. Verma et al. (2011), for instance, observe that the messages that contribute the most to situational awareness are also those that are expressed using objective (as opposed to subjective) language. Following this observation, they create a *stacked classifier* in which at one level certain characteristics of the message are modeled (e.g., by having a classifier that classifies messages as objective or subjective) and at the next level these characteristics are combined with other characteristics (e.g., writing styles such as formal or informal), and with features from the message itself. Verma et al. (2011) find that this approach performs better than directly using the input features on their dataset.

Along the same lines, in some cases there is background knowledge that can guide the creation of the model. For instance, Melville et al. (2013) use the pooling multinomials method (Melville et al., 2009). Pooling multinomials takes as input labels on items *and on features*. Following the example from the beginning of this section, if a priori we know that the word "shelter" is a good indicator of the category "emergency shelter," then instead of adding a hard rule that the word "shelter" automatically implies this class, we can pass this information to the learning algorithm to use it as part of the creation of the statistical models for the different classes.

Evaluation metrics. Comparing different classification systems is not a trivial task. With some exceptions, there are few reference collections in which to perform comparative evaluations.[4] As other information processing operations, classification is usually measured in terms of efficiency and effectiveness. Efficiency in this case is basically a matter of the speed of the system. Effectiveness can be measured in a number of ways, and depends on many factors, including the training data, learning scheme, target categories, and in some cases the language for which a classifier is built Zielinski et al. (2012).

A key concept to understand the effectiveness of an automatic classification system is its *confusion matrix*, which is a table representing correct and incorrect classifications. For instance, let's assume a classifier has been created to distinguish between messages containing information about "people," "infrastructure," or "other," and that we have external information that allows us to validate messages that actually belong to each of these categories (e.g., expert assessments over a subset of the data). In this case, the confusion matrix would be a 3×3 numerical matrix with the following structure:

	Actually about people	Actually about infrastructure	Actually about other
Classified as "people"	Pp	Ip	Op
Classified as "infrastructure"	Pi	Ii	Oi
Classified as "other"	Po	Io	Oo

Accuracy is probably the simpler metric for classification effectiveness. It corresponds to the probability that an item is classified correctly: $(Pp + Ii + Oo)/(Pp + Pi + Po + Ip + Ii + Io + Op + Oi + Oo)$. It is the sum of the values in the diagonal of the confusion matrix, divided by the sum of all cells. Classification accuracies reported in the literature of social media during crises range from 0.6 to 0.9 (Imran et al., 2015). Accuracy can be

---

[4] CrisisLex: collections and lexicons for analyzing crisis-related social media. http://crisislex .org/.

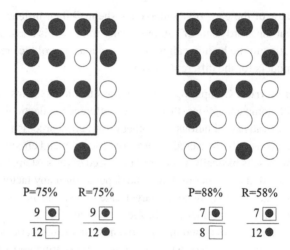

Figure 4.1 Visual depiction of precision and recall, comparing two hypothetical systems. Messages are represented by circles, and the messages classified as being relevant for a given class are depicted by large rectangles. Messages that are actually relevant are filled/black; irrelevant messages are empty/white. The system on the right has more precision (it has only one false positive), but it has lower recall (it has five false negatives).

misleading when dealing with imbalanced classes. For instance, suppose there are 100 messages in total, out of which one is about people, one is about infrastructure, and 98 are about other aspects. In this case, a classifier that always says "other" has $Po = 1$, $Io = 1$, $Oo = 98$ and all other values 0, which yields an accuracy of 98%, even if the classifier is blindly outputting always the same category.

Precision and recall are measures that can deal better with imbalanced cases. *Precision* (P) is a measure of specificity. It corresponds to the probability that an item that we have classified as belonging to a class, actually belongs to that class. Precision is measured on a per-class basis. The precision for the class "people" in the previous example would be: $Pp/(Pp + Ip + Op)$, that is, out of everything that was classified as "people," the fraction that was actually about people. *Recall* (R) is a measure of sensitivity. Recall is also measured on a per-class basis. It corresponds to the probability that an item that actually belongs to a class is classified by us as belonging to that class. The recall for the class "people" in the example given earlier, would be $Pp/(Pp + Pi + Po)$, that is, out of every element that was about people, the fraction that we actually classified as "people." A visual depiction of precision and recall is shown in Figure 4.1.

A popular metric combining both is their harmonic mean, known as the F_1 measure or simply F measure:

$$F = F_1 = 2\frac{PR}{P + R}.$$

A more general metric for combining precision and recall is the F_β measure, defined as:

$$F_\beta = (1 + \beta^2)\frac{PR}{\beta^2 P + R}.$$

By varying the parameter β we can achieve different trade-offs. For instance, F_2 favors recall at the expense of precision, and $F_{0.5}$ favors precision at the expense of recall.

Some supervised machine learning methods generate an output that is not a category label, but instead a score which is related to the probability that an element belongs to a class (or a set of classes). In this case, the score is usually thresholded at a particular value (e.g., zero) so that items with scores above the threshold are labeled as belonging to a class, and the items with scores below the threshold are labeled as not belonging to it. In these cases, there is more than once choice of threshold, which yields different trade-offs of precision and recall. In order to compare two systems irrespectively of the chosen threshold, a standard approach is to compute the area under the Receiver Operating Characteristic (ROC) curve. The ROC curve maps the performance of a classifier for every choice of threshold to a point in the plane, in which the false positive rate obtained with that threshold goes in the X axis, and the true positive rate in the Y axis. When the area under the curve (AUC) in the interval [0, 1] is 0.5, the classifier is not better than a random classifier, and when it is 1.0, the classifier is perfect. For an overview on the usage of ROC curves to compare classification systems, see Fawcett (2004).

4.3 Unsupervised Classification / Clustering

Clustering means grouping similar items together. Clustering is an *unsupervised machine learning method*, which is a large class of exploratory methods that search for patterns or structure in unlabeled data.

The input to a clustering algorithm is a set of items, in our case, vectors representing messages, and a way of measuring how similar two messages are, that is, a similarity function. A frequently used similarity function for text is the *cosine similarity* (see, e.g., Baeza-Yates and Ribeiro-Neto, 2011, ch. 6). In most cases, the input should also include the desired number of classes, although there are clustering methods that can apply some criterion to determine a "good" number of classes.

The output of a clustering algorithm is a mapping from items to classes, in which items in the same class are expected to be similar to each other, and items in different classes are expected to be different from each other. Depending on the specific algorithm used, the classes do not need to be disjoint, that is, a message can belong to more than one class. In this case, we speak of *soft clustering*, in contrast with *hard clustering*, where each message must belong to one and only one class.

Example hard clustering method: k-means. A popular clustering algorithm for documents is *k-means*, which is a centroid-based method. This algorithm operates by iterating between two steps. For the initialization, items can be assigned randomly to classes. In the first step, the algorithm computes the *centroid* of each class of items, that is, the item that minimizes the average distance to all of the items on that class. In the second step, documents are reassigned to the class whose centroid is most similar to them. The first and second step are repeated in sequence a number of times, until a certain stop criterion is reached. For instance, it can be done for a fixed number of iterations, or until the average distances to centroids stops decreasing, or do not decrease more than a certain amount per iteration. There are many other clustering algorithms in addition to k-means; for an overview, see Zaki and Meira (2014, part III).

Example soft clustering method: LDA. Latent Dirichlet Allocation (LDA), introduced by Blei et al. (2003), is often used to create a soft clustering of documents into a predefined number of topics. It assumes that every document reflects a combination of topics, in which the number of relevant topics for a document are a relatively small fraction of all the possible topics. It also assumes that every topic can be characterized by a small set of characteristic words that are highly probable for that topic, and that most words have the same probability across all topics.

LDA is a probabilistic model that considers documents as a result of a probabilistic process. Each document is defined by a probability distribution over topics, and each topic is defined as a probability distribution over words. To create each word in a document, we just need to sample from the topics according to the topic-distribution of that document, and then sample from the words of that topic according to that topic word-distribution.

The "L" in LDA stands for latent, which reflects the fact that while we can observe directly the words in each document, we do not know the topic-distributions or the word-distributions. These distribution need to be estimated using a probabilistic estimation method, such as Gibbs sampling (Wei and Croft, 2006). The "D" stands for the Dirichlet distribution, which is used to incorporate an assumption of sparsity, that is, that each document has few relevant topics and that each topic has few characteristic words. LDA is closely related to a method in Information Retrieval known as Probabilistic Latent Semantic Indexing (PLSI), described by Hofmann (1999).

The output of LDA is a probability distribution over topics for each of the documents. This distribution can be thresholded to read it as a soft clustering assignment, for instance, every document having a probability larger than a certain threshold of belonging to a topic, is assigned to that topic. Interestingly, words that have a high probability in the word distribution of a topic can be used as human-readable "summmaries" for the topic.

Clustering granularity. In the context of social media messages during crises, there are two prototypical scenarios in which clustering can be used. In some cases, we want to perform clustering to group together messages that refer to the same aspect of the crisis. In this case, typically a few large clusters are created, which we call the coarse-granularity setting. In other cases, we want to perform clustering to group together messages that convey basically the same information. In this case, typically many small clusters are created, which we call the fine-granularity setting.

A *coarse-granularity setting* (few large clusters) is used by Kireyev et al. (2009), which applies LDA to data from a 2009 Earthquake in Indonesia. The output of LDA includes broad topics that cover different aspects of the crisis such as one topic in which high-probability words are {*tsunami, disaster, relief, earthquake*}, and other topics represented by words {*dead, bodies, missing, victims*} and {*aid, help, money, relief*}. Nelson and Pottenger (2013) describe the usage of LDA for a similar application involving SMS messages in a coarse-granularity setting. Karandikar (2010) shows that LDA can be applied to compare data across different disasters (eight in their case), recovering important keywords which are characteristic of each disaster. Coarse-granularity clustering is also used for event detection, for example, by Berlingerio et al. (2013) and others, as described in Section 6.4.

A *fine-granularity setting* (many small clusters) can be used to help reduce the number of social media messages that need to be processed/examined by humans, for instance, by displaying multiple equivalent messages as a single item instead of multiple ones. This is the approach used by *CrisisTracker* (Rogstadius et al., 2013), which is a crowdsourced social media curation system for disaster awareness. The system, which collects data from Twitter based on predefined filters (i.e., keywords, bounding box), groups these messages into many *stories*, which are small clusters of tweets. These stories are then curated/classified by humans, which is much more efficient than repeatedly classifying messages that are almost equivalent to each other. The specific clustering method employed in this case is Locality-Sensitive Hashing (LSH), an efficient technique that uses hash functions to detect near-duplicates in data (Charikar, 2002).

4.4 Research Problems

Adapting/transferring classification models to new situations. A recurrent theme in the sociology of disaster literature is that, despite their superficial differences, disasters tend to have many elements in common with each other. Being able to reuse human-labeled and classification models can be very useful to produce results early on when a new disaster strikes. Indeed, Li et al. (2015) describe a domain adaptation approach that can be applied to Twitter data for disaster response.

Performing interactive taxonomy design. Designing content categories is an art that is difficult to master. Furthermore, sudden-onset disasters and emergency situations do not leave enough time to spend on creating new categorizations. The main source of uncertainty is that, while we may guess a priori which topics will appear in social media, the relative prominence of different topics is hard or impossible to estimate. Adaptive, interactive approaches in which experts interact with algorithms, data, and annotators to rapidly converge into an appropriate typology, could be very useful to accelerate the construction of an appropriate typology for a crisis.

Ranking. After categorizing messages, some categories may be very large; in this case one can attempt to summarize the category or to pick a few representatives of it. One form of choosing such representatives is by ranking, for example, by sorting elements in decreasing order of importance. Ranking is a very difficult problem in Information Retrieval; on the crisis domain, there are relatively few works dealing with ranking (Li et al., 2012).

4.5 Further Reading

For a high-level data mining perspective, Zaki and Meira (2014, parts III and IV) present algorithms for clustering and classification.

Ingersoll et al. (2013, ch. 6 and 7) focuses on text clustering and classification from a practical/practitioner perspective. Baeza-Yates and Ribeiro-Neto (2011, ch. 8) describes various algorithms on text classification, including aspects of feature selection and how to evaluate text classification methods. Joachims (2002) describes the general setting of text classification in its initial chapters, then presents in detail how to use Support Vector Machines (SVMs) for classifying text.

Many of the methods described on this section can be applied to other types of data beyond brief text messages, including blog and news content (Leetaru and Schrodt, 2014).

5

Virality: Networks and Information Propagation

The phrase "Twitter revolution" was coined in 2009 to describe the role of Twitter in "viral" calls to demonstrations against fraud in elections in Moldova and Iran. Since then, the rapid propagation of information through social media and mobile text messages has played an important role in the recruitment for protests in the Arab world, Europe, and America (González-Bailón et al., 2011). This rapid propagation has also been observed during disasters; for instance reposting activity has been observed to increase significantly in these situations (Starbird and Palen, 2010). A distinctive feature that is a consequence of these processes is the appearance of explosive "bursts" of messages that reach large masses of people in a relatively short time frame.

Sociograms, which are graphs in which nodes represent people and edges represent social connections, started to be recorded and analyzed systematically in the early 1930s (Moreno, 1934). Currently, sociograms having hundreds of millions of nodes, which we now identify with *social networks*, continue to fuel the growth of an enormous body of research that includes work by sociologists, psychologists, communication scholars, physicists, computer scientists, and interdisciplinary teams. In addition to holding connections among users, current social networking sites allow the creation of *information networks*, graphs in which nodes receive and disseminate information to other nodes through links.

Social networks are a defining element of social media, and graph theory provides a theoretical foundation for studying social networks, including aspects such as the mechanism for the formation of online connections and the propagation of information online.

This chapter studies two interrelated aspects of social media during crises from a graph-theory perspective. First, there are structural properties of social and information networks that allow us, for instance, to measure certain properties about the users or groups of users who create or propagate information (§5.1). Second, there are particular types of *information cascades* – the history

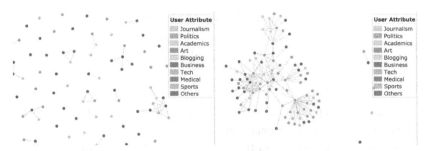

Figure 5.1 Comparison of an interaction-based network of social media users around the 2011 movements of Occupy Chicago (left) and Occupy Los Angeles (right). Figure from Sheth et al. (2014), reproduced with permission from the authors.

of propagation of a particular content on a network (§5.2) that can help us, for instance, determine the characteristics of messages, groups of messages, and users (§5.3).

5.1 Crisis Information Networks

Social media and other online systems include social networks in two ways: explicitly or implicit, also known as articulated or behavioral, respectively.

Explicit (articulated) social networks are created by people specifying who they are connected with, for instance by adding someone as a "friend," or by "following" someone in social media. These connections may include actual friends, family, acquaintances, colleagues, celebrities, and a large spectrum of people.

Implicit (behavioral) social networks are inferred from communication patterns, for instance, when people message or share content posted by others. Implicit networks may better reflect the online activities of a person than explicit networks which may include "inactive" connections.

Implicit networks are particularly interesting in the crisis scenario because many exchanges happen among people who were not connected before the crisis; indeed, crises can catalyze the creation of new (explicit) connections. We must keep in mind, however, that these are proxies for actual social connections: none of the two can be considered as an equivalent to the personal networks created by sociologists and psychologists through direct observation and questioning of participants (boyd and Crawford, 2012).

Figure 5.1, from Sheth et al. (2014), depicts two social networks emerging around users participating in the discussion about the 2011 Occupy movement in the United States. The left one corresponds to users in Chicago, and the right one to users in Los Angeles. Each node corresponds to a social media user, and links correspond to implicit connections: they associate users who have interacted with each other in some way, for instance, by sending each other a message, by mentioning each other, or by reposting content from each other. These examples allow us to introduce some general characteristics of graphs.

Connected components. In this case, the graph corresponding to Chicago has many *connected components*, which are sets of mutually reachable nodes. Furthermore, many nodes in the Chicago graph have no connections at all. In contrast, the graph corresponding to Los Angeles has most of its nodes participating in a single connected component. The existence of a "giant" connected component (i.e., a connected component having the majority of the nodes) once a sufficient number of edges exist is a characteristic feature of many theoretical models of graph growth, and it is observed in real-world graphs across many different domains (Bollobás and Riordan, 2003; Leskovec et al., 2005).

In directed graphs we further distinguish between weakly and strongly connected components, in which *strongly connected components* are such that all nodes belonging to one of them can reach each other by following directed links.

Degree distribution. We can also observe that the number of edges per node, i.e., the *degree* of the nodes, in one of the graphs of Figure 5.1 is relatively small, often zero, while in the other graph most nodes have at least one edge, and some have many more than that.

We also note that in the case of Los Angeles there are a few nodes that have many connections, that is, they have very high degree, whereas most nodes have a relatively small degree. This is a structural property common to all naturally occurring social networks, and places these graphs into a very specific class of network: those that have scale-free properties (Barabási, 2002; Watts, 2004). *Scale-free networks* have a skewed degree distribution, where a small minority of nodes have a very large degree, while the vast majority of nodes have a small degree.

The emergence of scale-free networks is usually explained through "rich-get-richer" kind of growth (also known as preferential attachment, which is a type of multiplicative process or Yule process), in which nodes having many connections actually acquire new connections at a faster rate than nodes having fewer connections (Barabási and Albert, 1999; Bollobás and Riordan, 2003).

Indeed, it may even be the case that social networks formed after an event have degree distributions that are even more skewed. Bhamidi et al. (2015) propose a "superstar" model for event networks, in which a single node (for instance, a user that is well known, or that provides novel or useful information) gains edges at a constant rate while the remaining nodes gain edges following preferential attachment. This phenomenon has also been observed in networks emerging after a crisis event (Mendoza et al., 2010; Bhamidi et al., 2015), where certain users gain prominence, for instance, in the sense of gaining many followers or being quoted very often. Bruns et al. (2012) also observed that a few accounts are involved in many connections in an implicit crisis network (in their case, mostly the accounts of large media organizations), while at the same time, there are many implicit connections among individuals that do not involve mainstream media, governments, or any large organization.

Centrality. In general, an heterogeneous network in which some nodes are very "well connected" and others not, which is the case of most social networks, lends itself to a type of analysis that attempts to classify users into different categories according to their position in the network relative to others. In a social setting, this corresponds to intuitive notions of what is a "well-connected" person.

The problem is that there are many definitions of being "well-connected" that match different intuitions. For instance, simply having many connections (e.g., many friends) can mean one is well-connected, except that it could be argued that being connected to "important" people might be worth more than having many connections. In that respect, an alternative definition is that being well-connected is having many connections to people that, in turn, are also well-connected. Another alternative states that being well-connected means reaching to many different groups of people, that is, being able to "bridge" social circles that do not often interact with each other.

It turns out that all of these definitions have been formalized in graph theoretical terms, along with many other similar definitions. Collectively, these are known as *centrality* measures for nodes on a graph. The most obvious centrality measure is the *degree*, that is, the number of connections of a node. The centrality measure that captures the intuition of "a well-connected node has many connections to other well-connected nodes" is known as *eigenvector centrality* and was introduced by Katz (1953) and popularized by the PageRank algorithm (Page et al., 1998). The metric that captures the ability of being the best "bridge" to connect people that are socially far apart is known as *betweenness centrality*; many other centrality metrics exist (see, e.g., Boldi and Vigna, 2014).

Centrality and crises. High-centrality users might be good sources of crisis-relevant information, and there are some studies in which this has been already observed. Sutton et al. (2012) study a set of accounts in Twitter corresponding to government agencies in the United States, such as @*FEMA* (the official account of the Federal Emergency Management Administration) or @*WhiteHouse* (the official account of the U.S. Presidency). The study covers the immediate aftermath of the 2010 Deepwater Horizon oil spill, one of the largest accidental marine oil spills in history. They observed that node degrees indeed have a skewed distribution, possibly a log-normal (i.e., the logarithm of the number of followers of government accounts follows a normal distribution). The accounts with the larger number of followers were also in general the most prominent institutions and more central in the graph in other ways. They also noted that accounts corresponding to institutions at different levels (e.g., federal vs. state) and accounts corresponding to difference sectors (e.g., health vs. law enforcement) in general did not interact with each other through social media, while they did interact with other institutional accounts of the same level or the same sector.

Similar results regarding node degree distribution and graph centrality of key organizations were obtained by Zhang and Comfort (2014) after analyzing data from Sina Weibo during the 2014 earthquake in Ya'an, China.

Purohit et al. (2014d) compute eigenvector centrality on a topic-specific user interaction (implicit) graph, to measure the influence of different users. In the graph used in their experiments, two users are connected if one of them replies, mentions, or reposts a message from the other on a given topic (e.g., medical needs), and edge weights are proportional to the number of interactions. Users who have high eigenvector centrality can be considered "experts" or "influential users" on the topic. These groups can be further refined by using a set of keywords found in the profile of users (e.g., "journalist" or "NGO").

Graph evolution and crises. It is important to note that graphs evolve over time, connections are created and destroyed, and new nodes appear. This means that centrality measures also evolve over time. For instance, among the most central social media accounts during a disaster we find a mixture of high-centrality accounts (e.g., media sources and prominent journalists), plus accounts that previously had very low centrality. Sometimes an eyewitness or an emerging news curator can be one of the most relevant sources of information during a crisis, even if that person did not have many connections or followers before the crisis started. In that sense, an analysis of social media during crisis does not necessarily need to be limited to official social media accounts, or to accounts that already have a certain prominence. Ideally, it should give special consideration to the network of connections and/or interactions that is formed during the crisis, as opposed to using only the preexisting network.

Crises may affect the way a social graph evolves. A study by Phan and Airoldi (2015) compared the connections and posting behavior of college students in universities affected by the 2008 Hurricane Ike, against the same characteristics in college students of unaffected universities. Their study spanned about three years of data. Among their main findings, they note that in terms of number of friends, both groups had similar behavior. However, students in universities affected by the hurricane had a stronger tendency to become friends with friends-of-friends. This is known as a *triadic closure*, the tendency to close "triangles" in evolving social networks (Easley and Kleinberg, 2010, sec. 3.1). Similarly, they also sent about the same number of messages to others, but students in affected universities tended to send messages to a smaller number of recipients. Both findings suggest that the effect of this disaster in the online social network of the students affected by it, was to create more tightly knit communities with stronger connections among their members. Kogan et al. (2015) observed a similar effect of dense network formation in social media among those affected by a disaster, but only during the response phase, not before or after. Bagrow et al. (2011, figure 3) showed a similar result for graphs describing mobile phone calls.

Other graphs. The structural analysis of social networks during crises does not need to be limited to networks in which nodes are users and connections are interactions among them. Other graphs can be defined and analyzed in similar ways. For instance, Le et al. (2014) study a *hashtag graph*, in which each node is a hashtag, and a link connects two hashtags if they co-occur – if they appear together – in at least one message. Their work focuses on the 2014 Boston bombings and shows that these graphs are also scale-free, and that they are also useful to follow the development of this crisis. Before the attacks, there was a strong co-occurrence of *#bostonmarathon* with *#marathonmonday*, followed by a strong co-occurrence of *#bostonmarathon* and *#prayforboston* immediately after the bombing, followed by a strong co-occurrence of *#boston* and *#lockdown* during the manhunt for the bombing suspects. Meladianos et al. (2015) study a similar graph that involves all words included in messages, not only hashtags.

A different graph is defined by Baba et al. (2015), who study a *co-retweet graph*, which is a bipartite graph in which nodes are users and tweets, and edges connect users with the messages they have posted or retweeted.

5.2 Cascading of Crisis Information

The possibility of reaching a potentially huge audience through word-of-mouth is a characteristic of social media that distinguishes it from other forms of online communication. It might be one of the main reasons why some people use social media at all during crises, for instance, this potential audience might be of particular interest to public information officers from emergency relief organizations.

The potential for content that "goes viral" has fascinated communications professionals across a wide range of disciplines, including product marketers, political campaigners, brand managers, and journalists. In its connection to the theory of information propagation in networks, there is ample evidence that viral propagation online actually resembles some of the models that have been proposed to abstract it, for instance, that people are more prone to act or propagate information if they receive it from multiple sources – until they receive the information from too many sources, at which point they may consider further propagating it superfluous (Spiro et al., 2012). At the same time, so far there is little evidence that viral phenomena can be engineered purposefully (Chen et al., 2013). In other words, the stage at which we are is to a large extent one of describing and analyzing information cascades, more than being able to provide a "recipe" for creating large cascades.

The main object of study of this type of descriptive research are *propagation histories*, which are trees describing how a piece of information is repeated by a population of users. The root of the tree is the original poster of a piece of information, each node corresponds to a user who shared this piece of information, and the parent of each node in the tree is the node to which the information propagation can be attributed. Figure 5.2 depicts one such tree, starting from an initial posting and continuing through reposts of information. The tree depicted here corresponds to an extraordinary case, as across all social media platforms for which data is available, most items do not propagate at all or have propagation histories that involve only two nodes: the original poster and a single sharer (Goel et al., 2012).

Cascade sizes are quite unpredictable, among other reasons, because the population of users is highly heterogeneous. A cascade may be large if it reaches a well-connected node that is willing to continue the propagation further, or may be small if that does not happen. Predictions may be possible when observing the development of a cascade over time, including its shape (Watts et al., 2007); in other words, it is easier to predict if and how a cascade will *continue* than whether a cascade will appear at all (Cheng et al., 2014).

Crisis cascades. As we discussed on Section 2.1, there are entertainment and political events that are much more visible in social media than disasters. For instance, Sakaki et al. (2010, 2013) showed that in comparison with cascades about a marketing event launching a video game, cascades of information about an earthquake and a typhoon were, on average, shorter. However, *during*

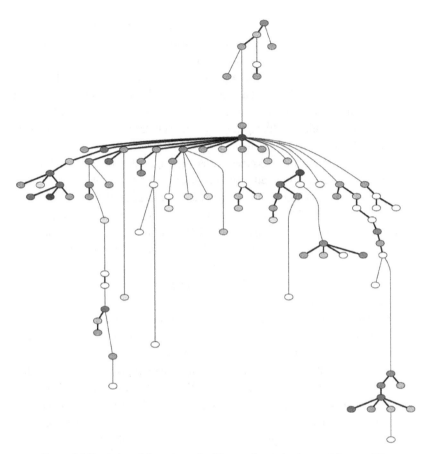

Figure 5.2 Depiction of the propagation history of a posting in a social networking site; the posting contained a photo from an environmental campaign. Every node is a user who posted or reposted this photo; the root of the tree is the original poster. Darker nodes are users with more followers, lighter nodes are users with less followers. Time progresses top to bottom, with edges representing reposting. Short edges are same-day reposts, and longer edges are delayed reposts. The entire propagation history is 60 days long. Figure from Ienco et al. (2010) reproduced with permission from the authors.

a disaster, messages related to the crisis are shared more than "off-topic" messages (Starbird and Palen, 2010; Sutton et al., 2013).

From an emergency response perspective, generating large cascades is important, particularly for warning messages, because people tend to verify with those around them if they should actually do something with respect to a warning, and may ignore it until they see others taking action (Sorensen, 2000).

According to Spiro et al. (2012), warning messages about hazards are shared faster than other messages, which may contribute to the fact that they are also shared more (i.e., generate larger cascades). Hui et al. (2012) and Tyshchuk et al. (2012) studied messages broadcasted in social media during the lockdown following an armed robbery at a university in the United States. Their studies show a dramatic difference between warning messages asking students and staff to "stay in shelter," which generated relatively large information cascades, and the "all clear" message, which did not.

In addition to hazard messages, other messages that have been shown to generate large cascades are advisory messages of caution (before a crisis happens), and those containing imperative, clear messages telling people what to do (Sutton et al., 2013). Messages from established media organizations are also shared more (Starbird and Palen, 2010; Bruns et al., 2012). The same happens with messages from accounts that have many followers (Starbird and Palen, 2010; Sutton et al., 2013), which highlight the importance, for emergency response organizations, of building a community around them in social media between crises.

The factors that induce people to share a message they see in social media can be studied systematically through user studies. Li et al. (2014) found that, among other factors, crisis messages that expressed anxiety (worries, concerns) and that were well-written and easy to read, were more likely to be shared than other messages. Chen and Sakamoto (2013, 2014) observed that messages expressing strong negative feelings were more likely to be shared than other messages. They also noted that people were more likely to share crisis messages if they were asked to imagine that they were near the affected area – hinting that maybe people who feel closer to a disaster are more prone to propagating disaster-related messages. A preliminary conclusion one could draw from these works, is that sharing behavior is promoted or inhibited by different emotional states of the people who receive these messages, or by the emotional content of the messages themselves. This, in turn, may contribute to the spread of false rumors: their propagation depends as much on emotional and subjective reasons than on an evaluation of facts. We will return to the topic of false rumors in Chapter 8.

5.3 User Communities and User Roles

User communities/groups. In Section 4.3 we described the clustering of content as an operation in which messages/documents are expressed as vectors, and a distance function among them is used to group similar elements together. Interestingly, a distance function is not required to perform clustering: a graph depicting arbitrary connections among nodes, weighted or unweighted, can also be clustered using *graph clustering algorithms*. For an overview of these methods, see Zafarani et al. (2014, ch 6).

Baba et al. (2015) assume that messages that are posted or reposted by similar groups of users are likely to be thematically similar. They exploit this assumption using graph clustering to uncover topical clusters on messages posted during the 2011 Great Eastern Japan Earthquake. Purohit et al. (2014c) also apply a graph clustering algorithm to identify thematically related groups of users among all the users who post information about a given topic (e.g., a developing crisis).

Roles based on structural properties. The centrality and connections of users, either in the whole network or inside a community, can suggest high-level characteristics of them. For instance, user-based metrics such as number of messages and unique messages can be combined with structural properties of the network to identify broad categories of users, such as "amplifiers" or "curators" (Tinati et al., 2012).

This type of generic, topic-independent role, can be described in terms of structural properties/centrality measures of a user in a social network, such as having a small number of connections but a relatively large number of friends-of-friends, or having a large betweenness centrality. Nodes having similar structural properties can be considered as playing similar roles in a network (Henderson et al., 2012). This can be extended to topic-specific sub-graphs (i.e., playing a particular role in the graph defined by a given topic); indeed user communities and roles can be discovered simultaneously (Ruan and Parthasarathy, 2014).

Roles based on information cascades. The observation of several information cascades can also lead to generalizations about the users who participate in those cascades. If some users participate in the diffusion of crisis-relevant information in a consistent manner, we could define user classes that are not exclusively determined by the relationships of a node with others in a social network (i.e., friends and other connections), but by the *influence* exerted by one node on others, as observed through a set of propagation histories.

Along these lines, González-Bailón et al. (2013) describe a series of roles for users participating in online calls for street demonstrations as part of the "*indignados*" movement in Spain in 2011 and 2012. These roles include (i) influentials, (ii) hidden influentials, (iii) broadcasters, and (iv) common users. These types of roles may be only partially exclusive to the crisis domain, as they overlap with similar user roles that have been described for news spreading. Cha et al. (2012) analyze the spread of news online to determine three groups of people who contribute to the spread of news online: (i) mass media sources; (ii) "evangelists," comprising opinion leaders, politicians, celebrities, and others; and (iii) ordinary users.

5.4 Research Problems

Graph theory has been perhaps the most common perspective adopted by researchers studying social media. There are many results that are domain-independent, while domain-specific results in the crisis domain are comparatively fewer.

Understanding factors affecting cascade size. Understanding what are the characteristics of messages that generate large cascades is important to be able to make some progress toward crafting high-impact crisis messages. An emergency relief organization may have something life-critical to communicate (such as a tsunami warning) and may need to know what is the best way of communicating it in social media to reach a large population of users.

Studying evolving crisis networks. More work is needed to understand a crisis from the perspective of an evolving network. Results such as the ones obtained by Phan and Airoldi (2015) involve a single crisis and a single social networking site. How are are connections created and destroyed during a crisis? How do communities emerge? Studies that consider the evolution of many crisis situations as communicated through social media may find interesting commonalities of graph properties that may complement the analysis of the texts.

5.5 Further Reading

The classic on scale-free networks by Barabási (2002) connects social networks to graphs in many other domains, providing a general high-level perspective on social networks. Easley and Kleinberg (2010, part I) describe algorithms for social networks from a link analysis perspective. Zafarani et al. (2014), provide a graph-based perspective to mining social media, including concepts and models of graph evolution, measures of centrality, community detection, and information diffusion.

The graph mining survey by Chakrabarti and Faloutsos (2012) describes graph patterns, generative models, and many graph mining algorithms and applications. The information propagation survey by Chen et al. (2013) describes widely used models for information cascades.

6

Velocity: Online Methods and Data Streams

One of the main reasons why social media is relevant for emergency response is because of its *immediacy*. For instance, the first reports on social media about the 2011 Utøya attacks in Norway appeared 12 minutes before the first news report in mainstream media (Perng et al., 2013), and in the 2013 Westgate mall attacks, social media reports appeared within a minute after the attack started, "scooping" mainstream media by more than half an hour.[1] People on the ground can collect and disseminate time-critical information, as well as data for disaster reconnaissance that otherwise would be lost due to the gap between a disaster and their arrival on site (Dashti et al., 2014).

On a lighter note, it has been speculated, jokingly but plausibly, that the damaging seismic waves from an earthquake, traveling at a mere three to five kilometers per second, can be overtaken by social media messages about them, which propagate orders of magnitude faster through airwaves and optical fiber.[2]

In this context, it is not surprising that people who associate social media with immediacy also expect a fast response from governments and other organizations, for instance, expecting help to arrive within a few hours of posting a message on social media (American Red Cross, 2012). Independently of whether those expectations are met or not in the near future, some capacity for rapid response to social media messages needs to be developed.

We recall from Section 1.5 that our main requirements are to create aggregate summaries about broad groups of messages (capturing the "big picture"), and to detect important events that require attention or action (offering "actionable insights"). We now add a new requirement: timeliness.

This chapter describes methods that ensure that the output summaries or insights are generated shortly after the input information required to create

---

[1] "How Useful Is A Tweet? A review of the first tweets from the Westgate Mall Attack." Nanjira Sambuli, *iHub Research*, October 2013. http://community.ihub.co.ke/blogs/16012/how-useful-is-a-tweet-a-review-of-the-first-tweets-of-the-westgate-attack.
[2] "Seismic Waves." Randall Munroe, *XKCD comic* #723. April 2010. https://xkcd.com/723/.

them becomes available. The way to achieve this low-latency or real-time data processing is to adapt a computing paradigm known as *online processing*, or equivalently, to consider that the input data is not a static object, but a continuously flowing *data stream*.

We begin by explaining how online processing differs from offline processing (§6.1), and present high-level operations on temporal data (§6.2). Then, we describe the framework of event detection (§6.3) and methods for finding events and subevents (§6.4). We also introduce the approach of incremental update summarization (§6.5), and end with a discussion of domain-specific approaches (§6.6).

6.1 Stream Processing

Computer algorithms can be divided into two broad classes: offline algorithms and online algorithms. In the context of crisis computing, they can be used to perform retrospective data analysis, live data analysis, or incremental data analysis.

- *Retrospective data analysis* uses an offline algorithm to process a batch of data relevant to an event, for instance, an archive containing social media messages posted during a certain time span. An example of a retrospective data analysis application could be to reconstruct a timeline of important events occurring during the first 48 hours of a disaster.
- *Live data analysis* uses an online algorithm to process a stream of data relevant to an event. Data is collected through a push/subscription/live API (see Section 2.2), and arrives after a delay in the order of a few seconds (i.e., with low latency), or a few hundred milliseconds (i.e., in "real-time"). An example of a live data analysis application could be to generate alerts of important events in a disaster as the disaster unfolds.
- *Incremental data analysis* lies somewhere in between retrospective and live data analysis. These methods often rely on algorithms that are run at regular intervals (e.g., every few minutes, every hour, or every day), processing small batches of data and keeping some memory/state in-between runs.

The trade-off between retrospective and live data can be described at a high level as a problem of accuracy versus latency. Intuitively, live data analysis is more difficult than retrospective data analysis, because we do not have the benefit of hindsight – algorithms are restricted to operate only on information from the past. We can acquire more information by waiting more, but waiting too long may not be desirable or acceptable in certain scenarios or for certain

Table 6.1 *Comparison of retrospective data processing and live data processing.*

	Retrospective Processing	Live Processing
Algorithmic setting	Offline	Online
Data acquisition	Download	Stream
Data selection	Search	Filter
Temporal context	Complete	Past only
Storage requirements	Prop. to data size	Bounded
Main benefit	Accuracy	Immediacy

users. For instance, emergency managers would prefer a shorter wait in order to respond to a situation as it unfolds; forensic analysts would be more willing to wait until a situation is fully resolved to obtain a more accurate picture of what happened. Table 6.1 compares retrospective data processing and live data processing from a high-level perspective. For development, historical data is typically used to *simulate* live data (e.g., Guo et al., 2013a; Aslam et al., 2013).

Online algorithms on complex data streams. In computing, an *online algorithm* is a series of discrete operations executed over discrete pieces of data, where the whole input is not available from the start. Online algorithms that operate on large data streams also follow the *streaming model of computation*, in which it is assumed that every item in the stream is seen only once, and it is not possible to store all the items in memory.

Large systems performing streaming computation often use *event-driven architectures*. In an event-driven architecture, a system receives external events (social media messages in our case), and passes them through a series of modules. Each module can, in turn, generate events to be processed by other modules or to be produced as output.

Additionally, computational systems in the emergency response space typically perform *complex event processing*, meaning that instead of processing a homogeneous stream of events from a single source, they must be able to process heterogeneous events from a variety of sources.

6.2 Analyzing Temporal Data

The analysis of temporal data seeks to find temporal patterns in the data. In general, the kinds of patterns that can be described depend on the dimensionality of the data, as depicted in Figure 6.1.

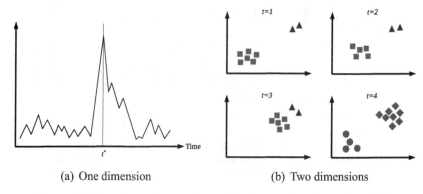

(a) One dimension   (b) Two dimensions

Figure 6.1 Illustration of time series analysis in one dimension and multiple dimensions (two in the figure). In the one-dimensional case, we are depicting an event happening at time t^*. In the two-dimensional case, we are depicting two clusters (squares and triangles) at $t = 1, 2, 3$ that merge at $t = 4$ (diamonds), plus a new, emerging cluster at $t = 4$ (circles).

Figure 6.1(a) depicts a *time series* – a sequence of observations in time – for a single scalar variable. The X axis represents the time, while the Y axis describes a quantity of interest. In crisis-related messages, this variable could be, for instance, the number of mentions of a certain keyword (e.g., the word "injured") or the number of messages that are classified within a certain category (e.g., messages reporting injured people). The operation on this series that will be our main focus of interest is the detection of *events*, which intuitively correspond to significant changes. In the figure, it can be argued that an event has occured at $t = t^*$.

Figure 6.1(b) depicts a two-dimensional time series at different moments in time, which could be minutes, hours, or days apart. In this series, objects are represented by two numerical values, which may correspond to different dimensions of the message after applying a topic modeling method (e.g., using LDA, see Section 4.3). This can be interpreted as the extent to which two topics are expressed in each message. Points that are close to each other should correspond to messages having similar characteristics. The multidimensional case is analogous to the two-dimensional case.

In Figure 6.1(b), a clustering method has been applied at every time step, and clusters at different time steps have been associated to each other by using symbols: squares, triangles, diamonds and discs. For instance, while the six messages posted at $t = 1$ and depicted by a square are not the same as the five messages posted at $t = 2$, they are both in the same region of the figure in similar time intervals, so we assume they correspond to the same theme or topic.

The operations of interest in this series are: to detect topics at each timestep, and to track those topics by mapping them across time steps, including noticing if they merge, disappear, or split.

Temporal Information Retrieval. The study of collections of documents having timestamps or other temporal information, is known as *Temporal Information Retrieval*. Traditionally, these studies used news articles as a data source; currently, many other types of documents are analyzed, including Web pages and postings in social media. Temporal Information Retrieval is more challenging in social media than in other document collections. Social media streams are larger and arrive at a faster rate than documents in other collections, and include short and unstructured content which is quite different from traditional news articles.

In general, the process of tracking how events develop and unfold over time in a timestamped document collection is known as *Topic Detection and Tracking* (TDT). Topic detection and tracking includes various techniques such as story segmentation, topic detection, new event detection, and topic tracking. Story segmentation is usually applied to continuous broadcasts such as newscasts on radio or television; it aims at automatically determining when a news story ends and the next story begins. Topic detection aims at grouping news articles into coherent stories. New event detection decides if an article is part of a new story or belongs to an already reported story. Topic tracking follows how an event unfolds over time. For a survey of topic detection and tracking, see Allan (2002).

6.3 Event Detection

An event is the occurrence of something significant at a specific time and in a specific location (Brants et al., 2003). Important events in social media are often characterized by an increase in the volume of messages associated to a specific topic, and/or to specific entities such as certain people or places (Dou et al., 2012). These increases are sometimes described as "trending topics" or "bursts" of activity.

Types of event. While significant events cause social media activity to increase, not all increases of social media activity correspond to significant events: the volume of messages in social media can also increase for other reasons.

Crane and Sornette (2008) distinguish increases due to external causes (*exogenous*) and increases that are due to viral propagation of a piece of information originating within a social media platform itself (*endogenous*).

Increases in activity due to exogenous causes are often described in the crisis computing literature as corresponding to "actual events" or "real-world events," for instance, an earthquake or a tornado. Increases in activity due to endogenous causes are in general not related to disasters. In Twitter, for instance, an endogenous event is the increase in frequency of a popular hashtag such as "*#musicmonday*," which is used to suggest music on Mondays, or "*#followfriday/#ff*," which are used to suggest people to follow on Fridays.

Events can be specified or unspecified (Atefeh and Khreich, 2013). The distinction is similar to the one between supervised and unsupervised approaches in machine learning. *Specified event detection* is concerned with detecting events of a specific type, for instance, an increase in messages about an infectious disease. *Unspecified event detection* is concerned with finding any kind of event in an input stream.

Events can be recurring or new. A *recurring event* is an event closely resembling a similar event observed in the past, such as the different games during a long sports tournament. A *new event* is different from past events (Yang et al., 2009), where this difference is quantified through a suitable metric (Kumaran et al., 2004).

Events and subevents. The word "event" for our purposes does not always mean a large-scale event, but sometimes a small-scale event or even a subevent of some larger situation.

Many disaster events, such as severe weather storms and earthquakes, can be detected and described accurately through meteorological observations and seismic sensors. In places having a good coverage of meteorological stations and seismic sensors, social media is probably not the first choice as a tool for detecting that one of these events has occurred. In these cases, event detection methods using social media may be used to complement existing sensor data (Musaev et al., 2014).

Crisis events spanning many hours or days include *subevents* of smaller scale. For instance, the 2012 shooting in Aurora, Colorado, in the United States, included at least the following subevents: (i) a shooting has taken place in a cinema, (ii) one person has been arrested, (iii) the arrested suspect has been identified, (iv) increased security measures have been taken in other cinemas (McCreadie et al., 2014). These are some of the subevents of interest that can be identified through automatic methods. In the following, we do not make a distinction between events and subevents except when necessary.

Describing events through multidocument summarization. After a system detects an event, it needs to describe it in a manner that makes sense to end-users. For instance, some organizations would like to receive event reports using a particular format or structure. Common elements across these reports include time, location, and a description of the event.

An heuristic that has been used for describing an event discovered in crisis-related social media, is to find named entities (Section 3.4), particularly locations (Mathioudakis and Koudas, 2010; Dou et al., 2012; Avvenuti et al., 2014). Other descriptors of an event obtained via information extraction include actors (people and organizations), actions, objects, and dates (Khurdiya et al., 2012; Nguyen et al., 2015).

The framework of *multidocument text summarization* provides a series of methods to generate a brief summary from a set of documents – in our case, from a set of messages. There are two basic methods for performing multidocument text summarization: *extracting* words or sentences from the input messages, and methods for *abstracting*, that is, synthesizing new sentences. A well-established method for extractive text summarization is to look for messages that are "central," that is, messages that are similar to many other messages. This heuristic is applied to the summarization of social media streams by Lee et al. (2013), among others. There are many methods for multidocument text summarization; for a survey, see Nenkova and McKeown (2011).

Delimiting phases/stages of a crisis. In addition to events, other time-sensitive elements of a crisis are its phases. Killian (2002, p. 51) describes four phases of emergency events: warning, impact, emergency, and recovery. Information needs are different in different phases. For instance, during the warning phase, the focus may be monitoring the situation, while, during the emergency phase, rescue and similar activities occur.

Event phases can also be observed in the social media response to a crisis. Supervised classification models can be used to classify messages according to the stages described earlier (Appling et al., 2014), or to a simplified version of it, such as *before*, *during*, and *after* an event (Iyengar et al., 2011). This can be of particular interest in the case of events that are not anticipated. The same classification can be attempted through lexical methods based on identifying discriminative words for each phase (Chowdhury et al., 2013).

6.4 Event-Detection Methods

Single-word frequency. A simple yet often effective method for detecting events is to assume that a sharp increase in the frequency of a word is indicative of an event. This method requires to maintain the frequency of words, such as counters of how many messages contain a given word in each discrete period of time. Typical periods of time can range from one hour to one day. An event is declared whenever the current counter for a word exceeds by a sufficient margin the previous counters, or some statistic computed from them, such as moving average or median. To avoid increasing indefinitely the memory usage over time, older counters can be discarded.

An example is the *TwitInfo* system by Marcus et al. (2011), which collects all tweets containing an input query (e.g., "earthquake"). The system maintains a historical average of the frequency of tweets per minute, and reports a new event whenever the current frequency is more than two standard deviations above the historical average frequency. Robinson et al. (2013b) continuously monitor Twitter for tweets geotagged in Australia and New Zealand and keywords related to earthquakes (e.g., *"earthquake"* and *"#eqnz"*), and trigger an alert through the Emergency Situation Awareness (ESA) platform (Cameron et al., 2012) whenever the observed frequency exceeds a certain threshold. Earle et al. (2011) trigger alerts based on a statistic dependent on Short-Term Averages (STA) and Long-Term Averages (LTA) of frequency: $C(t) = \frac{STA}{m \times LTA + b}$ where $m > 1$ and $b \geq 0$ are tunable parameters and an earthquake is declared whenever $C(t) > 1$.

Multiword frequency. A natural extension of methods based on the increase of frequency of a single word, is to consider groups of words. These methods also maintain per-word counters, that are then aggregated according to some similarity function between words. This similarity function can be computed based on time series correlations, or by other means, such as grouping together synonyms.

The *TwitterMonitor* system described by Mathioudakis and Koudas (2010) detects events by first finding individual words showing a sharp increase in frequency, and then by grouping together words by co-occurrence (i.e., if they frequently appear in the same messages). A variant of this method focuses on hashtags instead of general keywords (Corley et al., 2013).

This can be extended by creating a cross-correlation graph, in which each node is a frequently occurring keyword, phrase, or hashtag, and nodes are connected by weighted edges based on the cross-correlation of the time series of the keywords they represent (Sayyadi et al., 2009). Weng and Lee (2011) compute dense subgraphs in the cross-correlation graph, and detect an event whenever a relatively small subgraph exhibiting large cross-correlations among its words is found. The cross-correlation graph might be pruned to discard spurious words that are not related to an event, for instance, by applying k-core decomposition (Meladianos et al., 2015).

An alternative way of using the frequency of multiple terms to detect events is to look for changes in the distribution of frequencies. Events of high significance and disaster events tend to capture the conversation in social media, which exhibits more concentrated frequencies of hashtags and words (Kenett et al., 2014; Rudra et al., 2015, among others). In other words, these high-impact events are characterized by fewer hashtags and fewer words capturing a larger share of messages. Kenett et al. (2014) apply a concentration metric borrowed from economics, to evaluate the distribution of hashtags at different moments of time, and suggest to generate an alert when this concentration increases significantly.

Classification-based and clustering-based methods. These methods exploit the redundancy in crisis-related social media by grouping similar messages together, and reporting that a new event has occurred if: (i) a group of messages becomes "too large," or (ii) a message that is "unlike" any of the groups seen so far appears.

For the first case, a supervised classification method can be used to count the number of messages belonging to a particular class per unit of time. Significant peaks in this time series can be reported as new events (Avvenuti et al., 2014). Messages can also be classified in an unsupervised manner, clustered by applying an *offline clustering* method (e.g., LDA, see Section 4.3) on a set of recently seen documents. An event is reported whenever the number of messages per unit of time on one of these clusters exceeds a certain threshold, for instance, if it is larger by a certain margin measured in units of standard deviation of previous observations for that topic (Dou et al., 2012).

For the second case, it is common to use an *online clustering* method, that runs incrementally on each new message. One method for online clustering works as follows: a set of clusters is maintained, and every new message seen is compared to the current set of clusters, by performing a *nearest neighbor* search. If the message is similar enough to an existing cluster, it is added to it, and if it is not, a new cluster is created (Phuvipadawat and Murata, 2010). In this case, the creation of a new cluster indicates that something new, unlike what has seen before, can be a signal that an "event" has happened.

In addition to this nearest-neighbor based method, other clustering methods, such as density-based clustering (Lee et al., 2013), or self-organizing maps (Pohl et al., 2012) have been used for event detection in social media. In some cases, the clustering algorithms process specific aspects of the messages, instead of their entire text. Khurdiya et al. (2012) extract elements from messages such as actors, actions, dates, and locations; then similarity computation for clustering is done considering only these elements.

Regarding efficiency, a naïve implementation of an online clustering method can be very expensive, because every new item must be compared against many pre-existing items. A first idea to make this process more efficient is to maintain a cluster *centroid*, which is an hypothetical "average message" computed from the word vectors of the messages in a cluster. New elements are compared against this centroid, instead of against all elements in previous clusters (Becker et al., 2011). Another idea is to speed up the nearest neighbor search by reducing the dimensionality of the messages, by hashing them to a vector of a smaller dimension, and ensuring that two similar messages have similar hashes. This can be done by using LSH (Charikar, 2002), which has been applied to the detection of events and subevents in Twitter (Petrović et al., 2010; Rogstadius et al., 2013).

Spatial clustering corresponds to the identification of geographical areas exhibiting an abnormally high activity in social media during a relatively short time frame. Cheng and Wicks (2014) show that even without the content of the messages but merely by knowing that a message has been posted from a given location at a given time, one can detect events of interest. These events correspond to large clusters in a spatiotemporal sense, that is, large groups of messages posted from nearby places during a short time span. Chen and Roy (2009) note that, given the sparsity of geotagged messages, a spatial smoothing operation can be used to preprocess geographical information before event detection. Specifically, they apply the wavelet transform to transforms clouds of points into contiguous regions on a map.

Timeliness is an important consideration when performing online clustering, including the frequency-based and spatial cases. We are often more interested in clusters that represent recent messages, instead of clusters that represent all messages, where the exact definition of "recent" depends on the application (Aggarwal et al., 2003). In the case of social media messages during a crisis, and as expected when considering the different phases of a disaster situation (Baird, 2010), the topics that people speak about change as the crisis unfolds. In this scenario, it might be reasonable to consider that clusters reflecting the themes present in recent messages might be more relevant then clusters reflecting the complete set of messages posted during the entire crisis. Some event detection methods indeed incorporate the idea of demoting or removing older messages, or clusters that have not acquired new elements recently, from the computation of events (see, e.g., Lee et al., 2013).

Basic evaluation of event detection. In general, detection methods for crisis events in social media data are used to identify events that are *exogenous*, *specified*, and *new*. Their purpose often is to generate early alerts about changes

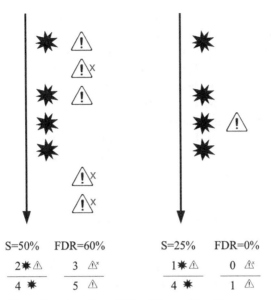

Figure 6.2 Visual depiction of sensitivity (S) and false discovery rate (FDR), comparing two hypothetical systems. The arrows represent time, the "explosions" are events, and the warning signs represent alarms issued. The system on the right has lower sensitivity, as it issues an alarm only in one of the four events. The system on the left is twice as sensitive, but it also issues three false alarms.

in social media motivated by a real-world development of a specific type that has important and immediate consequences for affected populations.

Evaluating the quality of an event detection system is not trivial. For systems that trigger an alarm whenever they believe an event has happened, a standard way of performing this evaluation is in terms of sensitivity and false discovery rate. The *sensitivity* is the fraction of events that are detected, for example, if there are four events in an area, and the system produces an alarm for only one of them, then its sensitivity is $1/4 = 25\%$. The *false discovery rate* is the fraction of alarms that are incorrect,[3] for example, if a system generates five alarms, but only two of those correspond to actual events, the false discovery rate is $1 - 2/5 = 3/5 = 60\%$. Figure 6.2 illustrates the concepts of sensitivity and false discovery rate. Compare with Figure 4.1 depicting precision and recall, which to be applied to event detection would require a definition of negative elements, for instance, "a day without events."

---

[3] This is not the same as the false positive rate, which is the probability of triggering an alarm every time a nonevent happens, which requires discrete time steps at which event detection can happen, or a discretization of time. In contrast, the false discovery rate can be defined even for continuous time.

There are trade-offs between these two aspects. Trivially, a system that triggers too many alerts may have good sensitivity but will also incur in a large false discovery rate. A system that triggers too few alerts will have poor sensitivity, but may also have a smaller false discovery rate. Usually a system allows for a number of choices in these parameters. The specific choice used depends on the costs associated to both types of errors – not triggering when we should, and triggering when we should not. These costs, in turn, depend on the actions that are taken as a consequence of the system's output. An evaluation of some event detection systems described on the literature according to these metrics is presented on Section 9.6.

6.5 Incremental Update Summarization

Current methods for temporal summarization aim at creating a *timeline* of information collected from a data stream (Aslam et al., 2013; Guo et al., 2013b) this is different from retrospective/offline text summarization.

An incremental update summarization method takes as input a stream of documents that are somehow topically related, for instance, they are received from a push API using a keyword-based query. Then, online processing or incremental data analysis is used to produce a sequence of relevant updates, in which each update contains information that is *relevant* and *novel* with respect to previous updates.

Example update summarization methods. Guo et al. (2013b) introduce a general online method for incremental update summarization. Every message that is received is broken down into sentences. Then, every sentence is scored individually using a regression model learned on historical data. Sentences which low scores are discarded. Each remaining sentence is considered a candidate update, and compared against previously issued updates. If the candidate contributes new information, it is written in the output as an update.

Incremental data analysis can also be used. McCreadie et al. (2014) perform incremental data analysis using fixed-size time intervals (e.g., one hour). From all the messages posted during each interval, a fixed number of diverse and representative sentences are extracted (e.g., ten sentences). These are candidate updates, which are filtered to remove those that are too similar to previously issued updates. Finally, a rank-cutoff method is used to decide how many of these updates are relevant enough to be included in the output, which consists of a variable number of updates per hour (from zero to ten).

Kedzie et al. (2015) also perform incremental data analysis using fixed-time intervals. In each interval, the salience (relevance) of all sentences is estimated using a regression model trained on manually annotated sentences. This model uses a series of features from the sentences, including superficial text features, query-specific features (such as the presence of the word "earthquake" and synonyms), geographical features, and temporal features. Next, a graph of sentence similarity is created for all sentences in the interval, and a variant of the Affinity Propagation (AP) clustering algorithm is used to group sentences (Frey and Dueck, 2007). The selection of pivots (exemplars) from each cluster is biased toward high-salience sentences. The generated sentences are candidate updates, which are then postprocessed to discard the ones that are too similar to previously issued updates, and to ensure a minimum degree of salience.

Rudra et al. (2015) also operate on fixed-time intervals. Their method first determines which messages in the interval contribute to situational awareness by using a supervised classification method. Then, it scores each word in the set according to its frequency, and generates a set of messages covering the highest-scoring content words. The total length of this set of messages is constrained, so the system tends to produce summaries containing few short messages.

Evaluating incremental updates methods. In addition to sensitivity and false discovery rate, metrics for evaluating systems for incremental update summarization include other elements such as verbosity, redundancy, and latency (Aslam et al., 2013; Kenter et al., 2015).

Aslam et al. (2013) describe the evaluation methodology used in the TREC 2013 Temporal Summarization track, in which participants must generate a stream of updates, corresponding to relevant subevents in a stream of documents. In their evaluation, a series of "nuggets" of information are extracted manually from each event as ground truth. Each information nugget is a piece of information that the system should generate, and it is associated to a time (the first time it appears in the stream) and a measure of importance (low, medium, or high). Under this evaluation framework, a good system should have high relevance (retrieve the high-importance nuggets), low verbosity (do not generate many updates, or updates that are too long and do not contain nuggets), no redundancy (do not repeat the same nugget again), and low latency (generate an update containing a nugget soon after the nugget's timestamp).

An evaluation framework can also consider multiple users that visit a system at different times. Concepts of latency and redundancy need to be modified in this case, because they have to be computed with respect to the other updates a user has seen since she logged in (Baruah et al., 2015).

Value tracking. Some quantifiable information about a disaster, for instance the number of people missing or displaced, cannot be known with 100% certainty as the disaster is unfolding (Neubig et al., 2011). These figures tend to be revised significantly as a crisis evolves, and hence require special processing to reflect the most recent – hopefully more accurate – estimate so far. The *value tracking* task, described in Aslam et al. (2013, sec. 2.2), corresponds to producing a sequence of estimations for a *specified* query (e.g., number of injured people), in which the estimation can be revised with each message that arrives. Experimentally, the evaluation of these systems is based on how close the estimation is to the actual value, which is gathered and validated after the fact.

Rudra et al. (2015) present a method to find *unspecified* quantities of interest. They apply a heuristic in which a POS tagger and a dependency parser are used to find numerals modifying a verb (e.g., "*67 missing*").

6.6 Domain-Specific Approaches

As in many applications involving noisy and ambiguous data, the application of domain-specific heuristics tends to improve the results obtained using open-domain methods. This is particularly applicable in our case given that activity in social media increases in response to various events that are not related to crises (as explained in Section 2.1).

Twitter-specific features. Heuristics based on observed behavior on a specific social media platform can be applied to improve the computation of candidate events or to postprocess them. For instance, when computing the similarity of two messages, Phuvipadawat and Murata (2010) boost the similarity of vector components corresponding to hashtags or usernames. In other words, hashtags in common between two messages are considered a stronger signal of similarity than keywords in common.

After applying an online clustering method, many spurious, nonevent clusters appear; Twitter-specific heuristics can be applied to remove such clusters. Becker et al. (2011) note that a high number of retweets typically signals an endogenous event, while a high percentage of user mentions is common during actual (exogenous) events. Similarly, multiword hashtags such as *#musicmonday* and *#followfriday* are also indicative of endogenous events. Phuvipadawat and Murata (2010) also postprocess the clusters and rank them according to certain heuristics, including whether they include names of people (extracted using a named entity tagger).

Crisis-specific features. Methods that exploit crisis-specific features often rely on a model to determine which are the clusters or candidate events of interest. This is typically a supervised model, created from messages posted in past events that have been deemed to be relevant. The type of model can be a simple lexical model (i.e., "a crisis event is one that contains a particular set of keywords") or a more complex statistical model, such as a machine-learned classification model (Section 4.2). At a high level, these methods scan social media for groups of crisis-relevant messages that are created approximately at the same time and approximately in the same location.

For instance, Sakaki et al. (2013) use a specific set of crisis-related keywords and a supervised classifier to find messages that are crisis-related, then use a statistical model of an event based on observations that are close by in time and space. This model is further refined in Sakai and Tamura (2015), and is designed based on observations from previous events, particularly from earthquakes. A similar method can be used to detect smaller-scale events, such as car crashes (Schulz et al., 2013). Rudra et al. (2015) also uses a supervised learning approach to filter messages of interest.

Crisis-specific features can also be used to rank updates or subevents. Verma et al. (2011) noted that the messages that can contribute to situational awareness tend to express facts more than opinions, and tend to be written in a formal, impersonal tone. These elements can be modeled computationally and combined to determine the probability that a sentence or message contributes to situational awareness. Li et al. (2012) consider a group of messages classified on a particular category and close by in time and space as a candidate event, and evaluate them as a set using a linear regression model. The model generates an "importance" score for the candidate based on aspects computed from all the messages in a candidate set, such as the number of people participating, and the frequency of certain keywords such as "killed" or "death." The parameters of the model are learned on previously seen crises.

A further extension is to consider more than one type of event. *SaferCity* (Berlingerio et al., 2013) identifies several types of public safety events in social media, classified using a supervised classification method into various types such as "traffic accident" or "theft and burglary," and clustered using a spatio-temporal approach that incorporates information about the content of the messages.

Incorporating multiple sources. Multiple heterogeneous data feeds can be processed simultaneously, engaging in complex event processing. For instance, *SaferCity* (Berlingerio et al., 2013) is intended to incorporate data from both social media as well as traditional news media. *STED* (Hua et al., 2013) uses data from traditional news media to reduce the amount of manual labeling required over social media messages, by propagating labels from news articles to social media messages.

LITMUS (Musaev et al., 2014) detects landslides using data collected from multiple sources, including seismic sensors, rainfall data, and social media.

Seismic data is obtained from the U.S. Geological Survey (USGS), rainfall data from NASA's Tropical Rainfall Measuring Mission (TRMM), and social media data from providers such as Twitter, YouTube, and Instagram.

6.7 Research Problems

Making predictions. A key aspect of time series analysis is *forecasting*, that is, making inferences about the behavior of a series in the future. In the crisis domain, even events that cannot be in general forecasted, such as a spontaneous demonstration or protest, can be anticipated to some extent by observing signals in social media and other data sources (Ramakrishnan et al., 2014).

Preserving privacy while mining. Recent studies have analyzed call detail records during emergencies, finding that there are anomalous patterns that are well correlated with crisis events such as an explosion in a factory (Aleissa et al., 2014) or a bombing attack (Young et al., 2014). Currently these approaches require access to private data that is only accessible to mobile telephony companies. A privacy-preserving data mining approach (Aggarwal and Philip, 2008) could be used to analyze this data and detect events without compromising the privacy of users (more on privacy on Section 11.1).

Performing effective text summarization at a scale. A general problem of dealing with crisis data from a system perspective is dealing with drastic variations in the flow of data. Ideally, a system is able to detect minor but significative changes in the flow of messages, while at the same time being able to cope with huge surges of several orders of magnitude, which are not uncommon. In particular, many algorithms for text summarization require a large number of comparisons between sentences or messages, often quadratic, which makes them prohibitively expensive for social media crisis data.

Quantifying without classifying. Results from the task of *text quantification* suggest that methods willing to quantify the amount of messages belonging to a certain category do not necessarily need to be optimized for categorization accuracy. Instead, one could try to directly estimate the number of messages in the category of interest (Sebastiani, 2014; Gao and Sebastiani, 2015).

6.8 Further Reading

The textbook on models and algorithms on data streams by Aggarwal (2007, ch. 2 and 3) describes clustering and classification on data streams. Allan (2002) surveys several aspects of topic detection and tracking. Atefeh and Khreich (2013) survey methods for event detection in Twitter, including unsupervised, supervised, and hybrid approaches – the latter applies a supervised classifier to determine the messages of interest, and then a clustering algorithm to group them.

The TREC Temporal Summarization track,[4] which is a long-running conference and competition in Information Retrieval, is a good source to track research developments on current methods for update summarization (Aslam et al., 2013).

---

[4] TREC Temporal Summarization track: http://www.trec-ts.org/.

7

Volunteers: Humanitarian Crowdsourcing

Crises and disasters are portrayed significantly in both legacy and online media, and attract the attention of millions of Internet users. Many of these users are willing to help humanitarian relief efforts remotely, through tasks that go from providing, curating, and synthesizing information about the disaster (Vieweg et al., 2010; Gao et al., 2011; Starbird, 2012a; Liu, 2014), to performing crisis mapping and all sort of *digital humanitarian* tasks (Meier, 2015).

While a seamless integration of digital volunteering efforts into professional/ formal response efforts has yet to be realized, volunteer groups have been successful in certain areas, such as creating maps that are useful for humanitarian organizations: "After Haiyan [November 2013 typhoon in the Philippines], many relief organizations, including the OCHA and the medical aid group Médecins Sans Frontières (also known as Doctors Without Borders), have gone into the Philippines carrying with them continually updated maps of the country generated by more than 1,000 OpenStreetMap volunteers from 82 countries" (Butler, 2013). A survey among officers from large humanitarian organizations found that many of them used some type of volunteer-processed social media data (Tapia and Moore, 2014).

Volunteering during disasters is not a product of new media or new technologies. Instead, it is an integral part of how communities react to disasters (Dynes, 1970). What is new today is that electronic communications have effectively redefined the boundaries of these communities. The "village" that feels, for instance, the devastating effects of a Typhoon in the Philippines, is indeed a *global village*.[1] People living half a world away can become actively involved, and even become key players in the response to an ongoing crisis (Carvin, 2013).

---

[1] "Global village" is a term popularized by philosopher Marshall McLuhan in the early 1960s.

In general, the involvement of volunteers has been described by formal organizations as a mixed blessing. Disasters involve the convergence of people, resources, and information. Naturally, some of the people, some of the resources, and some of the information are actually helpful in the disaster response, but not all of them (Fritz and Mathewson, 1957).

This chapter focuses on how large groups of people can contribute effectively, via the Internet, to response and relief efforts. In addition to obstacles regarding the integration of their contributions into the work of formal organizations, further challenges include recruiting volunteers, keeping them engaged, and ensuring a high-quality output. These problems are well known for researchers working in crowdsourcing and human computation, two concepts that are sometimes used interchangeably, but have different meanings. *Crowdsourcing* is an organizational framework, and corresponds to processes for procuring services from a large amount of people external to an organization, for example, from volunteers who are not affiliated with a formal agency in charge of relief efforts. *Human-based computation* is an information processing framework, and corresponds to methods for incorporating human intelligence into an information processing system, for example, volunteer annotation of large sets of images captured during a crisis.

In this chapter, we characterize digital volunteering (§7.1) and position digital volunteers individually and in groups in relation to formal organizations (§7.2). Then, we discuss elements of volunteer mobilization and motivation (§7.3). Next, we describe various types of volunteer tasks (§7.4) and systems integrating both human and computing processing (§7.5).

7.1 Digital Volunteering

Digital volunteering is the practice of performing volunteer work using digital technologies. While digital volunteering can be done to some extent without an Internet connection, it almost invariably involves Internet-connected devices and activities performed online. In this sense, digital volunteering is sometimes called online volunteering, and less often, virtual volunteering. One of the oldest examples of digital volunteering is Project Gutenberg, a large-scale book digitalization project established in 1971 that continues to this day.[2]

---

[2] "Online Volunteering Enters Middle Age." Jayne Cravens, *Non-Profit Quarterly*, June 2008. http://nonprofitquarterly.org/2008/06/21/online-volunteering-enters-middle-age/ – Project Gutenberg is actually older than the term "Internet" itself; while ARPANET existed in 1971, the term "internet" would not be used until the publication of the RFC 675 standard in 1974.

During disasters, digital volunteering is a general term used to describe a number of activities done online, which are not mutually exclusive with activities done "offline," such as clearing up debris from a road after a storm. Indeed, many volunteers are involved in both online and offline activities (Reuter et al., 2013). Digital volunteers typically perform a wide array of information processing tasks, such as data entry, geocoding, mapping, translation, classification, annotation, and curation, among others. Some of these activities may constitute by themselves actions of emergency or humanitarian response, or activities in support of those actions.

While, as noted earlier, the fact that members of the public participate in disaster response is not new, information and communication technologies enhance their contributions, greatly expanding their reach, making them much more visible than before (Palen and Liu, 2007; Palen, 2014).

Local digital volunteering. A primary digital volunteering activity during a crisis is to provide information, particularly eyewitness reports. The role of locals as information sources is well established in the humanitarian community. People located in the affected areas are well positioned to capture and process information about a developing situation (Zook et al., 2010). Their input can be particularly helpful in low- and middle-income countries, where authoritative demographic or geographical data collected by governments may not be accurate enough for the purposes of humanitarian response (Cinnamon and Schuurman, 2013).

At times, local volunteers are the only source of reliable information, for instance before responders can establish their presence in a disaster area. Their information gathering activities can be complementary to those of formal organizations: "Using crowdsourcing in a smart and careful way to remotely collect and aggregate data from the field can be useful where field presence is either not possible, or restricted. It can attract attention to specific areas, problems, or patterns to be further explored. When organizations have established a good field presence, crowdsourcing can help to corroborate data directly collected from the field" (ICRC, 2013).

Remote digital volunteering. The Internet enables remote volunteering as well, expanding the radius of possible volunteering activities and the audience for those activities well beyond the limits of a crisis-affected area (Palen, 2014). Remote digital volunteers are different from local digital volunteers, and these differences are expressed, for instance, in the way they create connections and repost content (Kogan et al., 2015).

An obvious disadvantage for volunteers located far away from a disaster is that they are not able to witness directly what is happening on the ground.

More importantly, many of them they may lack the context and background knowledge required to interpret correctly the information being produced at the place of the disaster.

However, "distant" volunteers also have some advantages. For instance, they may not be affected by power outages, adverse weather or other disruptions (St. Denis et al., 2012). They may also bring new expertise (e.g., technical skills and know-how), that may not be available immediately and in enough numbers among the locals that are able to help.

7.2 Organized Digital Volunteering

Dynes (1970) describes four types of organization during a disaster: established, extending, expanding, and emergent. *Established organizations*, such as a fire department, exist before an emergency and are tasked with the response to it. *Extending* and *expanding* organizations also exist before an emergency, but must deal with new tasks that are different from the ones they are used to perform (extending), or with new members and/or a different organizational structure from the one they had before (expanding).

Emergent organizations are formed spontaneously in the aftermath of a disaster. They are a natural, perhaps inevitable consequence of disasters, and not a symptom of lack of planning or an opposition to existing groups. Emergent groups are sometimes formed to achieve a specific goal, and sometimes to address the general needs of a group of people, in many cases performing a range of valuable activities that benefit affected populations (Stallings and Quarantelli, 1985).

Most emergent groups are short-lived, but occasionally some of them grow and develop over time. Gardner (2013) describes a small group of volunteers who were helping people affected by the 2005 Hurricane Katrina in the United States, initially by distributing grilled cheese sandwiches in a parking lot. Over time, this emergent group became a network of thousands of volunteers that operated several community relief centers for almost two years. Another significant example is the Red Cross movement itself, which grew from individual volunteer efforts (Dunant, 1862).

Emergent digital volunteering groups. Spontaneous digital volunteers working individually can join established or expanding organizations, or coalesce into new emergent digital volunteering groups (Palen and Liu, 2007). For instance, the self-organizing "voluntweeters" in the response to the 2010 earthquake in Haiti have the characteristics of an emergent group (Starbird and Palen, 2011).

Potts (2013) presents a description of emergent digital groups in disaster within the framework of Actor-Network Theory (ANT). In this framework, participants in these groups are "actors" performing a translation of data into information and knowledge. The process by which these groups form and mobilize can be described as having four stages: (i) problematization: the appearance of anchor actors who help define the situation, (ii) interessement: the sharing of this problem and the creation of a network, (iii) enrollment: the concentration of activity and recruiting of more actors, and (iv) mobilization: the movement to actions (Potts, 2013, ch. 2).

Emergent digital volunteering groups are similar to other crisis-related emergent groups described by sociologists of disaster. They tend to have "a somewhat small very active core; a larger supporting circle who can be mobilized for specific tasks; and a great number of primarily nominal supporters" (Stallings and Quarantelli, 1985). Internet communities in general, and digital volunteering groups in particular, usually follow a similar pattern. Content creators, contributors, and "lurkers" appear in a very asymmetrical ratio (the 90:9:1 rule[3]). These categories are not static, and a progression from simpler tasks and less commitment to more difficult tasks and more commitment has been observed in online social activities (Preece and Shneiderman, 2009), including some volunteer groups (Starbird and Palen, 2011).

Established digital volunteering organizations. Digital volunteer efforts can also become established organizations through various mechanisms. Emergent digital volunteering groups can reappear in different crises over time, growing in size, complexity and formality, and progressively becoming established organizations such as Humanity Road (HR) and the Standby Task Force (SBTF). In some cases, volunteer organizations form around systems used to enable volunteer activities, such as Sahana Foundation,[4] Humanitarian OpenStreetMap Team (HOT),[5] and other technology-centric volunteer organizations.

Alternatively, or sometimes additionally, existing organizations can help catalyze the creation of digital volunteer organizations. A Virtual Operations Support Team (VOST), in its original definition by emergency manager coordinator Jeff Phillips,[6] is a small and cohesive team of experienced, trusted volunteers brought together to expand the capabilities of an established emergency response organization, allowing them, for instance, to monitor a broad

---

[3] "What is the 1% rule?" Charles Arthur, *The Guardian*, July 2006. http://www.theguardian.com/technology/2006/jul/20/guardianweeklytechnologysection2.
[4] Sahana Foundation: http://sahanafoundation.org/.
[5] Humanitarian OpenStreetMap Team (HOT): http://hotosm.org/.
[6] History of virtual operations support teams: http://vosg.us/history/.

range of information sources during extended periods of time (St. Denis et al., 2012).

Humanitarian organizations refer to organizations of digital volunteers as Volunteer and Technical Communities (VTCs). These organizations have characteristics that include an open-source ideology, flexible structure and hierarchy, collaborative workflow, altruistic nature, desire to cultivate and disseminate technical skills, and enthusiasm for partnership (Capelo et al., 2012).

The characteristics of these organizations, as well as their structure, reflect to a large extent the motivations and values of the volunteers who participate in them. Their structure is dynamic, as there is a recursive relationship between the structure of an organization and the activities it performs, with technology and infrastructure also playing a role in the way an organization evolves, as noted by Starbird (2012a, ch. 6 and 8) and references therein.

Volunteer groups versus formal organizations. Just as volunteering is a constant in disaster response, the tension between volunteer groups and formal organizations is a long-standing issue in sociology of disasters.

Contrary to the expectations of many first-time volunteers, their help is not always well received. Stallings and Quarantelli (1985) noted that emergent citizen groups are frequently "ignored or rebuffed," and seen by formal organizations as "uninformed or narrowly biased about the issues, and unrealistic or simplistic in solutions proposed or goals sought." Some responders may even see them as a burden: "Like physical convergers and unwanted donations, digital convergers during crisis events can be viewed as another problem that emergency responders will have to manage" (Starbird, 2012b).

Additionally, it cannot be ignored that the mere presence of volunteers assisting on a key government function can have political implications. During disasters, governments and organizations are at risk of being perceived as inadequate or ineffective – generating opportunities for power relations to be restructured (Turoff et al., 2004). The actions of volunteers can be perceived as silently but vividly exposing government shortcomings or incapacity.

In this context, it is not surprising that results describing the effectiveness of the collaboration between volunteer organizations and formal organizations are mixed. A study by van Gorp (2014) found limited evidence of successful engagements due to a number of barriers, including: (i) limited resources, (ii) challenges managing volunteers, (iii) different levels of engagement and commitment by volunteers, (iv) different ways of working, and (v) limited knowledge of volunteers' expertise by aid organizations. Other researchers report a positive trend: as digital volunteering efforts become more organized and mature, they are increasingly integrated with formal organizations, sometimes in tight coordination with conventional humanitarian relief operations (Butler, 2013).

The relationship between volunteer and formal/professional organizations may improve as these organizations gain more experience dealing with each other. Indeed, volunteer groups and formal emergency response organizations have tried to document their experiences working together, to allow them to collaborate more effectively (see, for instance, Capelo et al., 2012; Waldman et al., 2013).

7.3 Motivating Volunteers

Digital volunteering efforts for crisis response often have relatively low barriers of entry for volunteers, who have swarmed into the fields of emergency and disaster response. A desire to help those in distress is a main motivating factor, as volunteers "perceive that there is something they can do which benefits others" (Tim McNamara from the Open Knowledge Foundation, cited in UN OCHA, 2012). However, volunteer motivations cannot be reduced to altruism alone.

There are many reasons why a person becomes or continues being a digital volunteer; these reasons are complex and context-dependent (Starbird, 2012a). Being a first-time digital volunteer, or a volunteer that has episodic participation, or a volunteer that has sustained participation, are different configurations that require different motivations and that provide different rewards. Similarly, being alone, or part of an emergent group, or part of an established organization, enables different elements of a complex motivation to be expressed differently.

Understanding why people volunteer can help design better systems for digital volunteering. The literature on this topic has described several elements, some of which are not trivial to anticipate or model. For instance, Clary and Snyder (1999) includes the following motivations in their framework for analyzing volunteering:

- Values: "I feel it is important to help others"
- Understanding: "Volunteering lets me learn through direct, hands-on experience"
- Enhancement: "Volunteering makes me feel better about myself"
- Career: "Volunteering can help me to get my foot in the door at a place where I would like to work"
- Social: "People I know share an interest in community service"
- Protective: "Volunteering is a good escape from my own troubles"

Table 7.1 *Example motivations described in six contexts: general volunteer work, community mapping, collective intelligence tasks, crowdsourcing initiatives, Volunteer and Technical Communities, and crowdwork. Monetary incentives appear in parenthesis, as in a strict sense they might not be applicable to volunteers.*

Clary and Snyder (1999) General volunteering	Coleman et al. (2009) Community mapping
• Values • Understanding • Enhancement • Career • Social • Protective	• Altruism • Professional or personal interest • Intellectual stimulation • Social reward • Enhanced personal reputation
Malone et al. (2010) Collective intelligence tasks	Carpenter (2011) Crowdsourcing initiatives

• (Money)
• Love
  – Enjoyment
  – Socializing with others
  – Contributing to a cause
• Glory
  – Recognition
	• Cause
	• Achievement
	  – (Cash prizes)
	  – Non-cash prizes
	  – Status
	  – Badges/levels/privileges
	  – Publicity
	  – Opportunities to contract
	• Social
	  – Interaction
	  – Identity
	• Efficacy and learning

Capelo et al. (2012) Volunteer and Tech. Communities	Starbird (2012a) Crowdwork
• Ideology • Personal satisfaction • Community • Humanitarian values • Desire to apply and improve technical knowledge	• (Economic capital) • Social capital: new friends and/or stronger relationships • Symbolic capital: reputation • Self-improvement: learning new skills • Benevolence: to benefit others • Entertainment

These elements plus the ones described by Malone et al. (2010) in the context of collective intelligence actions, Carpenter (2011) in crowdsourcing initiatives, Coleman et al. (2009) in community mapping, by Capelo et al. (2012) in Volunteer and Technical Communities, and by Starbird (2012a, ch. 8) in volunteer crowdwork are summarized in Table 7.1. Some of these works refer to both paid and volunteer work, and include monetary incentives as a motivation, which are written in parenthesis in the table. We can see a variety of motivations described across these studies, some of them common to all, such as ideology and values, social and community factors, and self-improvement and learning. They also have elements in common with volunteer motivations in Wikipedia and Free and Open Source Software developer communities, including the ideology of believing in the free provision of information to the world, as well as the enjoyment of belonging to a community (Benkler, 2006; Haklay and Weber, 2008).

All of these elements appear in some form in studies about the motivation of digital volunteers during disasters. For instance, a survey in 2011 of the Standby Task Force indicated that while the main motivation is the desire to help, a secondary motivation is a chance to learn new skills in technology use and hands-on crisis response (Hichens, 2011; Committee on Public Response to Alerts and Warnings Using Social Media, 2013). In a survey of 17 digital volunteers that helped during the Haiti earthquake in 2010, Starbird and Palen (2011) found that they many had some connection to the event (such as family or friends in the affected area), and that this type of digital volunteering was a strong part of their online identity – some of them identified themselves as volunteers (or "voluntweeters").

Understanding volunteer motivations is also important for retaining volunteers. Volunteers interviewed by Hichens (2011) said that in order to continue volunteering, they need to know in detail how their actions impact the volunteer effort, to see whether they were actually helping people.

7.4 Digital Volunteering Tasks

Digital volunteering during crises involves many tasks, such as sensing, tagging, mapping and curating information (Liu, 2014). These activities tend to happen both within and around social media.

Within social media. The basic activity is posting and sharing information, but it is not the only one. People also pass-along (reposting or "retweeting" content) and appraise information (e.g., up-voting or favoriting a message, or down-voting a message).

The specific actions that people can take are constrained by the features offered by each specific social media platform. Actions such as identifying and amplifying actionable information, routing information to specific people or groups, and to some extent verifying information, are digital volunteer actions that can take place within social media (Starbird, 2013).

Volunteers can perform more than one action. Starbird and Palen (2011) study the activity of "volunteer coding" in which people spontaneously translate social media messages from unstructured text to a hashtag-based microformat. They observe that many of the volunteers involved in this coding do much more than that, including brokering information about the event from different sources.

Around social media. Digital volunteers perform a variety of human computation tasks around social media, typically involving the processing of messages, photos, or video from social media or traditional news media. Information verification, when contrasting the information with other sources, is a digital volunteer activity that takes place around social media; structuring and synthesizing information to create informational resources, are other such activities (Starbird, 2013). Given that the input they receive is typically homogeneous, their operation can be described as a form of *crowd processing* (Geiger et al., 2011). The expected output of the volunteer work can be a set of images categorized into various types, or a spreadsheet summarizing various reports about relief operations. The prototypical tasks include correcting, categorizing, validating, comparing, searching, synthesizing, among others (Imran et al., 2013a).

Platforms for digital volunteering. Digital volunteering activities can be supported by a variety of different platforms.[7] As these platforms mature over time, they tend to be maintained, developed and operated by established volunteer organizations.

Crisis mapping is perhaps the application that popularized digital volunteering, and it is done through platforms such as OpenStreetMap (Haklay and Weber, 2008; Palen et al., 2015) and Ushahidi (Okolloh, 2009). In the former, volunteers trace and annotate roads and other structures on top of satellite images, sometimes guided by priorities or information gaps identified by on-the-ground responders. In the latter, volunteers geocode crisis reports by adding markers to an existing map. Collaborative mapping is more than drawing maps and geocoding: it may be a very complex process involving many steps such as aggregating, summarizing, and validating individual reports.

---

[7] For instance, see the list of partners of the Digital Humanitarian Network, http://digitalhumanitarians.com/partners.

MicroMappers is another example of a crowd processing platform for crisis information from social media, including crisis mapping.[8] It has been used to produce crisis maps by the Standby Task Force, for instance for the 2015 earthquake in Nepal.[9] MicroMappers enables several volunteer annotation tasks, including identifying different categories of messages in social media, categorizing photos to determine which ones contain reports of damage, and geo coding both messages and photos to display them on a map.

In addition to mapping, all kinds of platforms for digital volunteering can be envisioned, for tasks going from the very complex to the very simple. For instance, Barrenechea et al. (2015a) describe a digital volunteering system for matching photos of pets lost and found. Their system is designed to be very easy to use, so that children can also contribute to this task.

Training volunteers. In practice, most volunteers of emergent groups learn by themselves or receive some form of on-the-job training. Established organizations sometimes provide training between crisis situations, potentially contributing to expand the pool of prepared volunteers available for an emergency.

Emergency management exercises are an important component of emergency preparedness and a great opportunity for performing training. Large-scale exercises such as *Exercise24* can help to enhance coordination between different actors, including digital volunteers (Bressler et al., 2012). They can also be used to learn crisis information processing skills. Examples include the *ASU Crisis Response Game* (Abbasi et al., 2012) and the *Disaster In My Backyard* simulation (Meesters and van de Walle, 2013). In both of these cases, the simulation has been framed as a serious game. These simulations can sometimes be entirely digital, such as *Stop Disasters*, a video game developed for children nine to sixteen years old to learn about natural hazards and disasters (Felicio et al., 2014).

Software can also be tested through simulation, an approach that is common in Human Computer Interaction (HCI) research. For instance, Mao et al. (2014) describe experiments done with paid crowdsourcing workers, where social media data from a previous disaster is fed into a collaborative mapping tool. In this type of experiment, the software is heavily instrumented to record all actions and interactions of users, allowing researchers to measure several variables related to collaboration and effectiveness.

---

[8] MicroMappers, http://micromappers.org/, uses the PyBossa software http://pybossa.com/.

[9] "Disaster response gets boost from AI, crowdsourced data." Nicola Davies, *ExtremeTech*, June 2015. http://www.extremetech.com/extreme/208180-crowdsourcing-data-for-humanitarian-disaster-response.

In Section 11.4 we will come back to simulation exercises in terms of the ethical framework in which they should be conducted.

7.5 Hybrid Systems

Many systems for processing disaster-related data are hybrid, in the sense that they include both machine processing and automatic processing elements. A suitable combination of these elements can provide a better combination of speed, cost, and quality than running these systems separately or in cascade (Quinn et al., 2011). The design of hybrid systems is complex because of the mismatch between the different speeds, accuracy, and reliability which with these two types of element operate. Creating practices and standards for the design of these real-time crowdsourcing systems may shorten their development time and facilitate their evaluation.

Imran et al. (2013a) introduce a framework for *crowdsourcing stream processing*, which is crowd processing on a data stream, and apply it to a tool for processing crisis-related social media messages. In this framework, automatic and crowdsourced processing elements are composed in different ways. For instance, an automatic processing element may act as a filter that produces a reduced data feed for humans to analyze or validate, or a crowdsourcing processing element can produce training data for an automatic processing element to learn how to categorize further items.

In a hybrid system to process crisis-related media, one key design choice is to what extent human intervention is necessary on every item (i.e., on every social media message, news item, or photo/video). In some systems, a design constraint can be imposed that every item must be reviewed by a human. In other systems, this constraint can be relaxed. When every item must be reviewed by a human, given the volume of data that needs to be processed, either items will need to be dropped, or a backlog of items will be waiting for long periods of time for humans to look at it, reducing timeliness. When this is not imposed, a system can usually keep up with a much larger volume of data, but without human supervision, some items may not be processed correctly.

Cobb et al. (2014) also propose a hybrid approach, with a strong suggestion to integrate automatic processing into the normal workflow and practices of digital volunteers, instead of building separate systems. They advocate for automatic systems that passively observe and learn from the actions of human volunteers, perhaps occasionally nudging to provide training data, but avoiding replacing "real" work with work done only for the purpose of training an automatic system.

7.6 Research Problems

Enabling time-critical volunteer mobilization. While there are studies about how different payment modalities and schedules affect the quantity and quality of work in crowdsourcing systems (e.g., Mason and Watts, 2010), research on volunteer systems is more scarce. Additionally, research on volunteer motivations has been to date more descriptive more than prescriptive.

Volunteer and technical communities actively recruit digital volunteers through a variety of strategies, but not much has been done regarding systematic comparisons of the effectiveness of different strategies. An exception is the 2009 DARPA Network Challenge (also known as the "Red Balloon' challenge),[10] where several volunteer recruiting strategies were compared. The winner was a recursive recruitment strategy introduced by Pickard et al. (2011), in which people were incentivized not only to solve the challenge (in this case, spot one of the red balloons), but to recruit others who could solve it.

Retaining volunteers. In addition to methods for gaining new volunteers, retaining existing ones is an interesting research topic by itself. There are interesting parallels with the Wikipedia, where recruiting and retaining editors has been identified as both an important practical concern for its long-term viability, as well as an important research problem (Suh et al., 2009). In general, there are spaces that support participation, but others that make it harder for volunteers to participate (Potts, 2013, ch. 5).

A related aspect is to what extent digital volunteering may substitute other forms of volunteering instead of complementing them. For instance, some of the emergency managers interviewed by Reuter et al. (2013), indicated that their perception is that the engagement of nondigital volunteers is decreasing.

Reducing articulation work. Volunteer organizations have limited resources to spend in planning, coordination, monitoring, and similar activities, referred to as *articulation work*, or "work that supports other work" (Baker and Millerand, 2007). Reducing articulation work means freeing up resources for core activities, which is why digital volunteering organizations tend to develop some technological support for it. For instance, a large crisis mapping community can create a platform to divide a large area to be mapped into smaller cells that can be assigned to different teams (Palen et al., 2015). Manual work can be further reduced by applying methods for intelligent task assignment or task routing that have been proposed in recent years (see, e.g., Law and Ahn, 2011; Roy et al., 2015).

---

[10] "MIT wins $40,000 prize in nationwide balloon-hunt contest." *CNN*, December 2009. http://edition.cnn.com/2009/TECH/12/05/darpa.balloon.challenge/index.html.

7.7 Further Reading

Meier (2015) is a guide to digital volunteering, including an account of the creation and development of various digital humanitarianism initiatives. The PhD thesis of Starbird (2012a) is an in-depth study of digital volunteering during mass disruption events.

Liu (2014) describes many digital volunteering activities including OpenStreetMap, Ushahidi, the Standby Task Force, the Digital Humanitarian Network, and efforts by the U.S. Geological Survey to collect data from citizens about earthquakes. She also presents a framework for understanding crisis crowdsourcing based on answering questions of why, who, what, when, where, and how.

Benkler (2006, ch. 4), presents a discussion about intrinsic and extrinsic motivations of contributors. Hermida (2014, ch. 6), analyzes several scenarios in which people have shared crisis-related information online, including describing their possible motivations.

The relationship between volunteer and technical communities and formal humanitarian organizations has been addressed in two symmetric guides describing how to collaborate with each other: Capelo et al. (2012); Waldman et al. (2013).

Virtual Operation Support Teams (VOSTs) have published some guidelines about how to engage with social media, this is the case of the one in Colorado (COVOST, 2014) and New York State (Alley et al., 2015) in the United States.

Law and Ahn (2011) is an introduction to human computation covering the design of human computation tasks, and the algorithms used to route tasks to people and to aggregate results.

8

Veracity: Misinformation and Credibility

In August 2014, CBS News published a story and a cellphone photo of a bizarre meteorological phenomenon. The reporter used a photo provided by a tugboat captain, who stated that he was not a meteorologist but described the image as a rare "sideways tornado." The phenomenon is actually more than rare: it does not exist. The reporter could have consulted with the TV station's meteorologist, who later easily identified the photo as a shelf cloud. The story was pulled off their website and then amended, but the embarrassment for the news network did not go away.[1]

Hoaxes in media are centuries old. Noted satirists such as Jonathan Swift in the seventeenth century and Mark Twain in the eighteenth were successful at spreading them well before the Internet (Walsh, 2006). Disaster-related media hoaxes predate the Internet by decades. A famous example was the 1938 radio adaptation of the alien-invasion novel by H. G. Wells, *The War of Worlds*, which at the time caused numerous calls to newspapers and the police, and created a significant media backslash for (unintentionally, according to its producers) "deceiving" the listeners.[2] Social media simply places the tools necessary to create and spread all kinds of information, including hoaxes, on the hands of many.

This chapter deals with concerns about the presence of false information in social media, which are frequently cited as one of the major obstacles to its adoption by humanitarian and emergency relief organizations (Hiltz et al., 2011; Hughes et al., 2014b). Officers at these organizations have said that they

---

[1] "CBS News Falls for Hoax, Reports on Nonexistent 'Sideways Tornado'." *Gawker*, August 2014. http://thevane.gawker.com/cbs-news-falls-for-hoax-reports-on-nonexistent-sidewa-1617162073

[2] "The Myth of the War of the Worlds Panic." Jefferson Pooley and Michael J. Socolow, *Slate*, October 2013. http://www.slate.com/articles/arts/history/2013/10/orson_welles_war_of_the_worlds_panic_myth_the_infamous_radio_broadcast_did.html.

often find themselves wondering if they can trust a given piece of information from social media, or not. Some of them believe that social media are more likely than other sources to contain bad, false, unverified, or inaccurate information (Bressler et al., 2012; Vieweg et al., 2014). Emergency managers, who may also want to integrate information provided by the community, have also expressed doubts about the accuracy and reliability of social media (Merrick and Duffy, 2013). While disaster response organizations are used to operate with "good enough" information during emergencies, they seem to hold higher, even "unreasonable" standards of accuracy for data from social media (Tapia and Moore, 2014).

In social media during emergencies, it is easier to find a message describing something that is true, than it is to find a message describing something that is false (Mendoza et al., 2010). However, even if false information constitutes a minority of what is posted in social media, the negative consequences – practical, economical, legal, political – of trusting false information can be potentially large. Techniques such as human computation and machine learning can be used to provide more elements for experts to make this decision.

We begin this chapter with a general discussion of trust issues in social media during disasters (§8.1), explain how those are usually addressed within a policy-based model of trust (§8.2), and the difference between misinformation and disinformation (§8.3). Then, manually intensive methods based on crowdsourced verification are described (§8.4), followed by methods based on automatic supervised learning and hybrid methods (§8.5).

8.1 Emergencies, Media, and False Information

Criticism of media coverage of emergency situations is not new. A 1957 report published by the U.S. National Academy of Sciences raised serious issues about the way in which the media, specially the radio, informed and misinformed about disasters: "The methods of handling and reporting disasters by the mass media of communication have varied over a wide spectrum from the highly sensational, dramatic, false, and distorted at one end to the sane, verified, factual, and complete at the other" (Fritz and Mathewson, 1957).

The fact that reporters from mainstream media are increasingly relying on social media sources during crises, has opened a new front for criticism. Disclaimers indicating that information could not be independently verified, which tend to appear when social media photos or videos are used in news reporting, do not exempt media from being a target when those photos or videos convey the wrong information. For instance, in 2012 the BBC used an old photo from the war in Iraq to illustrate a more recent massacre in Syria.[3] In 2013, during the manhunt that followed the Boston Marathon bombings, the *New York Post* published on its front page the photos of two innocent bystanders who were mistakenly identified as suspects by the social media site Reddit. After the real culprits were located, U.S. President Barack Obama chastised the press: "In this age of instant reporting and tweets and blogs, there's a temptation to latch onto any bit of information, sometimes to jump to conclusions. But when a tragedy like this happens, with public safety at risk and the stakes so high, it's important that we do this right. That's why we have investigations. That's why we relentlessly gather the facts."[4] The Red Cross also advocates caution when dealing with unverified information: "Protection actors should take measures to minimize the risk of presenting a false or incomplete image of the issues they intend to address. In a crisis situation, a protection actor may feel under pressure to communicate findings that are not fully verified. When this happens, it is important to avoid hastily extrapolating firm conclusions, or being overly affirmative" (ICRC, 2013).

Social media provides a wealth of immediate information about developing situations, with multiple voices and perspectives that simply cannot be ignored by traditional news media and by humanitarian organizations. For these organizations, dealing with unverified information is often not a matter of choice, but a necessity. A degree of uncertainty is inevitable, and the extent to which information should be trusted is a matter that depends on weighting trade-offs that vary according to the situation (Tapia et al., 2013; Tapia and Moore, 2014). In other words, the risk of acting on incomplete information should not prevent an important operation from going ahead: "a lack of fully verified information is no reason for inaction when there are compelling reasons to suspect that violations have been committed, and might be repeated" (ICRC, 2013).

Timing is important for response and relief organizations: at the onset of a emergency response effort, when time presses but information is limited, there is more risk in ignoring social media information even if it has not been completely validated. As the situation evolves, the role of social media may be less central as other sources of information emerge.

Timing is also important for social media users. In time-critical situations, they have a preference for incomplete but early information over complete but late information. For instance, earthquake alerts from seismic sensors

[3] "BBC News uses Iraq photo to illustrate Syrian massacre." Hannah Furness, *Telegraph*, May 2012. http://www.telegraph.co.uk/news/worldnews/middleeast/syria/9293620/ BBC-News-uses-Iraq-photo-to-illustrate-Syrian-massacre.html

[4] "Statement by the President." *The White House, Office of the Press Secretary*, April 2013. https://www.whitehouse.gov/the-press-office/2013/04/19/statement-president.

are usually validated carefully by experts before they are issued, but a study by Comunello et al. (2015) indicated that users strongly prefer an immediate message in social media about an earthquake with a provisional estimate of its magnitude (marked "provisional estimate"), instead of a message ten to twenty minutes later, once the magnitude has been confirmed.

Additionally, social media information, as other types of information, is affected by *information expiration*, that is, something that was valid before but is no longer valid now (Vieweg et al., 2014). Internet users may contribute to this problem. For instance, more people posted about a warning message concerning a shooting at a university, than about the notification that this warning had been lifted (Hui et al., 2012; Tyshchuk et al., 2012).

8.2 Policy-Based Trust and Social Media

There are various ways in which we can approach the problem of trust, including: policy-based trust, reputation-based trust, and trust in information resources (Artz and Gil, 2007).

Policy-based trust means that only specific people and organizations are trusted for a given information category. Traditionally, governments, humanitarian, and emergency response organizations follow this model, which is to some extent mirrored by large Internet media dealing with emergency response. Information is trusted because it comes from an official source (Tapia and Moore, 2014). For instance, Twitter maintains a list of verified emergency-related accounts – only these accounts are authorized to push emergency notifications in case of a disaster.[5]

Reputation-based trust, or *source trust*, seeks to quantify to what extent we should trust on a certain source, based on the evidence we have collected so far. *Trust in information resources*, or *content trust*, seeks to quantify to what extent we should trust on a given piece of content, again based on the evidence we have collected so far. Source trust and content trust are inseparably linked: a trusted source produces and shares trusted content, and trusted content is produced and shared by trusted sources.

The main problem with policy-based trust in social media, is that it forces a binary decision (to trust or not to trust) on an issue that is a matter of degree. Trustworthy information is acquired by collecting and contrasting information from multiple sources, and seldom yields perfectly reliable information: "When

---

[5] "Twitter Alerts: Critical information when you need it most." Gabriela Pena, *Twitter Blog*, September 2013. https://blog.twitter.com/2013/twitter-alerts-critical-information-when-you-need-it-most.

in doubt, the information should be tagged as unverified. Several levels of reliability may be used when deciding to tag the reliability of information obtained through open sources" (ICRC, 2013).

Intelligence analysts in the NATO military as well as those of Australia and New Zealand use a two-dimensional scale to grade intelligence. This includes a dimension of reliability of the source, and another of credibility of the information; both are evaluated independently. Source reliability is expressed on a scale from "A" (source completely reliable) to "E" (unreliable source), with "F" being unknown source reliability; information credibility is expressed on a scale from 1 (confirmed by other sources) to 4 (improbable), with 5 being unknown credibility (U.K. Ministry of Defence, 2014).

Internet users often trust social media as much as they trust traditional news media sources, even for contentious issues such as political elections (see, e.g., ORI Market Research, 2012). People do not express feelings of being misled, suspicious or mistrustful about social media information, as often as they express that they find that information in social media is useful (Taylor et al., 2012). However, they also show a strong propensity for referencing traditional sources including high-reputation news media outlets, official government sources, and well-established nongovernmental organizations (Thomson et al., 2012; Reuter et al., 2015b).

To some extent, Internet users also operate on a policy-based trust model, but their trust policies are more fluid than the ones applied by emergency and humanitarian organizations, and more dependent on the context. For instance, users in Pakistan perceive social media as more truthful during disasters than traditional media (Murthy and Longwell, 2013), while Japanese users believe the exact opposite, and rate social media as much less trustworthy than traditional media (Hokudai Earthquake Project, 2011).

8.3 Misinformation and Disinformation

One of the simplest ways of operationalizing trust – and by no means the only way – is to consider three elements: competence, benevolence, and integrity (Gefen, 2002).[6] Competence refers to the ability to give accurate information, benevolence to the willingness to do the effort, and integrity to honest behavior. Essentially, the main concern with respect to social media is the lack of any of these elements, that is, people not being in the position to

---

[6] Some authors add a fourth dimension, predictability (McKnight and Chervany, 2001), and others use just two factors: ability and intent (Thomson et al., 2012).

provide precise information, not being willing to do so, or not being truthful about what they know.

Failures in the sense of competence are normally associated to *misinformation*, which is unintentionally spread; failures in integrity are normally associated to *disinformation*, which is deliberately spread (Stahl, 2006). Failures in benevolence may be related to obstacles or lack of incentives to provide information (bringing us back to the study of motivations of Section 7.3).

Misinformation tends to be more present than disinformation during natural disasters. Users may repost information that they have not verified yet, possibly weighing the cost of a false alarm versus the cost of not raising an alarm when they should.

Disinformation, while also present during disasters from natural hazards, tends to appear more often during human-induced crises. Lewandowsky et al. (2013) highlight that, given that perceptions of populations are becoming as important as the will of armies and governments to fight, controlling information is becoming a central aspect of modern warfare. In general, when there are two sides in conflict, or when there are legal liabilities or political consequences expected from an event, some people may have incentives to spread deceptive information.

In March 2015 it was uncovered that a group from Russia was using a number of "fake" social media accounts to propagate fake screenshots purporting to be of CNN reporting an explosion in Centerville, Louisiana, in the United States.[7] In June 2015 it was reported that this was an organization of about four hundred employees tasked with posting disinformation online.[8]

Some online disinformation campaigns involve a small set of identities interacting heavily with each other, but not with other, "regular" users. This type of campaign can be detected using graph-based methods, uncovering groups of users that are likely to be colluding (Ratkiewicz et al., 2011).

8.4 Verification Practices

Humanitarian organizations increasingly recognize that there is a trade-off between accuracy and speed (ICRC, 2013). Navigating this trade-off is an everyday activity for many journalists, who can provide valuable input to humanitarians regarding information verification practices. An ideal of

---

[7] "Russia Is Hacking Your News Feed." Leonid Bershidsky, *Bloomberg View*, March 2015. http://www.bloombergview.com/articles/2015-03-11/russia-is-hacking-your-news-feed.

[8] "The Agency." Adrian Chen, *New York Times*, June 2015. http://mobile.nytimes.com/2015/06/07/magazine/the-agency.html.

professional journalism is that "being right is more important than being first," but implementing this ideal in reality is far from trivial.[9]

Over the years, a series of practices have emerged regarding verification of social media during emergencies. Many of these practices can be found in the "Verification Handbook" edited by Silverman (2014), which is a guide co-authored by journalists and other professionals of the media and emergency relief sectors. This handbook includes among other elements a taxonomy of types of fake disaster-related information online: (i) real photos from unrelated events; (ii) art, ads, film, and staged scenes; (iii) digitally edited images, (iv) social media accounts impersonating someone else (fake accounts); (v) altered social media reposts; (vi) fake social media screenshots; and (vii) fake websites.

The Verification Handbook also outlines a verification process or checklist for verifying content. First, determine the first occurence of this content online, to establish its *provenance*. Second, identify the author to establish whether the *source* of the information is reliable. Third, look at key aspects of the *content*, including its location and date. There are numerous tools that can be used during this process, including for instance reverse image search systems, that allow to search the Web for similar images to a given one.

Common journalistic practices, such as contacting and interviewing sources, have also been applied by emergency managers to deal with social media content. Latonero and Shklovski (2011) interview the Public Information Officer of the Los Angeles Fire Department in the United States. In this interview, the officer recalls how he sent an e-mail to a person posting information, asking him to call back to his office at the fire department, and discussed on the phone the account of this eyewitness. "I felt I was able to add reasonable validation of what they were seeing, relayed that information to our responders in the field, and it turned out that there were people and property in danger in that area, things we couldn't see, that were over the horizon away from us."

Information verification platforms. Many verification practices can be codified in systems that assist users in evaluating the veracity of a claim posted in social media. Reuter et al. (2015a) describe a software where users can select and weight evaluation criteria from a predefined list, and use simple user interface elements such as sliders to combine ratings across these criteria. This software also integrates automatically computed elements that can help evaluate veracity, such as the distance between the location of a user and the place where the crisis is taking place.

---

[9] "Inside the BBC's Verification Hub." David Turner, *Nieman Reports*, July 2012. http://niemanreports.org/articles/inside-the-bbcs-verification-hub/.

The verification practices used by journalists, analysts, and emergency responders cannot scale to a large volume of information, as they are limited by factors such as the size of the staff in these organizations. However, these practices can be scaled up with the help of volunteers through crowdsourcing. In a crowdsourced verification platform, volunteers are invited to look at claims posted by journalists or emergency managers (e.g., a photo showing the consequences of severe weather), and are asked to provide evidence in favor or against that photo. An example of such system is Verily,[10] introduced by Popoola et al. (2013).

Visible skepticism. Messages containing false information are frequently discredited or questioned in social media (Sutton, 2010; Castillo et al., 2013; Resnick et al., 2014). These self-correction mechanisms of social media are valuable, but they do not solve the problem of misinformation, because many people are exposed to false information but not to the messages correcting it (Resnick et al., 2014; Carton et al., 2015). However, this suggests a way of dealing with false information in social media: by encouraging users to discuss about dubious content in social media itself. For instance, users can be encouraged to post messages about incorrect information, as has been done in several emergencies by using the *#Mythbuster* hashtag.[11]

There is a temptation to try to remove or censor false information, but this may not be the best strategy in comparison with the practice of *visible skepticism*: "Repeatedly allowing a rumor to surface and be corrected is different from correcting it once and then blocking it from surfacing again. The latter stops the rumor's spread within the current platform, but the former may do more to quell its spread through other channels, by challenging it as it comes up again and again" (Dailey and Starbird, 2014). When users are exposed to the refutation of a message simultaneously to the message itself, they are significantly less likely to share dubious content, and repeated exposure to information countering a rumor is more likely to reduce users' propensity to repeat that rumor than a warning such as "this tweet may contain misinformation" (Ozturk et al., 2015).

8.5 Automatic Credibility Analysis

Aristotle's *Rethoric* offered a blueprint of persuasion based on three key elements, which are often succinctly described as credibility (*ethos*), emotions

---

[10] Verily Crowdsourced Verification. http://veri.ly/.
[11] "Using #Mythbuster Tweets to Tackle Rumors During Disasters." Patrick Meier, *iRevolution*, January 2013. http://irevolution.net/2013/01/27/mythbuster-tweets/.

(*pathos*) and reason (*logos*). These elements can be used to describe methods for automatic credibility analysis.

Automatic reasoning. Only a few initial steps have been done on automating the verification of information based on patterns of reasoning, that is, the *logos* aspect in the *Rethoric*. Dong et al. (2015) introduced Knowledge-Based Trust (KBT), which is computed by automatically extracting facts from a Web page (i.e., triples of the form *<subject, object, predicate>*), and then determining to what extent those facts agree with facts posted on other Web pages. The main technical difficulty is that with current technologies, the error rate of information extractors is actually higher than the rate at which people introduce factual errors in content. Dong et al. (2015) address this problem by incorporating the error rate of the information extraction into the probabilistic framework used to estimate how much trust to place in an extracted fact.

Sharing, refutation, and questioning. While Mendoza et al. (2010) did not find a difference between how much truthful information and false rumors were retweeted in Twitter, they did note that information that turned out to be false was significantly more questioned and refuted. Questioning and refutation of information tends to appear at latter stages in the lifetime of a rumor. This was depicted by *The Guardian*'s study about the diffusion of news stories during the 2011 London riots.[12] A time slider can be used to interact with this visualization, making it evident that in many of these rumors, there is an initial period at which false messages "peak," followed by a period in which refutation messages are more prevalent, but in general in smaller quantities than the false messages that preceded it.

The fact that false rumors are more likely to be questioned and refuted can be used in automatic systems that detect credibility, by grouping messages belonging to the same story and then performing a per-cluster analysis of the data (Castillo et al., 2011).

Information credibility. The majority of research on automatic methods to help people decide how much to trust on a given content, has been based on the notion of *information credibility*, which is more closely related to the concept of *ethos* in the *Rethoric*. *Ethos* is established through the credentials of an author, bringing us back to policy-based trust – however, it is also established through tone and style.

---

[12] "Reading the Riots." *The Guardian*, December 2011. This visualization uses propagation histories, described on Section 5.2. http://www.theguardian.com/uk/interactive/2011/dec/07/london-riots-twitter.

Fogg and Tseng (1999) describe information credibility as the quality of information being believable, and emphasize that this is a perceived quality that is made from multiple elements. Automatic systems that can emulate human perceptions of credibility, that is, predict whether a person would say that she believes in a given message, are well within grasp of current computational methods, particularly supervised learning. Two main elements are required: being able to collect ground truth from users, and being able to computationally model credible content. Ground truth for credibility is easier to obtain than from most other aspects of content trust. Determining if a piece of content is true or false may be extremely time consuming and often requires a great amount of background knowledge or context. In contrast, determining if a piece of content is believable is something we do every day on an intuitive basis, and hence tends to be a relatively fast operation.

Textual features. Basic methods to distinguish between credible and non-credible messages use a series of textual features computed from the text. These are similar to the stylometric features used by the NLP community for problems related to authorship attribution (Stamatatos, 2009).

To model the credibility of information on Twitter during emergencies, Castillo et al. (2011, 2013) use a series of content-based, user-based features, and propagation-based features which are used as input for a supervised classifier using a decision tree algorithm. As preprocessing, messages that are not deemed of interest by another automatic classifier are discarded from the set. Gupta and Kumaraguru (2012) use content- and user-based features as inputs to an SVM classifier. Their dataset consists of 14 crisis events, and their system is implemented as a browser plugin in Gupta et al. (2014). Some of the features used in these works are listed in Table 8.1.

These methods depend on human annotation for training, and as such, assume that people can to a certain degree agree on whether a message is credible or not. McCreadie et al. (2015a) note that this is in general true, but the degree of agreement depends on the type of message and the way in which a question is framed. For instance, asking people whether a message contains controversial or disputed information tends to elicit less agreement than asking people whether a message states a fact.

With respect to the evaluation of methods for estimating information credibility, ideally this should be done on publicly accessible collections. *CREDBANK* (Mitra and Gilbert, 2015) is a reference collection of social media messages annotated with credibility assessments.

Topics and expertise. A different research direction attempts to model explicitly a form of source trust, that is, the expertise of authors on different topics,

Table 8.1 *Partial list of features used in automatic information credibility systems for Twitter, from Castillo et al. (2011, 2013); Gupta and Kumaraguru (2012); Gupta et al. (2014).*

Type	Examples
Content	Features computed from the content of the message, such as: (1) Length of the tweet, (2) number of words, (3) number of unique characters, (4) number of hashtags, (5) number of retweets, (6) number of swear language words, (7) number of positive sentiment words, (8) number of negative sentiment words, (9) tweet is a retweet, (10) tweet is a reply, (11) number of special symbols [$, !], (12) number of emoticons [:-), :-(], (13) Number of @-mentions, (14) number of retweets, (15) time lapse since the query, (16) has URL, (17) number of URLs, (18) use of a URL shortener service
User	Features computed from the author of the message, such as: (1) registration age of the user, (2) number of messages posted, (3) number of followees, (4) number of followers, (5) ratio of followers to followees, (6) number of user-created lists in which it is included, (7) number of user-created lists created, (8) is a verified account, (9) length of self-description ("bio"), (10) length of screen name, (11) has a URL
Propagation	Features computed from a message's reposting history, including aggregates computed from content and user features, such as: (1) fraction of tweets that contain URLs, (2) fraction of tweets with hashtags, (3) fraction of sentiment words, positive and negative, (4) depth of reposting tree, (5) number of reposts

and assign more credibility to the messages they write on topics in which they are likely to be experts. Expertise modeling can be done, for instance, by studying the contents users produce and how those contents propagate (Tang et al., 2009). These models of expertise have been used to identify and rank potentially credible or trustworthy users for a given topic (Canini et al., 2011; Zielinski et al., 2013).

With respect to crisis-related messages, Ito et al. (2015) describe a method for computing credibility using topics discovered by unsupervised methods. This is done by first running LDA to compute the topics of a user and the topics of a message. Two types of basic features can be derived from these, to measure the concentration of topics (e.g., whether the user repeatedly posts about the same topic) and to measure the correspondence of topics (e.g., whether the user's previous posts match the topic(s) of the current post).

Some people take advantage of the popularity of a certain hashtag, which means many people are searching for that hashtag, to write messages publicizing certain products (Earle et al., 2010). Spam detection methods for social media can be applied to remove these messages (Benevenuto et al., 2010), as well as bots (as described on Section 2.3). This is also related to methods for finding false product reviews, which is a well-studied subject that has many elements in common with the problem of determining whether a crisis-related message in social media should be trusted. Methods for detecting false product reviews are overviewed in Liu (2012, ch. 10).

8.6 Research Problems

Extending automatic verification methods. Content-based methods for verification are an interesting research direction, but they require multiple reports referring to the same situation, which may or may not be available at a given time. Logical inconsistencies in a message are one potential sign that the information is incorrect, but they are only one of many possible reasons in which information may be incorrect. More research is needed to understand to what extent these methods can contribute to verify claims done on social media during crises.

Creating new human verification methods. Rumors are a problem-solving strategy, a way of rapidly improvising an interpretation of an ambiguous situation (Shibutani, 1966); as such, they are inherent to sense-making. Understanding the verification practices used by professional journalists and/or emergency response organizations is key to be able to assist them. Verification practices for social media should also evolve as the technology matures.

Modeling the credibility of other contents generated by the public. Many types of emergency-related communications have to deal routinely with false information. For instance, every year there are literally millions of false calls to 911, the main emergency number used in the United States.[13] In the United Kingdom, the Metropolitan Police receives tens of thousands of misuse or hoax calls every year.[14] Computing methods developed for social media can be extended to deal with these types of false information during emergencies.

---

[13] See, e.g., "City flooded with nearly 4 million inadvertent 911 calls on cell phones a year." Juan Gonzalez, *New York Daily News*, May 2012. https://www.nydailynews.com/new-york/city-flooded-4-million-inadvertent-911-calls-cell-phones-year-article-1.1074752 or "Fake 911 calls aren't cheap." Ed Boyle, *CBS News London*, June 2012. http://www.cbsnews.com/news/fake-911-calls-arent-cheap/.

[14] "999 'time wasters': Where do emergency services draw the line?" Alex Homer, *BBC News*, August 2014. http://www.bbc.com/news/uk-england-28562807.

8.7 Further Reading

Artz and Gil (2007) present a brief conceptual framework for trust research in computer science. Sherchan et al. (2013) present a survey on trust in social media.

Hermida (2014, ch. 8), describes misinformation and disinformation in social media from the perspective of journalists and online content producers. Meier (2015, ch. 7 and 8) addresses verification of crisis data using human and machine intelligence.

9

Validity: Biases and Pitfalls of Social Media Data

In 2008 Google launched Flu Trends, showing that the search volume of certain terms in a region was strongly correlated with levels of flu activity in that region.[1] They also found that the increase in the usage of flu-related terms happened days before health care authorities were able to report an increase in cases of flu. The reasons are twofold: there are delays in the official data collection done from hospitals, and people search for symptoms before visiting a doctor. Despite the success of Flu Trends, it was not beyond criticism. Lazer et al. (2014) highlighted a series of issues with its predictions, including a systemic bias that produced an overestimate in 100 out of the 108 weeks analyzed during a two-year period. As a more general criticism, Lazer et al. denounced this as an example of *big data hubris:* the assumption that a large dataset can be a substitute, rather than a supplement, to a traditional analysis method. The popular press has lambasted "big data fundamentalism," the idea that larger datasets imply more objective results.[2]

Researchers performing social science research have embraced and criticized, sometimes at the same time, the usage of large-scale datasets from social media. Social media, as a reflection of social interactions at large scale and in digitally accessible formats, provides a larger quantity of data at a much lower cost than alternative datasets, such as surveys or direct observations. However, the infamous "streetlight effect" may be at play here: scientists inclined to search for evidence where it is easier, instead of where better evidence is likely to be found.[3]

---

[1] Google Flu Trends. http://www.google.org/flutrends/.

[2] "Why Big Data Is Not Truth." Quentin Hardy, *International New York Times*, June 2013. http://bits.blogs.nytimes.com/2013/06/01/why-big-data-is-not-truth/.

[3] See, for instance, "Why Scientific Studies Are So Often Wrong: The Streetlight Effect." David H. Freeman, *Discover Magazine*, December 2010. http://discovermagazine.com/2010/jul-aug/29-why-scientific-studies-often-wrong-streetlight-effect.

The representativeness of social media and other types of digital traces, and their lack of context, are often cited as key factors to distrust conclusions based solely on them. "Just because you see traces of data doesn't mean you always know the intention or cultural logic behind them. And just because you have a big N doesn't mean that it's representative or generalizable."[4] For instance, methods to use trends found on Twitter data as direct predictions of political election results, have been to a large extent debunked (Gayo-Avello, 2012).

This chapter warns against a naïve interpretation of results obtained from social media data from emergencies. The quality of social media data for this purpose is affected by at least two types of factors. First, using social media as a data source introduces a series of biases that are difficult to evaluate and that can change rapidly over time. Second, automatic processing methods, particularly probabilistic ones, may introduce errors that might distort the results.

These concerns do not mean that we cannot answer relevant questions using this data, but instead that we should be cautious about the inferences drawn from the data, and the way those inferences are communicated to end users who make decisions at least partially based on them. It is important to continuously understand the biases being introduced and to validate results obtained through social media data against other sources of information. This chapter presents research that goes in that direction. First, example works comparing data obtained from social media with data from "offline" phenomena are presented (§9.1). Second, issues of sampling bias due to social (§9.2), contextual (§9.3) and technological (§9.4) problems are discussed, including methods for validating and contrasting this data with other sources. We then go deeper into spatial (§9.5) and temporal (§9.6) aspects of this validation.

9.1 Studying the "Offline" World Using "Online" Data

The comparison done by Google Flu Trends of an "online" variable (searches for flu-related trends) with an "offline" variable (visits to hospitals for flu-related symptoms) provided a template for a series of works that performed similar comparisons. Researchers turned their attention to all kinds of user-generated data, including logs of online searches, blog postings, news articles, and social media messages, among other types of data. Correlations between time series extracted from these media and other variables were found for the

---

[4] "Big Data: Opportunities for computational and social sciences." Blog post by danah boyd, April 2010. http://www.zephoria.org/thoughts/archives/2010/04/17/big-data-opportunities-for-computational-and-social-sciences.html. "Big N" is an informal way of describing a large dataset, for instance, a large number of people or a large number of messages.

stock market (Bollen et al., 2011), the market of jobs (Ettredge et al., 2005) and cars (Choi and Varian, 2012), the box office revenue of movies (Asur and Huberman, 2010), the sales of music and video games (Goel et al., 2010), and results in political elections (Tumasjan et al., 2010).

Scientists were quick to point out, however, that there are many limitations to these predictions. First, in a large group of time series, significant correlations among random pairs of series are likely to be observed. For instance, in the 2000–2009 period, the U.S. per-capita consumption of margarine and the divorce rate in the U.S. state of Maine were correlated at $r = 0.99$ (Vigen, 2015). Second, for media products (e.g., music), sometimes there are public data sources, such as Billboard Top 100 lists, that produce predictions of record sales that are similar or better than those obtained with large online datasets (Goel et al., 2010). Third, in the political arena, serious issues were observed regarding the generalizability of results obtained for one country in one type of election, to a different country, and/or a different type of election (Gayo-Avello, 2011).

De-biasing can be done to some extent, under certain circumstances (Zagheni and Weber, 2015), but in general no resampling methodology can be used to reproduce faithfully the results of a different study using a different survey methodology (e.g., phone surveys vs. social media). These problems are compounded when datasets over which this research is done are not publicly available, making it harder to disprove wrong conclusions (Lazer et al., 2014; Ruths and Pfeffer, 2014).

Data from online and social media data can be interpreted as a type of survey done over an opt-in "panel" of Internet users. However, there are many distortions in this data, including people who have multiple accounts and accounts used by multiple people, and the fact that online social connections are an inaccurate reflection of actual interpersonal ties (boyd and Crawford, 2012). More worryingly, the participation and topical coverage of this type of data is not only unrepresentative of the general population, it is also much more dynamic and less predictable than conventional survey panels: "In short, if online and social media data are to be treated as surveys, they must be treated as imperfect surveys indeed" (Diaz et al., 2016).

For many practitioners of humanitarian and emergency response, the distinction between "offline" and "online" may be relevant, but perhaps a more important distinction is between the "traditional" datasets they have used for years, such as weather reports, and "new" and emerging datasets, such as social media. A general problem of attempting to answer questions about society using online data, is that online data sets are big, but there is no guarantee that they are representative of the behavior of the general population. During a crisis, the presence of a social media message about a particular situation depends on many factors, including the person being willing and able to post information about the situation, his/her availability of a device able to post that message, the availability of network connectivity, and in the case of a geotagged message, the capability and intention of the device owner to include these geotags. Each of these factors introduces a new bias in the data.

The questions we explore next are basically about the extent to which datasets created from social media can be useful for research and practice on disaster response, about the systematic issues these datasets have, and the consequences of those issues.

9.2 The Digital Divide

The ICRC highlights two issues stemming from biases in crisis data. First, they can result in unintentional discrimination, leaving out some participants "owing to language ability, political affiliation, educational level, access to communication means when using crowdsourcing, or other factors." Second, even when there is no discrimination, "sampling bias hampers an accurate understanding of the situation and distorts the resultant protection response" (ICRC, 2013).

The *digital divide* is the enormous disparity that exists in terms of access to information and communication technologies among people living in different countries, as well as people living within the same country. A related concept is the *data-divide:* the lack of availability of high-quality data that affects low- and middle-income countries (Cinnamon and Schuurman, 2013). Worryingly, a large portion of research on social media for emergency management has been focused on populations that have widespread access to mobile social media. With some exceptions, there is little work on how access to these technologies impacts the results obtained by researchers (Hughes et al., 2014b).

According to 2015 data, about 60% of the world has no access to the Internet. Furthermore, access is very uneven across the world. There is a huge gap between average levels of access in developed countries (78%), in comparison to developing countries (32%).[5] In many countries, many people do not have easy access to mobile phone and the Internet, they have a vulnerable structure that can be easily destroyed or interrupted, and they lack a reliable electricity supply (Whipkey and Verity, 2015).

Within countries there are also huge differences. For instance, in 2011 a Gallup poll of mobile phone users in 17 African countries revealed that mobile

---

[5] International Telecommunications Union (ITU) Statistics: http://www.itu.int/en/ITU-D/ Statistics/.

phone usage was significantly more common among the urban, affluent, and educated.[6] The same has been observed in China, where historically the Internet penetration in rural areas is less than one-third of that in urban areas (White and Fu, 2012 citing data from CNNIC[7]). Even in urban areas, within a city different neighborhoods may have vastly different levels of Internet access.[8]

The fact that huge differences exist in terms of access to social media and mobile devices, does not mean that these channels should not be used. The situation has some similarities with what happened when the system supporting the emergency phone number 911 was set up in 1968 in the United States. Many municipalities did not provide the service until the 1980s and it was not until the 1990s that it was widely adopted. Still, it is hard to dispute the utility of this service on the grounds that it was not universally accessible during its first two decades; never in history everyone has had access to the same communication technologies at the same time.[9]

In general, new technologies are less available for elderly people, less educated people, people with low income, people in rural areas, people belonging to a linguistic minority, and people with disabilities.[10] The latter group is particularly vulnerable during emergencies when information is communicated through social media, as Bricout and Baker (2010) note, because computing technologies are in general less adapted for people with disabilities than other forms of media, such as the television.

As noted by Castells (2001) among others, the digital divide is not simply a matter of Internet connections per person across different groups of people, but about the consequences of having or not having a connection. Analyzing annotations in Google Earth after the 2005 Hurricane Katrina, Crutcher and Zook (2009) noted a strong divide along racial lines: neighborhoods with large African American populations were less likely to have volunteered geographical annotations, even when those were as affected or more than other neighborhoods. Elwood (2008) also warns about volunteered geographical information systems as potential contributors to inequalities. For instance, census data undercounts people in places were there are more homeless or informal settlements, and a neighborhood perceived as vibrant by a minority group may

---

[6] "Mobile Phone Access Varies Widely in Sub-Saharan Africa." *Gallup Poll*, September 2011. http://www.gallup.com/poll/149519/mobile-phone-access-varies-widely-sub-saharan-africa .aspx.

[7] China Internet Network Information Center: http://www1.cnnic.cn/IDR/ReportDownloads/.

[8] "Map the iPhone Users In Any City, And You Know Where the Rich Live." Emily Badger, *CityLab*, June 2013. http://www.citylab.com/work/2013/06/map-iphone-users-any-city-and-you-know-where-rich-live/5961/.

[9] "Big Data for Disaster Response: A List of Wrong Assumptions" Patrick Meier, *iRevolution*, June 2013. http://irevolution.net/2013/06/10/wrong-assumptions-big-data/.

[10] Duke University Digital Divide Microsite: http://sites.duke.edu/digitaldivide/.

be perceived as a dangerous neighborhood by those who do not belong to that minority. The way in which people contribute new information may contribute to increase or decrease power imbalances due to this data.

Coming back to the consequences of the digital divide, on the one hand, even if only few people in an affected area can send an SMS or post an update on social media, the fact that these messages reach relief workers can be potentially very helpful for the entire community. On the other hand, technologists must constantly remind themselves and users of their systems of all the gaps in their data, including the communities that are underrepresented or excluded (Crawford and Finn, 2014).

9.3 Content Production Issues

People selectively choose what to share online, and even the ones who seem to disclose "everything" online, and perhaps particularly them, in reality engage in a performance and presentation of a carefully edited self (Marwick and boyd, 2011; Marwick, 2013, ch. 5).

During a crisis, there are many reasons why someone may decide to post, or not to post, certain pieces of information online. For instance, in cases of armed conflict, some people may self-censor themselves to avoid becoming a target of violence (we come back to this in Section 11.2). In the same situation, others may engage in the spread of disinformation (as discussed in Section 8.3).

Depending on the specifics of a crisis, some types of information are rarely posted or absent from social media. Saleem et al. (2014) note that, for instance, lists of names of emergency-related casualties are in general not shared early during a crisis. Additionally, the information expiration problem discussed in Section 8.1 is a serious issue with respect to the information people share online during an emergency. People are more prone to indicate that a danger exists or that an item is needed, than that a danger no longer exists or that an item has already been supplied – contributing, for instance, to the "second disaster" of having to deal with donations that are no longer needed by those affected.[11]

The way in which a situation is described by the public also depends on each individual's capacity to communicate effectively. In an ideal case, their messages should use the same terms and expressions used by emergency management agencies – but there is no indication this is, indeed, the case. Semantic technologies can contribute to some extent to solve this mismatch (as discussed on Section 3.7).

---

[11] "The 'Second Disaster': Making Well-Intentioned Donations Useful." Pam Fessler, *NPR*, January 2013. http://www.npr.org/2013/01/12/169198037/the-second-disaster-making-good-intentions-useful.

Quantitative information is also scarce. Purohit et al. (2014a) note that quantifiers in social media regarding emergency resources are extremely rare, for instance, basically no message about an emergency shelter in their data mentioned how many people could that shelter accommodate. Saleem et al. (2014) observed in the 2013 Alberta floods in Canada that most eyewitness reports of water level used figurative or vague language rather than standard units of length – however, they also note that photos depicting the water level were used extensively and could be interpreted (with manual labor) to estimate flood heights. Sellam and Alonso (2015) were able to find a few thousand tweets containing useful quantitative information in a corpus of millions, Crutcher and Zook (2009) cite volunteer-provided annotations about the 2005 Hurricane Katrina in Google Earth that speak about water levels of "5 inches" or reaching the "2nd story," and Earle et al. (2010) report that some people try to guess the magnitude of an earthquake, although frequently confusing intensity and magnitude (e.g., *"Minor earthquake. Maybe a 4"* and *"just felt an earthquake here . . . 5.5?"*).

9.4 Infrastructure and Technological Factors

Connectivity. After the 2010 earthquake in Haiti, cell phone towers were still operational enough for people to send and receive SMS messages, which has shown to be a quite resilient technology across disasters (Liu, 2014). However, disasters can certainly cause disruptions such as energy and communications blackouts, particularly in less-developed countries (Whipkey and Verity, 2015). In some crisis situations, mobile networks have shown to be less resilient than expected. Jennex (2012) studied the 2011 blackout in San Diego, observing that more than 90% of people either lost mobile Internet access or experienced a degradation of it, with only about 35% of mobile users retaining some sort of Internet access; 17% of those who attempted to update their Twitter status were able to do it without problems. Depending on the type of application, this may or may not be sufficient to obtain a general picture of the needs and concerns of those in the affected area.

In other cases, such as the 2012 Hurricane Sandy in the United States, mobile phone voice service was interrupted in some areas, while Internet communications continued – causing people to flock to Internet-based telephony to communicate with others about their situation (Whittaker, 2012). When Internet connectivity survives a disaster, it has the potential to provide crisis communications, particularly in places where other infrastructure is poor (White and Fu, 2012).

Even without Internet access due to a disaster or because of human intervention (e.g., an intentional Internet blackout mandated by the government during a demonstration), alternative network topologies may be used. "Mesh" networks in which devices connect to each other instead of to centralized servers, have been implemented in popular mobile apps that provide online messaging services independently of the availability of Internet.[12]

Damages to transport infrastructure can also affect the generation of content by mobile phone users. If the population is immobilized, for instance, during a flood situation where roads are dangerous, people do not have access to vantage points and instead will post from wherever they find themselves at that moment (Saleem et al., 2014).

Technology factors. Different platforms are used by different people for different purposes, and have different interaction modalities. For instance, some of them allow people to "dislike" or "downvote" content, while others do not. Different interaction modalities reinforce the fact that different platforms appeal to different demographics. In other words, the choice of a social media platform as a data source obviously affects the results that are obtained.

The data collection interfaces offered by social media platforms also introduce biases. Researchers do not know the exact sampling, ranking, and filtering methods used by the publicly available data consumption interfaces provided by social media (boyd and Crawford, 2012), and do not even know if those are stable or change over time. Undisclosed changes in sampling rates can be deceiving, for instance an increasing trend might be the result of an actual decrease in the data and a higher sampling rate. Morstatter et al. (2014) showed discrepancies between Twitter's public API and full datasets obtained from this service.

The usage of inference-based methods to enrich textual data, such as geocoding, is useful but may also introduce errors in the data. For instance, "someone might text the crisis map's phone number to report something they saw earlier, possibly texting from a shelter about a bridge that collapsed 10 miles down the road." (Gao et al., 2011).

9.5 The Geography of Events and Geotagged Social Media

Malik et al. (2015) studied whether geotagged tweets were spread in the United States following population patterns, in other words, whether they were representative of the locations of people. While at a very high level a map of geotagged tweets looks similar to a map of large metropolitan areas and cities, when looking in detail they observed that socioeconomical and demographic

---

[12] "Why a messaging app meant for festivals became massively popular during Hong Kong protests." Amar Toor, *The Verge*, October 2014. https://www.theverge.com/2014/10/16/6981127/firechat-messaging-app-accidental-protest-app-hong-kong.

factors play a much bigger role than population densities in the density of geotagged tweets. Anecdotally, the largest density of geotagged tweets in the United States was observed from Las Vegas Strip, several large airports, and Walt Disney World; and several densely populated areas, such as prisons, had no geotagged tweets.

After this result, one could wonder if there is any chance that social media activity around a given place can be correlated with crisis or disaster events in that place. Actually, a number of researchers have documented that such correlations exist.

The U.S. Geological Service (USGS) has done a a multiyear, multidisciplinary effort to determine to what extent Twitter can be used as a social sensor for earthquakes (Earle et al., 2010; Guy et al., 2010). Their starting point is the empirical observation that conversations in social media including the word "earthquake" are rare, except in times and places where an earthquake has happened. Their studies have produced a number of increasingly more elaborate methods to interpret increases of social media activity.

Earthquakes have a typical distribution of intensities with an area of high intensity, and a radial pattern where intensities attenuate as the distance from this area increases. This distribution of intensities is usually matched by the activities observed in social media (e.g., by Evnine et al., 2014 for Facebook). This distribution can also be used to resolve ambiguities in the data. Robinson et al. (2015) present an example where they compare the distribution of social media messages posted in Australia and New Zealand in response to an earthquake in Melbourne (which was very concentrated around Melbourne) and the reaction in the same countries to an earthquake in Indonesia (which was much more spread).

As we noted on Section 2.1, earthquakes not only affect how users produce online information but also how they consume it. Bossu et al. (2008) show that the location of visitors to the most prominent website providing seismological information in Europe,[13] obtained from their IP address, can be used as a proxy to understand where an earthquake was felt.

Floods are other type of disaster where agreement with social media has been observed. Smith et al. (2015) compare water levels during 2012 inundations in different parts of Newcastle, England, against activities in Twitter measured through a relatively small sample of geocoded tweets, observing these are somewhat correlated. Dashti et al. (2014) observe a similar correlation between flood hazard zones determined using historical flood data in the county of Boulder in the United States, and tweets about the floods affecting the county in 2013.

---

[13] European-Mediterranean Seismological Centre: http://www.emsc-csem.org/.

Herfort et al. (2014); de Albuquerque et al. (2015) study floods during June 2013 in the river Elbe in Germany. They observe that flood-related messages in Twitter are indeed concentrated around cities close to the river, particularly Magdeburg. The similarity in geographical distributions is noticeable, and can be seen in Figure 9.1.

This bias toward cities is also observed by Sakaki et al. (2013) in their system for tracking the spatial movement of a phenomenon, such as a typhoon. They observe lower accuracy in determining geographical regions when the events happen on a sparsely populated area, such as an earthquake with an epicenter in the middle of the sea, or a typhoon happening far from the coast.

Additionally, geographical correlations have been observed in other nondisaster phenomena, including sightings of the Aurora Borealis which match well with geophysical data from geomagnetic storms (LaLone et al., 2015).

Data from social media can also be fused with other geographical data. For instance, the concentration of mobile phones in a given area, considered together with authoritative information about road networks, can be helpful during an evacuation for identifying bottlenecks or roadblocks (Oxendine et al., 2014).

Besides social media messages, data collected by mobile service providers has also been used to study geographical variables of disasters (Bagrow et al., 2011). Bengtsson et al. (2011) describe how information about the position of mobile phones, obtained from mobile service providers, was used to observe the movement of people out of Port-au-Prince in the aftermath of the 2010 earthquake in Haiti. Indeed, the estimations using mobile phone data were more accurate than those obtained by volunteers on the ground using surveys of buses and ships leaving the city, as confirmed by a detailed analysis done weeks after the disaster.

Intensity. While determining the geography of an incident using social media data may be addressed to some extent with current approaches, determining the intensity of the phenomenon in different areas seems to be quite difficult. In general, the frequency of postings about an emergency situation in different areas cannot be used as a proxy for the severity of the situation in those areas. Negative results in this sense include Saleem et al. (2014), who observed that particularly dangerous areas may not be covered by tweets during an ongoing crisis, and Vieweg et al. (2014), who compared the number of tweets containing hurricane-related terms in different islands in the Philippines, finding only a weak correlation between the number of messages posted on each island, and variables such as number of people affected or number of houses destroyed.

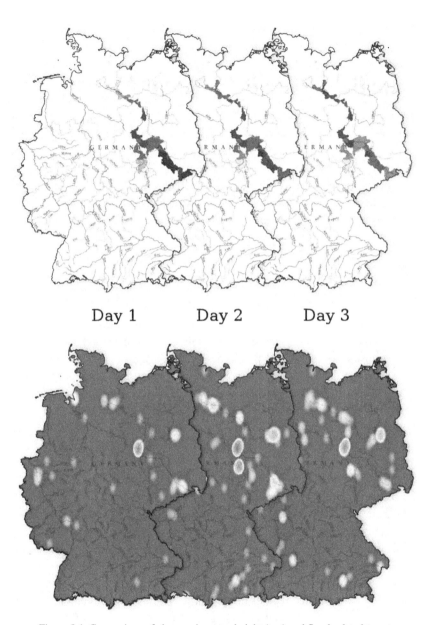

Day 1   Day 2   Day 3

Figure 9.1 Comparison of changes in water height (top) and flood-related tweets (bottom), during floods in the river Elbe in Germany from June 8, 2013 to June 10, 2013. Adapted from Herfort et al. (2014), using World Hydro Reference as overlay map. Reproduced with permission from the authors.

Promising results were reported by Chen et al. (2014) in the prediction of the Air Quality Index (AQI) in four large Chinese cities, considering variables computed from term frequencies in messages in Sina Weibo. These terms are related to coughing, wearing a mask, having sore throat or cold symptoms, and can be combined into a prediction of the AQI using a function learnt from historical data. Mei et al. (2014) extended these results in various ways. First, they considered all the words in each message, learning a regression model of the AQI based on the presence or absence of each word. Second, they assumed an element of spatial continuity, in which nearby areas should have similar air quality at a given time. Third, they assumed temporal dependencies in the form of a Markov process, in which the air quality at a given time depends on the air quality in the time interval immediately preceding it.

9.6 Evaluation of Alerts Triggered from Social Media

In Section 6.4, two metrics for evaluating event-detection methods were described: sensitivity (the fraction of events that are detected), and false detection rate (the fraction of alerts that are false). These metrics have been used in the evaluation of several prototypes and deployed systems for generating crisis alerts from social media. There are few reference datasets for evaluating event detection methods (McMinn et al., 2013 is one exception), so in general evaluations of different methods are done on different collections, making them difficult to compare. In general, the results show that existing systems offer a range of trade-offs between sensitivity and false detection rate, and they tend to perform better for large-scale events that are clearly perceived by the affected populations.

Earle et al. (2011) compared simple keyword-based approaches to measure the number of crisis-related messages in Twitter over time (e.g., counting how many messages contain "earthquake" and related terms), with data from seismological sensors. They found that although many earthquakes were not tweeted about, when people tweeted about an event, detections took in most cases less than two minutes, "considerably faster than seismographic detections in poorly instrumented regions of the world." During a five-month period and when compared to validated seismological data, the sensitivity of their system was nominally low: it detected 48 out of 5,175 earthquakes. However, most of the events it did not detect were of smaller magnitude and not actually felt by human populations, which means they had less potential to cause damage. Additionally, they false discovery rate was about 4%: only 2 out of the 48 detections were spurious.

Avvenuti et al. (2014) compared their system, *EARS*, against data from the Italian National Institute of Geophysics and Vulcanology (INGV). Similarly to Earle et al. (2011), they also reported that earthquakes of low magnitude (lower than 3.0) are very hard to detect using social media because they are basically detected only by physical sensors, but not felt by people. For earthquakes of magnitude 3.5 and above (20 in their sample of 70 days), their sensitivity is around 80% and their false detection rate, around 15%.

Robinson et al. (2013b) evaluated an earthquake detection system for Australia and New Zealand based on Twitter data. They report a sensitivity of 81% (17 alarms on 21 events over a 12-months period), and a false detection rate of 55% (a total of 31 alarms, out of which 17 were correct). They used a simple heuristic of imposing a minimum support of three tweets before triggering an alarm, which further reduced the false detection rate.

Power et al. (2013) study an alert system for fires based on automatic classification of Twitter messages. The system generated 42 fire alerts over a four-months period, of which 20 were related to actual fires (false discovery rate of 52%), which is a smaller number of false alarms than another system they describe, which was based entirely on keywords.

Merging social media data with other sources. *LITMUS* (Musaev et al., 2014) is an advanced system for detecting landslides that integrates data from multiple sources, including physical data measuring seismic activity and rainfall, and social media data from Twitter, YouTube, and Instagram. First, the world is divided into geographic cells covering 2.5 minutes of latitude and longitude each. Then, signals from each data source in each cell are aggregated using a weighted sum, in which the weights of different signals are calculated using a separate training set, and are related to the accuracy of each source independently when detecting a landslide. The authors show that the false discovery rate of this method is lower than one relying exclusively on physical sensors, at the expense of a loss of sensitivity of around 20%.

Merging data sources is a promising approach, but it also presents some challenges. Data integration problems may arise, which require systems that can interoperate. This is one more argument for the use of semantic technologies, and for the development of appropriate data standards that allow unambiguous data fusion.

9.7 Research Problems

Measuring the impact of bias. In crisis situations, some activities require high-quality data, whereas in other cases "good enough" data suffices (Zook et al., 2010; Tapia and Moore, 2014). Organizations used to take decisions with incomplete information, rarely come back to retrospectively evaluate to what extent their decisions were affected by incomplete or erroneous information, and what were the costs of those decisions.

The responsibility of measuring and countering the bias introduced by a new source of information lies with those who provide the information. Evaluating the extent to which bias affects decisions is necessary to enable the creation of reliable decision-support systems.

Estimating reliability. Similarly, more research is needed to be able to estimate the reliability of different predictions done with this data. For instance, systems that trace the geographical boundaries of a phenomenon using data from social media can provide a more accurate picture by also displaying the uncertainty of those boundaries. Systems that generate automatic alerts can benefit its users by exposing what is the estimated reliability of each of the alerts.

Understanding the value of disclaimers. Communicating the reliability of an inference, or reminding users of the lack of those reliability estimates, are also important to make the output of computational tools more valuable as decision-making elements. Crisis maps produced by the Standby Task Force during Typhoon Ruby carry the following footnote: "Social media is not necessarily representative or verified. Please keep this in mind when interpreting the crisis map."[14] This follows recommendations by organizations including the ICRC, which states that "Any external report should mention the reliability of its contents in general terms. Incidents that are not yet fully established can be included, as long as the level of reliability is clearly disclosed" (ICRC, 2013).

However a disclaimer that some information cannot be independently verified may not be effective at stopping an image from being widely circulated as "true," as we saw for the case of the photo of Iraq being used to illustrate an event in Syria by the BBC (Section 8.1). More research is needed to understand how journalists, emergency managers, and the public, interpret and act upon different types of disclaimer.

9.8 Further Reading

Crawford and Finn (2014) examine many limitations, both in terms of biases and ethical questions, of using social media data about disasters. Tufekci (2014)

---

[14] MicroMappers map for Typhoon Hagupit, 2014. http://maps.micromappers.org/2014/hagupit/tweets/.

exposes several methodological issues and interpretative pitfalls of research using social media data. boyd and Crawford (2012) identify general issues in current "big data" research, particularly the one that uses social media and online data.

Mejova et al. (2015) address several applications of Twitter data analysis to problems in the domains of health care, political opinion, city sensing, socioeconomic indicators, and disaster response. Their main focus is how messages on Twitter correlate with variables on these domains. Zagheni and Weber (2015) describe methods for reducing the bias introduced by using nonrepresentative populations extracted from the Internet. Reliable external information can be used to calibrate the measurements, and in some cases even without external information, if all one cares about are trends, even biased data can be used to some extent.

Hughes et al. (2014b) includes a practitioner's view of social media during emergencies, including several issues related to data reliability connected to the topics of this chapter.

10

Visualization: Crisis Maps and Beyond

"What can speed humanitarian response to tsunami-ravaged coasts? Expose human rights atrocities? Launch helicopters to rescue earthquake victims? Outwit corrupt regimes? A map." Patrick Meier's pioneering work in crisis mapping capitalizes on two key advantages of crisis maps: they act as a focus for digital volunteering efforts, and they provide information in a way that is familiar and easy to digest by relief agencies.[1]

Previous chapters have described several methods for filtering, classifying, consolidating, and extracting trends from social media messages. A last but not least step of this process is to present this information in a way that is helpful to its intended users. Emergency managers often express the requirement to incorporate social media messages into a Geographical Information System (GIS), using a map-based display (Hiltz et al., 2014). Beyond maps, other visualizations have been used to highlight other aspects of the data, such as temporal trends, themes, topics, or connections.

This chapter describes current practices in the presentation of crisis data extracted from social media. It builds upon the various methods to process and consolidate social media messages presented in previous chapters. The emphasis is on crisis maps, which is probably the most popular paradigm used by volunteer communities and social media users to present information about disasters (§10.1). The chapter also analyzes other visual elements that are present in existing "dashboards" about social media during crises (§10.2), including their interactive elements (§10.3).

10.1 Crisis Maps

Figure 10.1 depicts various types of maps, which we describe on this section. The choice of which type of map to use depends on the requirements of end

---

[1] Patrick Meier, Profile at *National Geographic Explorers.* http://www.nationalgeographic.com/explorers/bios/patrick-meier/.

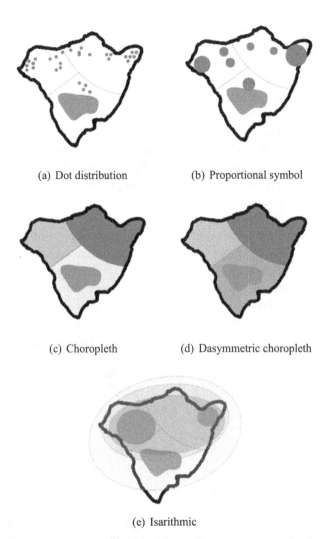

(a) Dot distribution   (b) Proportional symbol

(c) Choropleth   (d) Dasymmetric choropleth

(e) Isarithmic

Figure 10.1 Depiction of various types of map described on this section. The term "heatmap" is ambiguous: while it is often used to describe isarithmic maps, it is also used to describe choropleth maps.

users. At a high level, we continue using the breakdown presented in Section 1.5 between user requirements seeking "actionable insights," and user requirements capturing the "big picture." This distinction can be used to select an appropriate type of map for a given application.

Actionable insights. End users interested in actionable insights would prefer representations in which information items are presented individually, or grouped in small clusters. This requirement can be satisfied using a dot distribution map, or a proportional symbol map.

A *dot distribution map* uses dots or other types of symbols to mark the position of specific elements. In a one-to-one dot distribution map there is one dot for every element. For example, if there are 100 geo-referenced damage reports from a city, there will be exactly 100 dots, each one in the location associated to one report. If there are too many reports, a subsampling (one-to-many) strategy can also be used, in which each dot represents a fixed number of elements (e.g., one dot for every 100 reports). If the number of items to be depicted increases further, and/or if the items are spread over a large geographical area, a different visualization strategy is required.

A common problem in some dot distribution maps are markers that are exactly in the same position, or too close to each other to be distinguished visually. This may be an intrinsic characteristic of the data, or an artifact of coarse-grained geocoding, for instance, when several reports are known to come from one area (neighborhood, area, city), but it is not known exactly from where in that area. Markers can then be aggregated, creating a proportional symbol map, or they can be dispersed, following a marker dispersion strategy.[2]

A *proportional symbol map* shows symbols of different sizes where the size is proportional to the number of items. Symbols can be an abstract shape such as a circle/disk, a figurative symbol such as a fire icon, or a word or phrase. Proportional symbol maps are helpful to reduce visual clutter. For examples in the literature see, for instance, Earle et al. (2010, figure 2), and Evnine et al. (2014, figure 1).

The "big picture." End-users interested in a high-level description of a situation might be more interested in maps where regions or areas of interest are marked – not only specific points. These representations include choropleth, dasymmetric, and isarithmic maps.

In a *choropleth map*, predefined regions are colored according to a certain variable. When the variable to be plotted is ordinal (i.e., a number or an ordering), an ordered mapping from a gray scale or color scheme is used to depict the variable. The predefined regions are usually administrative regions such as countries, states, municipalities, or neighborhoods. The schemes used to map the variable of interest to colors are called *color progressions*. Color progressions are basically divided into single-hue color progressions, in which the hue is kept constant but the luminosity and/or saturation varies (which includes the

---

[2] See, for example, "Disperse Markers (Cartography)" *ArcGIS Help* section 10.2. March 2014. http://resources.arcgis.com/EN/HELP/MAIN/10.2/0070/00700000002n000000.htm.

grayscale case), and multi-hue color progressions, in which multiple hues are used at different levels of the scale.

A *dasymmetric map* is a variant of a choropleth where extra information is used to create a subdivision of regions that allows for a better representation of the data to be depicted. For instance, let us suppose a region of the map includes a large area without population, such as the lake depicted in Figure 10.1(d). In a dasymmetric map, those areas can be colored separately to indicate that, for instance, no reports have been received from them because no population actually lives in those areas. This, in turn, may affect the calculation for other areas, as in the example in Figure 10.1(d) where the region surrounding the lake is now darker, because the density of reports per square kilometer in the newly-defined area is higher.

An *isarithmic map*, also known as a *contour map*, represents a continuous variable through curves having a constant value. In an isarithmic map, regions are not fixed on the map but are computed from the data itself, and correspond to different intervals of data values. The term *heat map* is used commonly to indicate an isarithmic map in which the areas inside contour curves are colored according to the value at the edge of the contour; however, the term is also used sometimes incorrectly as a synonym of choropleth, which is arguably a less-known term.

Caveat: population and device density. As discussed in Section 9.6, the geographical distribution of reports provided by the public are distorted by the locations of people with the capability of generating such geotagged reports (Malik et al., 2015). This tends to introduce a bias toward large urban centers, which is apparent in many crisis maps. In the case of choropleths, a way of reducing this bias is to normalize by population, for example, by applying colors related to the number of reports per 100,000 habitants. In the case of dot distribution maps and proportional symbol maps, the bias is harder to avoid. To mitigate its effects, users can be shown for comparison the same map representing population density, to allow them to appreciate the similarities and differences. In general, users should be warned about this and other biases as they might be misled to the wrong conclusions.[3]

Example Crisis Maps

Dot distribution and proportional symbol maps. The *Traffic Observatory* (Ribeiro Jr. et al., 2012) and the *Dengue Observatory* (Gomide et al., 2011)

---

[3] An humorous take on this topic can be found in: "Heatmap" by Randall Munroe, *XKCD comic* #1138, November 2012. https://xkcd.com/1138/.

are two maps based on social media data. The dengue map[4] is used to track the dengue fever, an endemic tropical disease. It displays a dot distribution map in which every dot represents a Twitter message containing the keyword "dengue." *LITMUS* (Musaev et al., 2014) shows another example of a dot distribution map, in which there are five sets of symbols/markers, which also have different colors, to represent each one of the different data stream it aggregates: seismic sensors reporting an earthquake, rainfall sensors reporting heavy rains, and messages in Twitter, YouTube, and Instagram with landslide-related keywords.

Ushahidi (Okolloh, 2009), one of the most well-known examples of volunteer-provided geographical information, is a flexible community mapping platform that can be used for a number of purposes. The default maps are based on proportional symbols ("bubbles"), where each symbol's size is proportional to the number of reports in an area; often the number of reports is also overlaid in the symbol. Clicking on one of the "bubbles" zooms into the map and displays smaller bubbles with counters of reports, or individual data points.[5]

The *Social Media Sentiment map* (Lu et al., 2015) displays side-by-side dot distribution maps corresponding to messages having positive sentiment (blue dots) and messages having negative sentiment (red dots). In their examples, both types of messages appear to be clustered around densely populated cities.

Choropleth maps. The *Social Big Map* (Choi and Bae, 2015) displays a choropleth based on administrative regions. Each region is colored according to the frequency of messages reporting a particular disaster. The color scheme is multihue, with blue indicating less reports and red indicating more reports.

10.2 Crisis Dashboards

Most existing systems are built around the metaphor of a *dashboard*, that is, a set of visual displays that provides a visual summary of temporal, spatial, and thematic aspects of crisis-related messages. Many dashboards described in the literature are integrated with other data sources besides social media: they are

---

[4] *Observatório do Dengue, Instituto Nacional de Ciência e Tecnologia para a Web*, Brazil. http://www.observatorio.inweb.org.br/dengue/.
[5] Ushahidi: http://www.ushahidi.com/.

examples of *mashups* (Liu and Palen, 2009) or more technically, *collational interfaces* (Tucker et al., 2012).

Each visual element in a dashboard is a small "widget." Typically, the largest or dominant widget on a crisis dashboard is a map. Other common elements across crisis dashboards include:

News feeds. A news feed is a time-sorted itemization or *timeline* of recent or important social media messages. A news feed can be presented as a list or as a table. It can be presented in textual form or it can incorporate other forms of media, such as images or video.

News feeds can include one item per message, or group the messages into clusters or categories. For the grouping, topic models are sometimes used, as they have been shown to improve usability of social media dashboards (Bernstein et al., 2010). When messages are grouped, sometimes summaries or headlines, created manually or automatically through text summarization, are included.

Multimedia feeds. A particular type of news feed is a multimedia feed, where photos or videos are offered. For instance, a multimedia feed can be used to display recent user-posted photos about a developing crisis. Each multimedia object is often represented by a smaller/low-resolution version of it (a thumbnail), which can be clicked to see a larger version. In the case of videos, some video preview functionality can be offered on mouse over. Multimedia feeds can be displayed as a gallery of images via a rectangular grid of images or a set of stacked cards of various sizes, or as a carousel display/slider.

Time series. A time series graph, such as the one depicted in Figure 6.1(a), is a graph representing the volume over time of a hashtag, word, phrase, or concept. For instance, it can be used to indicate the number of messages about a disaster over time. Time series can also be used to represent positive or negative sentiment over time, usually by depicting positive sentiment as positive values, and negative sentiment as negative values. Crisis-related time series typically exhibit peaks of activity, which can be annotated either automatically through event detection methods or manually.

Distribution chart. A distribution chart can be used to represent the relative volume of different classes of messages on a graph. For instance, it can indicate the proportion of different emergency resources requested in crisis messages (e.g., food, water, shelter, etc.). Typical choices for depicting a distribution are pie charts and bar charts. Other types of chart used in crisis dashboards are tree maps, in which the proportion of different classes of messages is represented by the areas of rectangles in a mosaic. Distributional charts should allow users to quickly compare the magnitude of different categories of information. This is not the case for pie charts, which require people to compare angles placed in disarray with respect to each other. Pie charts have been heavily criticized and in general, for a small number of categories, a table is a better alternative (Tufte, 2001).

Tag cloud. A tag cloud is a visual display of hashtags, words, phrases, or (less often) category labels of messages in a collection or a subset of a collection. For instance, it can be used to highlight the most common words present in crisis messages. A selection of the elements to display is usually done based on frequency, that is, a tag cloud includes the most frequent elements in the chosen set. A tag cloud can depict these frequencies, usually by applying different font sizes, and less commonly by applying different colors. The layout of the tags can be sequential (e.g., alphabetic), circular (most important in the center), or clustered (grouped by similarity). The choice of layout depends heavily on the task we want the users to perform using the tag cloud, for instance, whether we want users to quickly identify the most frequent tag, or we want them to quickly determine if a given tag they have in mind is present among the most frequent (Lohmann et al., 2009).

Network. A network represents relationships between actors, concepts, or events in visual form. For instance, it can describe follower-followee or repost relationships among important social media users during a crisis. Network-based visualizations of high-density networks with anything above a handful of nodes, are usually very complicated to understand. In most cases they just look like a "hairball," conveying no useful information. Aggressive filtering to reduce the number of nodes or edges (e.g., by picking only high-weight edges) can be used to simplify this visualization. Interestingly, a network-based visualization can be done over a network that is estimated from repeated observations of similarly posted content. A content-driven network visualization of "who-copied-from-whom" during the 2011 Fukushima earthquake appears in Rodriguez and Leskovec (2014).

Flows. A diagram depicting information flows can be used to describe distributions that are related to each other. For instance, Thom et al. (2015) represent the number of messages in different categories, or conjunctions ("and") of categories by means of a flow diagram with symbols of different sizes. *RumorLens* uses a Sankey diagram to illustrate the number of people who post a rumor (or counterrumor) and the number of their followers who are exposed to it (Resnick et al., 2014; Carton et al., 2015).

Example Crisis Dashboards

Table 10.1 provides examples of systems that display crisis-relevant information from social media, and sometimes from other sources. The systems included on this list have varying degrees of maturity; some have been deployed in real-life situations, typically with the support of a government or nongovernmental organization, while others remain as experimental prototypes.

In addition to the systems listed in Table 10.1, there are many commercially available tools designed to perform visual analytics of social media data. Crowe (2012, ch. 6) describes the usage of some of these tools in the context of emergency management.

10.3 Interactivity

Interactivity is an effective way of combining many types of visualizations, switching among them based on input from users.

Details on demand. When used online, most crisis maps feature some degree of interactivity. The classical interaction paradigm for this interactivity is *details on demand*. This means that actions such as clicking or zooming on a place of interest display more information. For instance, clicking on a marker in a dot distribution map may show the specific message or messages associated to that marker, clicking on a symbol in a proportional symbol map may de-aggregate the information of that symbol into smaller symbols or individual markers, and clicking on an area in a choropleth may display some statistics about that area.

Filtering. A survey by Bellucci et al. (2010) of systems for displaying crisis information from different sources, found a common weakness among basically all the ones they analyzed: displays are too cluttered. Part of the answer to this visual clustering is to allow users to filter along different dimensions of interest, for instance to restrict the presentation to a specific concept, geographical region, or time period.

Liu and Palen (2009) stress that time and space are the most important variables that we use to make sense of a developing event. In that sense, allowing users to filter by time is not only useful for reducing visual clutter, but can allow users to learn from the past and to identify vulnerable geographical areas. Filtering by time can be done by inputing two time ranges or by using an on-screen temporal slider allowing users to go back and forth in time. These allow before-and-after comparisons and sometimes the visualization of movement or trajectories.

Table 10.1 *Example systems described in the literature that extract crisis-relevant information from social media. Some example capabilities are listed for each system. Sorted by year of earliest reference in the literature.*

Sahana Eden	Prutsalis et al. (2010)
Data	Data inputed directly, SMS (via import)
Capabilities	Maintain registries of organizations, persons, shelters, and relief resources
Visualizations	Dot distribution maps
URL	http://sahanafoundation.org/products/eden/
Twitris	Sheth et al. (2010); Purohit and Sheth (2013)
Data	Twitter
Capabilities	Semantic enrichment, automatic classification, geocoding
Visualizations	Dot distribution map, news feed, multimedia feed, distribution chart, tag cloud, network
URL	http://twitris.knoesis.org/
SensePlace2	MacEachren et al. (2011)
Data	Twitter
Capabilities	Geotagging, named entity extraction
Visualizations	Dot distribution map, news feed, time series, tag cloud, network
URL	http://www.geovista.psu.edu/SensePlace2/
TwitterReporter	Meyer et al. (2011)
Data	Twitter
Capabilities	Topic detection
Visualizations	Dot distribution map, news feed grouped by topics
URL	https://github.com/3RiverDevelopment/TwitterReporter
TweetTracker	Kumar et al. (2011)
Data	Twitter and SMS
Capabilities	Geocode, extract keywords and hashtags, detect events
Visualizations	Dot distribution map, news feed, distribution chart, tag cloud
URL	http://tweettracker.fulton.asu.edu/
ESA	Yin et al. (2012); Cameron et al. (2012); Power et al. (2014)
Data	Twitter
Capabilities	Detect and profile events, classify, cluster, geocoding
Visualizations	Dot distribution and proportional symbol map, news feed, time series, tag cloud
URL	https://esa.csiro.au/

Table 10.1 *(cont.)*

Twitcident	Abel et al. (2012a); Terpstra et al. (2012)
Data	Twitter and TwitPic
Capabilities	Semantic enrichment, classify
Visualizations	Dot distribution map, news feed, time series, distribution chart, tag cloud
URL	http://wis.ewi.tudelft.nl/twitcident/
CrisisTracker	Rogstadius et al. (2013)
Data	Twitter
Capabilities	Cluster, annotate manually
Visualizations	Proportional symbol map, news feed, distribution chart
URL	https://github.com/jakobrogstadius/crisistracker
ScatterBlogs	Bosch et al. (2013); Thom et al. (2015)
Data	Twitter, Instagram, YouTube
Capabilities	Custom classification
Visualizations	Dot distribution and proportional symbol map, news feed, distribution chart, tag cloud
URL	https://www.scatterblogs.com/
TweetComp1	Zielinski et al. (2013)
Data	Twitter
Capabilities	Filtering, classification, trustworthiness analysis, and geocoding
Visualizations	Dot distribution map and choropleth map
URL	http://tridec.server.de/geoserver/ (defunct)
EARS	Avvenuti et al. (2014)
Data	Twitter
Capabilities	Data filtering, event detection
Visualizations	Dot distribution map, news feed, time series
URL	(Not operational)
Tweedr	Ashktorab et al. (2014)
Data	Twitter
Capabilities	Classify automatically, extract information, geocoding
Visualizations	Dot distribution map, news feed
URL	https://github.com/dssg/tweedr
AIDR	Imran et al. (2014a)
Data	Twitter and SMS
Capabilities	Automatic and manual classification
Visualizations	Timeline
URL	http://aidr.qcri.org/

(cont.)

Table 10.1 *(cont.)*

Social Big Board	Choi and Bae (2015)
Data	Twitter
Capabilities	Classification by keywords
Visualizations	Choropleth maps, news feed, time series
URL	http://sns.ndmi.go.kr/

ScatterBlogs	Thom et al. (2015)
Data	Twitter
Capabilities	Subevent detection by spatiotemporal anomalies
Visualizations	Dot distribution and choropleth maps, news feed, time series, distribution chart, tag cloud
URL	https://www.scatterblogs.com/

EPIC Analyze	Barrenechea et al. (2015b); Anderson et al. (2015)
Data	Twitter
Capabilities	Filtering and annotation
Visualizations	News feed, time series, distribution chart, tag cloud
URL	http://epic.cs.colorado.edu/

HIRA	
Data	Twitter, news, and reports
Capabilities	Receive manually entered reports
Visualizations	Choropleth map, distribution chart, time series
URL	http://data.unhcr.org/hira/

Direct manipulation. Some visual displays can be extended to allow more elaborate forms of interaction by users, resulting in the *direct manipulation* of informational elements.

News feeds are particularly adapted to this type of interaction. For instance, *CrisisTracker* (Rogstadius et al., 2013) allow users to delete/hide spurious stories that do not correspond to actual subevents in a crisis, and *SensePlace2* (MacEachren et al., 2011) allow users to promote/demote stories to alter their relevance. Users can also perform higher-level operations, such as grouping messages together creating interactive clusters of elements, as done by Mao et al. (2014) in their proposed tool for crisis mapping.

Other types of display can also support direct interaction. The *CrowdSA* proposal by Salfinger et al. (2015b) displays crisis events in a format that can easily be made interactive by allowing users to manage crisis objects and relations. *ScatterBlogs* (Thom et al., 2015) allows fine-tuning of parameters in an automatic classifier via a visual interface.

10.4 Research Problems

Visualizing in context. It is impossible to design an effective visualization without understanding the situation and context in which the information will be consumed. Emergency and humanitarian workers must deliver results fast, and usually work under high pressure, with no time for anything unrelated to dealing with the crisis (Turoff et al., 2004). They also frequently experience information overload, which has been documented by researchers. For instance, Kurkinen et al. (2010) discuss an application for helping police officers see citizen reports from a police car, and notes how cluttered the dashboard of a modern police car already is, including cameras, radio, GPS, and a computer. Introducing better data visualization methods requires more research to understand the different contexts in which emergency and humanitarian work happens.

Designing crisis dashboards through participatory methods. Users can be involved in the design of visualizations for them through the methodology of *participatory design*, where they discuss and even develop low-fidelity prototypes, for instance by sketching and creating mock user interfaces using paper, pens, and scissors. Hughes (2014) describes one such exercise (a participatory design workshop) with a group of public information officers, which produced a wealth of data about their concerns, priorities, and expectations. Participatory design workshops typically require several hours of face-to-face interaction of people having very packed schedules, but are an invaluable source of input for better systems and better visualizations.

In addition to participatory design sessions, software designers and developers of disaster-related systems may become embedded participants in the groups they are designing solutions for (Potts, 2013). In many cases there are no significant obstacles for doing so, for instance, through some volunteer groups, and this experience can yield important insights that may not be obtainable through other methods.

Evaluating visualizations. Determining whether visualizations have impact in emergency operations and humanitarian relief ultimately depends on the extent to which they enable better, more effective decisions by the public, by volunteer groups, or by formal organizations. This is hard to prove, in part because of the difficulties in quantifying this type of effort. The current situation is one in which basically there have been no measurement of the impact of these platforms. McClendon and Robinson (2013) indicate that while geospatial media platforms have captured the public interest and media attention "there are few specific examples of the information leading to different decision-making patterns, widespread allocation of resources, or information leading to the rescue of disaster victims."

Some work has been done at evaluating crisis dashboards using Human-Computer Interaction (HCI) methods. These evaluations usually involve specific tasks that need to be completed using a visualization interface, for example, determining where an incident has happened and describing the incident. The tasks are evaluated with metrics including comprehension, time, and accuracy, obtained either via instrumentation of the application, observation of the participants, or interviews. Other components of these evaluations include questions about usability and utility of different interfaces, such as "I think I would use this application frequently," which are answered on a Likert scale (strongly disagree, disagree, neutral, agree, strongly agree). Examples of this type of experiment include Tucker et al. (2012) and Robinson et al. (2013a).

To ensure that the evaluations of different systems are done in a consistent same way, standards for specific tasks and metrics have been proposed (Diaz, 2014).

Supporting decisions and making predictions. A long-term ambition is the development of *decision support systems* for crisis response that incorporate social media data (Hristidis et al., 2010; Virtual Social Media Working Group and DHS First Responders Group, 2014). One capacity of an advance decision support system is the capability of generating predictions, for instance, helping predict epidemic transmission of diseases based on geographical proximity as reported in social media (Brennan et al., 2013). The dashboards we have described in this chapter are only a small part of such envisioned systems.

10.5 Further Reading

Turoff et al. (2004) introduces a framework for the design of an information system for emergency response management, based on empirical observations from existing systems. They present numerous insights from experience including a set of nine premises that have been highly cited in the design of newer systems.

Salfinger et al. (2015a) surveys and compares current crisis-sensing systems from various perspectives, including how they present situational awareness information to users, and how users interact with these systems. Onorati et al. (2013) is another survey in which systems are evaluated according to a series of interactive principles.

Various community-powered mapping platforms, including Open-StreetMaps, Wikimapia, Ushahidi, and others, are surveyed in Roche et al. (2013) and White (2011, ch. 7).

The Geographical Information Systems wiki (http://wiki.gis.com/) is a community-powered encyclopedia of concepts related to geographical information systems, including maps.[6] Graham et al. (2015) includes a chapter on visualization of textual information from an historian's perspective.

A good resource for developers is Kumar et al. (2013a, ch. 5), which describes how to create various visualizations of Twitter data using JavaScript and the D3 library.

---

[6] See, for instance, information about map types: http://wiki.gis.com/wiki/index.php/Category:Map_types.

11

Values: Privacy and Ethics

"This is the paradox: effective response in the 'Networking Age' requires open data and transparency, but the more information that is shared the more risks and challenges for privacy and security emerge" (UN OCHA, 2014a). Disasters and emergencies create situations of vulnerability for affected populations that often leave them more exposed to harm. There are many ways in which data scientists and analysts can do harm, for instance, by exposing the private lives of people, or by putting response operations in danger.

Privacy and security concerns should not be used as a reason not to apply new communication technologies during emergencies, but they should be taken into account (UN OCHA, 2012). At a high level, researchers and practitioners need to find the right spot between full opacity and full transparency, finding a balance between security concerns and operational needs. Given their risk aversion, it may be impossible to engage with some organizations, particularly the ones that operate at a national level or at an international level, without some formal agreements in place, particularly related to personal data protection standards.

Social media brings more complexity to emergency and disaster situations by reducing the amount of control that responders and relief workers have. For instance, emergency incident scenes have traditionally been delimited and closed by barriers such as the proverbial "yellow tape" used by the police in many countries. Social media and mobile phone cameras can nearly evaporate this traditional scene control (Crowe, 2012, ch. 5). Rescue personnel, including firefighters, police officers, and others who physically converge on the scene have responsibility and legal codes to respect. As the public also enters the scene (physically or virtually), they must adhere to ethical standards they may be unfamiliar with. Technology can be used to weaken or to strengthen those standards.

This chapter is an attempt to highlight some of the ethical concerns around processing social media data during emergencies. Some of these concerns have elicited some degree of self-regulation, for instance, in the form of ethical guidelines, while others have not.

We start with widely agreed-upon areas in which the practitioner community has already developed some guidance, including privacy (§11.1) and human conflict (§11.2). Then, we venture into territory where the questions are newer and hence less guidance can be provided, such as the protection of digital volunteers (§11.3), and issues related to experimentation (§11.4) and data sharing (§11.5).

11.1 Protecting the Privacy of Individuals

In August 2009 Typhoon Morakot became the deadliest Typhoon to hit Taiwan in recorded history. A forum was created to collect reports from the public, and it received thousands of reports during just a few days of activity. Wu et al. (2011) analyzed data from this forum in April 2011 (twenty months later) and found it to be a rich source of personally identifiable information, including the full names, phone numbers, and address of almost two thousand people. As of May 2015, more than five years after the disaster, that information was still there – it was removed at some point in mid-2015, but data remains cached in the Internet Archived and possibly in other repositories. This personal data could be used in a discriminatory context for employment, property, and health insurance (Crawford and Finn, 2014).

It is often the case that applications that are open for the public for reporting are also open for the public for viewing (Gao et al., 2011). Even if safeguards are in place to avoid the type of disclosure that happened during Typhoon Morakot, such as obfuscation of personally identifiable information, data from different sources can be linked to deanonymize a person, systems can be hacked or compromised, and data leaks may occur due to a number of causes, including physical theft of computers due to reduced security during a crisis situation (Herold, 2006).

The humanitarian community has decades of experience managing analog or nondigital crisis information, and take privacy very seriously: "the privacy and confidentiality of the affected population . . . is the cornerstone of humanitarian ethics" (Whipkey and Verity, 2015). Some humanitarian organizations have brought their experience into guidelines for dealing with digital crisis information. In the rest of this section, we outline data protection guidelines provided by the Red Cross and United Nations.

Red Cross' Guidelines. The International Committee of the Red Cross (ICRC) offers eighteen principles for the management of sensitive information by protection actors (ICRC, 2013). They seek to address a number of risks to which the people who provide information are exposed, including retaliation from authorities or other groups, loss of control over their own personal data, and vulnerability to misuse or fraud.

At a general level, these principles establish that the entities that collect data must make sure, before they start any data collection, that they have the capacity and processes in place to manage the data properly. The evaluation, understanding, and mitigation of the potential threats that data collection entails are their responsibility. The principles suggest a minimalistic approach in which no more data is collected than needed for a particular purpose, the level of detail with which data is collected matches the purpose, and aggregated data is preferred whenever it is possible. They also establish processes and data flows that should be transparent for affected populations, particularly when soliciting information from them through digital channels.

The notion of *informed consent* is important to achieve this transparency. Informed consent means that people receive in advance clear information about who is collecting the data, for what purpose, what are the risks and benefits, where and for how long will the data be stored, and so on. After receiving this information, the people whose data will be collected explicitly give their approval subject to those conditions. To be true to this definition, informed consent cannot be construed to be a check box next to a long document with opaque legalese.[1]

ICRC guidelines establish that informed consent is also a requirement when collecting data posted on the Internet. According to ICRC (2013), the fact that a piece of information is posted online does not mean its author consented to this information being posted on the webpage of a third party without the necessary precautions: "When such consent cannot be realistically obtained, information allowing the identification of victims or witnesses, should only be relayed in the public domain if the expected protection outcome clearly outweighs the risks. In case of doubt, displaying only aggregated data, with no individual markers, is strongly recommended." The maps produced by the Standby Task Force follow this recommendation.[2]

---

[1] Infamously, the terms of service of PayPal were noted at some point to be longer than Shakespeare's *Hamlet*. http://conversation.which.co.uk/technology/length-of-website-terms-and-conditions/.

[2] "Typhoon Hagupit: UN using crowdsourcing platform to help assess damage" Caroline Bannock, *The Guardian*, December 2014. http://www.theguardian.com/world/2014/dec/09/typhoon-hagupit-un-using-crowdsourcing-platorm-to-help-assess-damage.

UN OCHA's Guidelines. The United Nations Office for the Coordination of Humanitarian Affairs approaches privacy issues from an arguably practical standpoint (UN OCHA, 2014a). They seek a balance between the imperative to save lives and the responsibility to do no harm: "Absolute protection would make humanitarian response impractical by not allowing the collection of any information, while the public listing of personal details would likewise endanger lives." For people in distress, protecting their "private data" may be a much lower priority than gaining help or locating loved ones (Crawford and Finn, 2014). The UN OCHA guidelines assume that individuals seeking lifesaving assistance will often be unable to assert whether they want to share their data in a certain way or not. Therefore, it is the responsibility of the humanitarian organizations to handle the data responsibly.

These guidelines define four types of information of concern from the point of view of privacy: (i) information about places and objects (e.g., the location of an emergency food stock), (ii) personally identifiable information (e.g., the name of an individual), (iii) community identifiable information (e.g., the name of a group), and (iv) metadata (e.g., the time at which a message was sent). They include nine guidelines, stressing compliance with all relevant legislation, and minimalism in terms of collecting only the information needed for a specific purpose and retaining it only during the time needed. The guidelines also call for undertaking the appropriate safeguards to keep the data secure, and to ensure data quality, including the right of people to access, rectify, and object to the data held over them.

UN OCHA (2014a) also takes an adversarial perspective in which political, criminal, and sectarian attacks may seek to undermine the safety of digital operations and the data stored by them. This is particularly important in areas of limited statehood, where crisis mapping can be useful to supplement the lack of institutional procedures,[3] but where contributors may also be less protected from violence or other forms of retaliation if they are perceived as a threat.

Enabling surveillance and increasing state and corporate control over citizens, are valid concerns that research on big data arises (boyd and Crawford, 2012; Tufekci, 2014). Government surveillance is explicitly considered by UN OCHA to be a potential source of this type of threat, following their experience in past years: "In conflict situations or other highly polarized environments, privacy concerns can become paramount. Information can be used by authorities or non-state actors to target those who provide it, or other individuals. Governments often seek to monitor online dissent and information

---

[3] "Crisis Mapping in Areas of Limited Statehood" Patrick Meier, *iRevolution*, February 2014. http://irevolution.net/2014/02/13/crisis-mapping-areas-of-limited-statehood/.

sharing." (UN OCHA, 2012). These actions may endanger the free "humanitarian space" that humanitarian relief workers need to perform their work (Wagner, 2005).

11.2 Intentional Human-Induced Disasters

Human-induced disasters are caused by anthropogenic hazards, which are of two types: technological (accidental) and sociological (intentional), as presented in Table 1.1. Large-scale sociological human-induced disasters, such as a bombing, a riot, or a war, are expressions of conflict between groups or factions. This conflict creates a particularly challenging environment for disaster response, including digital response activities.

Digital volunteering and human conflict. Libya's crisis map in 2011 was one of the first large-scale community mapping efforts to operate during an armed conflict. To prevent this data from becoming harmful, two maps were maintained: a public one, which included a delay of twenty-four to forty-eight hours and presented a filtered view of the data, and a private, password-protected one, which included more information.[4] In addition, volunteers who processed and mapped the incoming reports were vetted following a strict (but ad hoc) process to avoid being infiltrated by any of the factions in conflict (Meier, 2015).

Some digital volunteering organizations avoid getting involved in human conflict situations entirely. They do this by either expressly declaring that human conflicts are outside the scope of their organizations, or sometimes simply by inaction (Starbird, 2012a, sec. 6.5.1).

Protecting victims and responders during armed attacks. During the attacks in Norway in 2011, as the public found out about the attack while the attacker was still at large, it was discussed in social media that even the alert tone of a phone could reveal the position of hidden survivors from the attacker: "DON'T CALL friends in Utøya! It can endanger them. Wait for them to call you, even if it is intolerable" (tweet quoted in Perng et al., 2013).

With the widespread of social media usage during terrorist attacks and armed conflicts, state actors have often asked people to refrain from disseminating certain information online. Sometimes there is a tension between the right of the public to learn on a timely fashion about how their governments

---

[4] "The [unexpected] Impact of the Libya Crisis Map and the Standby Volunteer Task Force." Andrej Verity, *Standby Task Force Blog*, December 2011. http://blog.standbytaskforce.com/2011/12/19/sbtf-libya-impact/.

are responding to a crisis, and the effectiveness of that response. There are also political reasons for controlling the flow of information. For instance, while the U.S. Army regulates the usage of social media by its members, insights from uncensored videos posted by soldiers deployed in Iraq and viewed by many, have contributed to questioning U.S. foreign policy (Andén-Papadopoulos, 2009). Sometimes the boundary at which withholding information constitutes censorship requires understanding intentions, which are very difficult to judge.

Oh et al. (2011) claim that information relayed by the media and the public through Twitter during the 2008 attack in Mumbai, India, enhanced the capabilities of the terrorist group that staged the attack: "unregulated real time Twitter postings can contribute to increase the level of situation awareness for terrorist groups to make their attack decision." In 2013, the police of Kenya asked reporters and social media users to delay information about military movements during the siege of the Westgate Mall in September of that year. The police asked a Twitter user to delete a picture of helicopters readying to launch an attack on the mall, and the Ministry of Interior urged people to "be responsible when you share information" (Simon et al., 2014).

11.3 Protecting Citizen Reporters and Digital Volunteers

In all kinds of crises, whenever they are reporting from the ground, citizen reporters are as exposed as regular journalists to danger, and might not enjoy the legal protections or social recognition of their work to protect them from harm. Indeed, large media organizations that receive citizen reports sometimes include prominent warnings asking people to avoid putting themselves in danger.[5] However, some people put themselves at risk anyway, even for something as mundane as taking a "selfie" next to a dangerous event.[6]

In authoritarian regimes, social media may facilitate retaliation against those who provide information: "Iran's Revolutionary Guard and the paramilitary Basij used Twitter to hunt down and target Iranian pro-democracy activists" (Burns and Eltham, 2009). In general, in armed conflicts, information gathering efforts can provide intelligence to armed groups and endanger the safety of the people issuing the reports, as well as the safety of relief workers (Gao et al., 2011).

---

[5] For instance, the BBC asks people submitting images or videos not to put themselves or others in danger, or taking unnecessary risks. http://www.bbc.com/news/world-10776546.

[6] "Why you shouldn't take a selfie in front of a fire." *KITV Channel 4*, March 2015. http://www.kitv.com/national/hearst-video/why-you-shouldnt-take-a-selfie-in-front-of-a-fire/31829114.

Distal exposure. For remote digital volunteers, *distal exposure*, that is, being exposed to a disaster from afar, can also be harmful, especially when the exposure is repeated (Bonanno et al., 2010, p. 23). Media about disasters needs to be handled carefully to reduce harm due to repeated exposure to traumatic content. The "rawness" of social media messages from disaster areas gives them an intense affective dimension (McCosker, 2013). Some volunteers interviewed by Starbird and Palen (2011) indicated feeling "emotionally drained," and others reported having nightmares because of the calls for help that were left unanswered. Digital volunteers are particularly exposed to this type of harm when performing image or video annotation tasks, and should be spared from needless repeated exposure, among other practices designed to reduce harm (see "tips for coping with traumatic imagery" by Rees, 2014).

When soliciting volunteer annotations on unknown images, digital volunteers should be warned in advance that some images may be disturbing. If the images are already known to contain graphic or potentially traumatic content of a specific type, people can be warned using conventional mechanisms, such as "TW" which stands for "trigger warning." For instance, "TW: violence" next to a link indicates that a violent image or video will be shown if one clicks that link.

11.4 Ethical Experimentation

One step toward reducing the risks associated to deploying a new technology during an emergency, is to thoroughly test such technology beforehand, for instance through a simulation exercise (Abbasi et al., 2012; Bressler et al., 2012; Meesters and van de Walle, 2013), as pointed out in Section 7.4. The *ASU Crisis Response Game* (Abbasi et al., 2012) was a simulation involving 75 students divided into groups including victims, first responder teams, and filtering teams. Coordination for the creation of rescue "missions" was done through publicly available social media channels. This type of simulation exercise can produce a wealth of information about how people may interact and coordinate during an actual crisis. However, this experimentation also entails risks, such as causing unnecessary alarm or disruption. In the case of the ASU game, volunteers were asked to prefix all messages with *"NOT REAL THIS IS A GAME!"* to prevent this.

As a general guideline, researchers who plan to conduct experiments involving human subjects, including online and remote data collection and experimentation, should seek approval by an Ethical Review Board or an Institutional Review Board (IRB). This is a requirement in research grants of many national and international funding agencies, a common practice in the human factors and collaborative work communities, and increasingly a requirement for publications in conferences and journals in the space of social media. While it does not guarantee that the outcome will be free from criticism,[7] it does mean the prospective authors of a study will need to answer a number of key questions before an experiment takes place, and think critically about their research (boyd and Crawford, 2012).

Bowser and Tsai (2015) propose a framework for these questions that forms the basis of an ethics review process for Internet research. There are many elements in this framework, with two fundamental questions posed early in the process: whether users participating in the experiment are giving explicitly their consent to participate, and whether the experiment, in any form, deceives or misleads them. Both elements might be critical in the case of experiments involving people placed on a simulated crisis response scenario.

11.5 Giving Back and Sharing Data

Disasters have a strong emotional dimension. They are exceptional circumstances, often including dramatic increases in social solidarity (Fritz and Mathewson, 1957). In times of crisis, negative and cynical content in social media is reduced significantly in favor of positive, helpful commentary (Charlwood et al., 2012). People try to help others through social media not only through practical information advice but also by providing emotional support (particularly to anxious and frightened people), which builds community resilience and makes people feel connected, useful, and supported (Taylor et al., 2012).

Researchers and practitioners using social media during a disaster should keep in mind that they are entering a space of *conversation* that cannot be treated as yet another data source. "Communication, whatever the medium, is fundamentally a social activity rooted in social and cultural mores, needs and structures, and the value of a conversation lies as much in its importance for trust and relationship building as in the relaying of information in either direction" (Robinson and Wall, 2012). Researchers and practitioners should approach this community with an empathic frame of mind, and give as much thought to the question on how they can give back to the community, as to the question on how much they can take from it.

---

[7] "How an IRB could have legitimately approved the Facebook experiment – and why that may be a good thing." Michelle N. Meyer, *Harvard Bioethics Blog*, June 2014. https://blogs.harvard .edu/billofhealth/2014/06/29/how-an-irb-could-have-legitimately-approved-the-facebook-experiment-and-why-that-may-be-a-good-thing/.

Traceability and interoperability. For social media users to be able to verify and validate information, they need to be capable of tracing data across systems, for instance, by annotating and creating links between pieces of information. The existence of segregated technological spaces that neither allow these annotations nor interoperate with each other makes this task much harder (Potts, 2013). This technological segregation can be alleviated by exposing public APIs that allow different systems to exchange information.

Being able to trace data across systems is also necessary to maintain data accessible to its contributors. Sutherlin (2013) explains how crowdsourcing translation of messages from Arabic into English during the 2011 revolutions in the Middle East render them inaccessible to many of its original contributors. If a connection between the English translations and their Arabic originals is not kept, a person who does not speak English may not be able to find the translation of his/her original messages, much less challenge or give feedback on the way they are being used.

In established, formal organizations, problems regarding interoperability have been described as involving discrepancies of data structures, taxonomies, and ontologies (Virtual Social Media Working Group and DHS First Responders Group, 2014), which can be at least in part addressed through the application of semantic technologies (as we described in Section 3.7).

Data sharing. One way in which researchers can give back is by understanding that crisis-relevant information is a basic need that can contribute to create value if shared widely and freely (UN OCHA, 2012). One of the largest challenges when looking for data relevant to humanitarian response is often not lack of data but the fact that governments and other partners are unwilling to share the data that they already have (UN OCHA, 2014a). However, data sharing can become an ethical imperative if it makes the response more effective, reduces the duplication of efforts, and avoids placing and unnecessary burden on victims, witnesses, and communities (ICRC, 2013; Whipkey and Verity, 2015). Data sharing also enables different agencies to respond in a consistent manner to a disaster, which is essential during a disaster (Turoff et al., 2004).

Standards for *Open Humanitarianism* have been developing, which include as goals: (i) increasing the availability of information about humanitarian aid, (ii) supporting communities' participation, and (iii) increasing access to new technologies (Olafsson, 2012).[8]

An important element of increasing the availability and shareability of this information is the usage of open content licenses. The Humanitarian Data

---

[8] Open Humanitarianism: http://openhumanitarianism.info/.

Exchange (HDX),[9] a project by UN OCHA, is the largest repository of open and accessible humanitarian data. HDX accepts a plurality of open licensing options, including Creative Commons and Open Data Commons licenses, as well as data released in the public domain. In the case of social media, the release of open datasets for disaster response and humanitarian relief requires the cooperation of social media platforms, particularly the ones that have restrictive terms of service regarding data redistribution.

11.6 Research Problems

Enhancing the privacy of data contributors. The fact that people affected by a disaster post private information publicly in social media during a crisis, does not imply that they have agreed that others can take this data out of context. People would be concerned to find their data being gathered and stored by third parties (such as governments and other organizations) for extended periods of time or used for different purposes. The guidelines by the Committee on Public Response to Alerts and Warnings Using Social Media (2013, ch. 5), discuss issues related with the privacy of these messages, but more research is needed to understand the public's expectations of privacy in these situations, and how those expectations measure against the needs of humanitarian organizations accessing this data.

Developing safe data practices. Problems with information security can be aggravated during emergencies (Harnesk and Hartikainen, 2011). Crisis computing systems should ensure that the data that is collected and contributed is secure. For instance, Wu et al. (2011) suggest obfuscating contact information and/or providing forwarding services so that people can be contacted without disclosing private data, such as their e-mail address. Similar practices may emerge as standards as these systems mature.

Developing inclusionary practices. Emergency managers recognize "the growing need to provide support and communication for citizens with functional or special needs" (Crowe, 2012). However, with few exceptions, very little research has been done regarding the role of social media for communicating disaster-relevant information to people with disabilities (Bricout and Baker, 2010; Fu et al., 2010).

Developing legal standards. What happens if a member of a digital volunteer group negligently releases information that causes a disaster victim to be

[9] Humanitarian Data Exchange (HDX): https://data.hdx.rwlabs.org/.

injured? Robson (2012) recommends that digital volunteering organizations obtain indemnification from potential liabilities from the governmental agencies or NGOs requesting their services, and indeed suggests that in the absence of new legal standards covering this type of operation, work only with agencies that agree to that indemnification.

Understanding "disaster tourism" and "digital voyeurism." Disasters breed curiosity and attract a crowd of people who want to see the disaster site and the response activities firsthand (Hughes et al., 2008). This attraction encourages a form of what de Waal (1987; 1997) characterized as "disaster tourism." The convergence of people on a disaster site, digitally or physically, can become an opportunity if some of the people who converge become a helper when the need arises, but it can also hinder rescue, relief, and recovery operations (Hughes et al., 2008)

In March 2015, 'Sola Fagurusi was the only survivor of a fatal car crash in which the other three occupants of his car died: "I passed out and regained consciousness to find my limbs numb. Just as I managed to look around, there was already a crowd ... I was shortly glad they were trying to call for help. I saw a flash briefly and it occurred to me they were either taking pictures or shooting videos while I laid there helpless." The people who used their phones to take pictures and videos of the accident did *not* call the emergency services, which were summoned instead by another vehicle that went past the scene.[10]

On the one hand, this story can be seen as a reflection of the "Bystander Effect" or "Genovese Effect," named after the famous case of the murder of Catherine "Kitty" Genovese in New York, where 37 witnesses did not call the police (Gansberg, 1964). On the other hand, this story can also be seen as the duty to rescue being tramped by either digital voyeurism, "disaster porn,"[11] or the need to perform a "journalistic" act. Is social media contributing to weaken the duty to rescue? What can practitioners and researchers do to make sure people first notify the emergency services and provide all the assistance they can lend *before* posting in social media?

11.7 Further Reading

Privacy is a very complex topic; Solove (2013) presents a compelling argument about the value of privacy, particularly against the assertion that privacy is only

---

[10] "I'm dying, they're tweeting." by 'Sola Fagurusi. *PUNCH (Nigeria)*, March 2015. http://www .punchng.com/i-punch/i-am-dying-they-are-tweeting/.

[11] "The dangers of turning the Japanese tragedy into addictive 'disaster porn'." Cristina Odone, *The Telegraph*, March 2011. http://blogs.telegraph.co.uk/news/cristinaodone/100080078/ the-dangers-of-turning-the-japanese-tragedy-into-addictive-disaster-porn/.

for people who have "something to hide." Crawford and Finn (2014) build upon Solove's and other arguments to provide a critical view of the usage of social media and mobile data during crises.

Bonanno et al. (2010) present a broad survey on the psychological effects of disasters, including both people directly affected, as well as those exposed through mass media.

The codes of conduct of the largest professional societies related to computing, ACM and IEEE, stress the importance of avoiding harm and injury to others in the context of the computing profession.[12] The ethics guidelines from the Association of Internet Researchers address issues including privacy, autonomy, vulnerability, and risks/benefits trade-offs.[13]

Many of the points mentioned in the data protection standards of the ICRC and OCHA are related to privacy directives and related legislations in many countries. As starting points for the interested reader, Lindsay (2011) cites several federal-level legislation on this topic in the United States; for the European Union, see the Data Protection Directive of the European Parliament and Council (1995).

---

[12] ACM Code of Ethics and Professional Conduct: http://www.acm.org/about/code-of-ethics. IEEE Code of Ethics: https://www.ieee.org/about/corporate/governance/p7-8.html.

[13] Association of Internet Researchers, Ethics Guide 2012. http://ethics.aoir.org/index.php?title=Main_Page

12

Conclusions and Outlook

As noted by many bloggers and journalists, many of the Syrians refugees fleeing from the war in 2015 were carrying smartphones. One of them told an AFP reporter: "Our phones and power banks are more important for our journey than anything, even more important than food." Smartphones provide a guide, a map, and help refugees navigate many issues, including asylum bureaucracy. In extreme circumstances, a message with geographical coordinates sent from a sinking boat can be the difference between life and death.[1]

The question on whether people will continue using social media during crises, is really a question on whether they will continue using social media at all; in times of crises, people use the tools that are most familiar to them (Potts, 2013). As long as people use mobile technologies and social media, these technologies will continue playing a key role in the way they communicate during disasters and humanitarian crises.

Different emergency response and humanitarian relief organizations make different choices with respect to how to be part of this conversation. Some have embraced social media, others have remained in the sidelines, most are somewhere in between. Individuals in these organizations also make their own choices, which follow to some extent – but seldom completely – whatever is mandated by organizational policies. Individuals with more interest and/or competencies on social media have been driving forces to change their organizations and their policies.

Computing researchers and practitioners, specially during the early years of crisis informatics, often developed methods with little or no input from the crisis and disaster management community. This has changed in recent years, as more interdisciplinary research projects appear, both big and small. These projects can be very rewarding, but they are also very challenging for all involved.

---

[1] "The most crucial item that migrants and refugees carry is a smartphone." Hanna Kozlowska, *Quartz*, September 2015. http://qz.com/500062/the-most-crucial-item-that-migrants-and-refugees-carry-is-a-smartphone/.

This chapter integrates part of the discussion of the previous chapters by using two paradigms: information quality (§12.1) and peer production (§12.2). Next, we address two emergent topics: using technology to support institutional communications, (§12.3) and processing user-generated videos for crisis response (§12.4). We conclude outlining relevant factors for future developments on this field (§12.5).

12.1 The Quality of Crisis Information

Many data-related problems we have described are essentially information quality issues. We are trying to find high-quality information in communication platforms designed with information quality as just one of many design goals, and probably not the most important one. Commercial social media platforms are designed to be easy to use, enjoyable, and to promote engagement and content sharing. As everything else on the Internet, they enable a broad range of quality to be expressed – which is not necessarily a weakness (Agichtein et al., 2008).

The literature on information quality describes it as a complex characteristic composed of many facets. Eppler (2006, table 10), lists 70 information quality criteria, including comprehensiveness, accuracy, clarity, neutrality, objectivity, coherence, timeliness, and many others. The framework proposed by Wang and Strong (1996) describes four basic groups of information quality facets: intrinsic quality (e.g., believability or accuracy), contextual quality (e.g., value-added, timeliness and completeness), representational quality (e.g., ease of understanding, concise representation), and accessibility.

The relative importance of information quality factors is essentially a subjective matter, which requires user input to be validated. This input can be obtained from user studies, for instance, several aspects of quality can be shown explicitly to users, asking them to weigh and comment on their relative value during a crisis situation (Ludwig et al., 2015b).

Conciseness and clarity seem to be important criteria for emergency managers, followed by accuracy and timeliness, according to interviews with a group of experts by Friberg et al. (2010, 2011). Research on social media for crises so far has addressed mostly intrinsic quality aspects (e.g., as discussed in Chapters 8 and 9) and to some extent representational issues (as discussed in Chapter 10). Much more research is needed to understand and model a larger set of information quality criteria.

Studying systematically *contextual information quality* is particularly challenging. Understanding, for instance, the value added by social media information requires to observe the actual operations of an emergency or humanitarian relief team, learning about the other information sources they use, and how they use them. In this case, studies performed in the lab cannot replace field studies.

12.2 Peer Production of Crisis Information

Many aspects of digital volunteering can be understood as a form of commons-based peer production, a framework proposed by Benkler (2006) to analyze communities such as Wikipedia editors and Free/Libre Open Source Software developers. These communities tend to coordinate work mostly in an horizontal fashion, with little hierarchy. They use inputs that are open to all, including social media and other information sources; they also generate outputs that are open to all, and often explicitly embrace values related to open data (Palen et al., 2015). In the case of digital volunteering communities, the output is an informational product, sometimes very specific and well defined (e.g., a map, or a spreadsheet), and sometimes much more general, such as "a better understanding of the situation on the ground."

Successful peer-production communities tend to be highly modular: work is divided into small units that can be easily integrated with each other. This is consistent with the way large, established, and mature digital volunteering organizations operate in time of crises.

Emergent organizations tend to start with loosely defined goals that become more specified as they evolve. Tasks may be also ill-specified at the beginning; greater routinization of tasks and division of labor can be achieved as an organization grows and mature (Stallings and Quarantelli, 1985). This evolution has been observed in digital volunteering contexts (Starbird and Palen, 2011; White et al., 2014).

Peer production and the humanitarian sector. Peer-production communities can involve both volunteer and paid participants, and operate across institutional boundaries. This allows peer production to be integrated with industrial sectors, as it has been the case for software development. There are many large software companies that contribute (sometimes full-time) employees to work in open source software projects.

In the humanitarian sector, we could envision a similar situation (which has already happened to some extent with VOSTs). When a tighter integration between volunteer and formal organizations is achieved, members of formal organizations can indicate what are their information priorities, or directly ask the volunteer community to answer specific questions relevant to an operation (Ludwig et al., 2015a).

12.3 Technologies for Crisis Communications in Social Media

Humanitarian agencies that adopt an integrated approach to communicating with disaster-affected communities are viewed more positively by their intended beneficiaries (Gleed, 2011). Best practices on how to achieve this by communicating effectively are continuously being developed; see, for instance, White (2011), Committee on Public Response to Alerts and Warnings Using Social Media (2013, ch. 2), the resources by Communicating with Disaster Affected Communities (CDAC),[2] and the recommendations by Charlton (2012). While most of the technologies presented in this book are about collecting information from social media toward formal organizations, some research has also been done about the dissemination of messages from formal organizations.

One key aspect of communicating effectively in social media is to pay attention to how messages are written, to make sure they are understandable and useful for the public. Messages should be clear, specific, accurate, certain and consistent (Sutton et al., 2013). User studies can be done to determine how to operationalize these criteria in practice, for instance by testing in detail several variations regarding wording, date formats, usage of hashtags, and other aspects. (Comunello et al., 2015). In addition to user studies, automatic text analysis can uncover regularities in the way messages perceived as clear or unclear are written, which may lead to automatic readability criteria that can alert about messages that might be hard to understand (Temnikova et al., 2015).

Technology can also be used to measure and to some extent predict the impact of a message in social media using information cascade analysis (Chen et al., 2013). Additionally, it can help manage multiple communication channels at the same time, for instance, *XHELP* (Reuter et al., 2015b) allows users to post crisis-related messages (such as requests for information about missing persons) in multiple social media platforms, aggregating the responses and allowing responders to manage multiple conversations at the same time – saving valuable time for other activities.

12.4 User-Generated Images, Video, and Aerial Photography

Photos and videos are posted by users in social media for a variety of purposes. Most often, they document the hazard itself, its effects, and the postimpact response. There are also some surprising uses, such as people performing a

---

[2] CDAC: http://www.cdacnetwork.org/.

quick inventory of their belongings for insurance purposes before evacuating a property (Liu et al., 2008).

Systems such as *Twitcident* (Abel et al., 2012a,b) surface pictures extracted from social media streams, but in general they do not perform content-based retrieval on such images. Most current systems that deal with multimedia data perform *context-based multimedia retrieval* – they index, aggregate, and search based on tags, dates, and other metadata associated to the images or videos, not the visual or audio content itself. Systems performing *content-based multimedia retrieval* of multimedia posted in social media, in which the actual images and videos are analyzed, are much more rare.

A rich, emerging source of user-generated video footage are Unmanned Aerial Vehicles (UAVs). Prices for consumer-grade UAVs have plummeted in recent years and continue to fall rapidly, as devices become easier to fly, more autonomous, resistant to impact, and lighter. UAVs have been used in a variety of crisis-related applications including documenting the effects of a disaster on cities and farms, as well as other applications for social good, such as monitoring fauna in national reserves (Meier, 2015, ch. 4 and 6). Specialized communities using UAVs during humanitarian crises are starting to emerge.[3] These communities will contribute to increase the demand for the development of new technologies able to process crisis photos and videos.

12.5 Outlook

Humanitarian computing is to some extent a neglected area of applied computing.

In for-profit industrial research labs, research projects in this area are only possible within large or more forward-looking labs, because profits are not short-term. In academic university labs, the obstacle is that working on this topic requires long-term relationships with institutions that have urgent needs, and in many cases need continuous engineering support.

Possibly the largest source of funding for these projects are governments; in the United States, the United Kingdom, Europe, Japan, and Australia, among others, there are multiyear research projects involving many researchers at a time. Irrespective of the source of funding, the development of this research topic depends to a large extent on the capacity of researchers to prove the value of these technologies. This, in turn, requires to deal with both organizational and technical challenges.

---

[3] See, for instance, the UAViators community: http://uaviators.org/.

The challenges of interdisciplinary research. Research that claims to be of practical value cannot be substantiated by merely pointing out that a certain computing method "may" be of interest or valuable for emergency or disaster response. Instead, claims of practical value for a particular sector, in this case the emergency response and humanitarian sectors, need to be substantiated by actually delivering results to those users.

This can only be achieved through *interdisciplinary* research. As such, its success hinges on the extent to which the objectives from the different partners can be aligned. However, these objectives can be very different. Computing researchers seek to develop new computational methods, publish them on a conference or journal, and perhaps create a simple demonstrator to show those advances. Established organizations, both formal and volunteer-based, often seek robust solutions that can support their operations; ideally mature and stable software with 24/7 technical support. These objectives are hard to reconcile.

To a large extent, the needs of organizations involved in emergencies and disasters are short-term, practical, and more a matter of engineering than advanced computing. For a successful engagement, computing researchers need to demonstrate practical value, and it needs to be clear at the onset what is the time frame in which that value will be demonstrated. In some cases, a short-term value delivery on a core need of the organization (possibly based on existing developments, without a strong research component) may pave the way for delivering long-term value with a stronger research component. Compromises are sometimes necessary, and communication is key to manage expectations.

Engaging in a productive technological or scientific project with an organization is as much a matter of relationships as it is a matter of results. The best time to establish a relationship with an organization is between operations.[4] Crises are environments full of energy and creativity, and people may be inspired to find new solutions (Starbird and Palen, 2011). However, it may be counterproductive to try to start a collaboration in the middle of an emergency, when emotions run high and people are under stress.[5] Trying to introduce new technologies during an active operation can be disruptive and ineffective (Harvard Humanitarian Initiative, 2011, p. 36).

Waldman et al. (2013) provide a guide for engaging with formal humanitarian organizations. This guide recognizes many problems that volunteer and

---

[4] "Social media for emergency managers can't start when the emergency does." Joseph Marks, *Nextgov,* November 2011. http://www.nextgov.com/technology-news/2011/11/social-media-for-emergency-managers-cant-start-when-the-emergency-does/50103/.

[5] "How to survive as an aid worker without losing your soul." *The Guardian,* March 2015. http://www.theguardian.com/global-development-professionals-network/2015/mar/23/how-to-survive-as-an-aid-worker-without-losing-your-soul

technical communities willing to work with these organizations may encounter, which computing researchers are also likely to face.

The speed of technology adoption. Today, social media is not a primary communication channel for emergency managers, but it is used as an alternative or additional communication channel (White, 2011). While the humanitarian community increasingly discovers the value of social media, "too many agencies still believe that engaging with beneficiaries via the latest communication technology is something they can do at some vague point in the future, when they are 'ready'." This clashes with the reality of a communications revolution that has been going on for years (Robinson and Wall, 2012). The first recommendation that the Queensland Police gives in their report about social media during disaster is "If you are not doing social media, do it now. If you wait until it's needed, it will be too late" (Charlton, 2012).

Today, social media for emergencies may be in a similar stage as Wikipedia was as an educational resource in its early years. It was looked on with both excitement and suspicion. Wikipedia did not become an educational resource by decree but instead by the coevolution of the educational community and the community of Wikipedians. The educational community saw long-lasting value in interacting with Wikipedia content, and the content became simply too good to be ignored.

The same may happen with social media in disasters. Technological adoption is very difficult to anticipate, but as a generation that was born with social media replaces a generation that was not, it would be surprising to find less openness to social media in humanitarian and emergency response organizations.

To encourage this adoption, many training courses and certifications are now being offered, helping local agencies to adopt social media in their response and recovery processes (Hughes et al., 2014b). Efforts aimed at training responders about the usage of social media are only partially about the technology itself, after all, popular social media platforms are designed to be easy to use, and are already used by billions of people.

Instead, the main objective should be to create a new mind-set, in which collaboration with the public and collective intelligence are in the foreground (White, 2011). This change depends on many factors, including the extent to which computing researchers can demonstrate the practical value of our contributions.

Bibliography

Abbasi, Mohammad-Ali, Kumar, Shamanth, Andrade Filho, Jose A., and Liu, Huan. 2012 (Apr.). Lessons learned in using social media for disaster relief - ASU crisis response game. Pages 282–289 of: *Proceedings of 5th International Conference on Social Computing, Behavioral-Cultural Modeling and Prediction.*

Abel, Fabian, Celik, Ilknur, Houben, Geert-Jan, and Siehndel, Patrick. 2011. Leveraging the semantics of tweets for adaptive faceted search on Twitter. Pages 1–17 of: *The Semantic Web.* Springer.

Abel, Fabian, Hauff, Claudia, Houben, Geert-Jan, Stronkman, Richard, and Tao, Ke. 2012a (June). Semantics + filtering + search = Twitcident. Exploring information in social Web streams. Pages 285–294 of: *Proceedings of 23rd Conference on Hypertext and Social Media Hypertext.* ACM, Milwaukee, Wisconsin, USA.

Abel, Fabian, Hauff, Claudia, Houben, Geert-Jan, Stronkman, Richard, and Tao, Ke. 2012b (Apr.). Twitcident: Fighting fire with information from social Web streams. Pages 305–308 of: *Social Web for Disaster Management (SWDM), Companion: Proceedings of 21st International Conference on World Wide Web Conference (WWW).* ACM, Lyon, France.

Acar, Adam, and Muraki, Yuya. 2011. Twitter for crisis communication: Lessons learned from Japan's tsunami disaster. *International Journal of Web Based Communities*, **7**(3), 392–402.

Adams, David S. 1970. *Policies, programs, and problems of the local Red Cross disaster relief in the 1960s.* Tech. rept. University of Delaware, Disaster Research Center.

Aggarwal, Charu (ed). 2007. *Data streams: Models and algorithms.* Advances in Database Systems. Springer.

Aggarwal, Charu C, and Philip, S Yu. 2008. *A general survey of privacy-preserving data mining models and algorithms.* Springer.

Aggarwal, Charu C., Han, Jiawei, Wang, Jianyong, and Yu, Philip S. 2003 (Sept.). A framework for clustering evolving data streams. Pages 81–92 of: *Proceedings of 29th International Conference on Very Large Databases*, vol. 29. VLDB Endowment, Berlin, Germany.

Agichtein, Eugene, Castillo, Carlos, Donato, Debora, Gionis, Aristides, and Mishne, Gilad. 2008 (Feb.). Finding high-quality content in social media. Pages 183–194 of: *Proceedings of 2008 International Conference on Web Search and Data Mining.* ACM, Berkeley, California, USA.

De Albuquerque, João Porto, Herfort, Benjamin, Brenning, Alexander, and Zipf, Alexander. 2015. A geographic approach for combining social media and authoritative data towards identifying useful information for disaster management. *International Journal of Geographical Information Science*, **29**(4), 667–689.

Aleissa, Faisal, Alnasser, Riyadh, Almaatouq, Abdullah, Jamshaid, Kamran, Alhasoun, Fahad, Gonzalez, Marta, and Alfaris, Anas. 2014. Wired to connect: Analyzing human communication and information sharing behavior during extreme events. Pages 12–15 of: *KDD-LESI 2014: Proceedings of 1st KDD Workshop on Learning about Emergencies from Social Information at KDD'14*. New York, USA: ACM.

Allan, James. 2002. *Topic detection and tracking: Event-based information organization*. Springer.

Alley, Alys, Mori, Mariko, Vitullo, Amanda, and Wallace, Janelle. 2015 (June). *Social media monitoring for emergency managers*. Tech. rept. Syracuse University (Student Report).

American Red Cross. 2012 (August). *More americans using mobile apps in emergencies*. Online and phone survey.

Andén-Papadopoulos, Kari. 2009. US soldiers imaging the Iraq War on YouTube. *Popular Communication*, **7**(1), 17–27.

Anderson, Kenneth M., and Schram, Aaron. 2011 (May). Design and implementation of a data analytics infrastructure in support of crisis informatics research (NIER track). Pages 844–847 of: *Proceedings of 33rd International Conference on Software Engineering*. ACM, Honolulu, Hawaii, USA.

Anderson, Kenneth M, Aydin, Ahmet Arif, Barrenechea, Mario, Cardenas, Adam, Hakeem, Mazin, and Jambi, Sahar. 2015. Design challenges/solutions for environments supporting the analysis of social media data in crisis informatics research. Pages 163–172 of: *Proceedings of 48th Annual Hawaii International Conference on System Sciences (HICSS)*. Kauai, Hawaii, USA: IEEE.

Ao, Ji, Zhang, Peng, and Cao, Yanan. 2014. Estimating the locations of emergency events from Twitter streams. *Procedia Computer Science*, **31**, 731–739.

Appling, Scott, Briscoe, Erica, Ediger, David, Poovey, Jason, and McColl, Rob. 2014. Deriving disaster-related information from social media. Pages 16–22 of: *KDD-LESI 2014: Proceedings of 1st KDD Workshop on Learning about Emergencies from Social Information at KDD'14*. New York, USA: ACM.

Artz, Donovan, and Gil, Yolanda. 2007. A survey of trust in computer science and the semantic Web. *Web Semant.*, **5**(2), 58–71.

Ashktorab, Zahra, Brown, Christopher, Nandi, Manojit, and Culotta, Aron. 2014. Tweedr: Mining Twitter to inform disaster response. In: *Proceedings of 11th International Conference on Information Systems for Crisis Response and Management (ISCRAM)*. University Park, Pennsylvania, USA: ISCRAM.

Aslam, Javed, Ekstrand-Abueg, Matthew, Pavlu, Virgil, Diaz, Fernado, and Sakai, Tetsuya. 2013 (Nov.). Overview of the TREC 2013 temporal summarization track. In: *Proceedings of 22nd Text Retrieval Conference (TREC)*.

Asur, Sitaram, and Huberman, Bernardo A. 2010. Predicting the future with social media. Pages 492–499 of: *Proceedings of IEEE/WIC/ACM International Conferences on Web Intelligence and Intelligent Agent Technology WI-IAT*, vol. 1. Los Alamitos, California, USA: IEEE Computer Society.

Atefeh, Farzindar, and Khreich, Wael. 2013. A survey of techniques for event detection in Twitter. *Computational Intelligence*, 132–164.

Avvenuti, Marco, Cresci, Stefano, Marchetti, Andrea, Meletti, Carlo, and Tesconi, Maurizio. 2014 (Aug.). EARS (Earthquake Alert and Report System): A real time decision support system for earthquake crisis management. Pages 1749–1758 of: *Proceedings of 20th ACM SIGKDD International Conference on Knowledge Discovery and Data Mining*. ACM, New York, USA.

Baba, Seigo, Toriumi, Fujio, Sakaki, Takeshi, Shinoda, Kosuke, Kurihara, Satoshi, Kazama, Kazuhiro, and Noda, Itsuki. 2015. Classification method for shared information on Twitter without text data. In: *Proceedings of Social Web for Disaster Management (SWDM), at WWW 2015*. Florence, Italy: ACM.

Baeza-Yates, Ricardo, and Ribeiro-Neto, Berthier. 2011. *Modern information retrieval: The concepts and technology behind search*. 2nd edn. Addison-Wesley Professional.

Bagrow, James P., Wang, Dashun, and Barabasi, Albert-Laszlo. 2011. Collective response of human populations to large-scale emergencies. *PloS One*, **6**(3), e17680.

Baird, Malcolm E. 2010. *The "phases" of emergency management*. Tech. rept. Vanderbilt Center for Transportation Research (VECTOR).

Baker, Karen S., and Millerand, Florence. 2007. Articulation work supporting information infrastructure design: Coordination, categorization, and assessment in practice. Pages 242 of: *Proceedings of 40th Annual Hawaii International Conference on System Sciences (HICSS)*. IEEE.

Baldwin, Timothy, Cook, Paul, Lui, Marco, MacKinlay, Andrew, and Wang, Li. 2013. How noisy social media text, how diffrnt social media sources. Pages 356–364 of: *Proceedings of 6th International Joint Conference on Natural Language Processing*. Nagoya, Japan: ACL.

Barabási, Albert-László. 2002. *Linked: The new science of networks*. 1st edn. Perseus Books Group.

Barabási, Albert-László, and Albert, Réka. 1999. Emergence of scaling in random networks. *Science*, **286**(5439), 509–512.

Baron, N. S. 2003. Language of the Internet. Pages 59–127 of: Farghali, A. (ed), *The Stanford Handbook for Language Engineers*. Stanford, CA, USA: CSLI publications.

Barrenechea, Mario, Anderson, Kenneth M., Palen, Leysia, and White, Joanne. 2015a. Engineering crowdwork for disaster events: The human-centered development of a lost-and-found tasking environment. Pages 182–191 of: *Proceedings of 48th Annual Hawaii International Conference on System Sciences (HICSS)*. Kauai, Hawaii, USA: IEEE.

Barrenechea, Mario, Anderson, Kenneth M., Aydin, Ahmet Arif, Hakeem, Mazin, and Jambi, Sahar. 2015b. Getting the query right: User interface design of analysis platforms for crisis research. Pages 547–564 of: Cimiano, Philipp, Frasincar, Flavius, Houben, Geert-Jan, and Schwabe, Daniel (eds), *Engineering the Web in the Big Data Era*. Lecture Notes in Computer Science, vol. 9114. Springer International Publishing.

Baruah, Gaurav, Smucker, Mark D., and Clarke, Charles LA. 2015. Evaluating streams of evolving news events. Pages 675–684 of: *Proceedings of 38th International*

Conference on Research and Development in Information Retrieval (SIGIR). Santiago, Chile: ACM.

Becker, Hila, Naaman, Mor, and Gravano, Luis. 2011. Beyond trending topics: Real-world event identification on Twitter. Pages 438–441 of: *Proceedings of 5th International AAAI Conference on Weblogs and Social Media (ICWSM)*. Barcelona, Spain: ACM.

Belkin, Nicholas J., and Croft, W. Bruce. 1992. Information filtering and information retrieval: Two sides of the same coin? *Communications of the ACM*, **35**(12), 29–38.

Bellucci, Andrea, Malizia, Alessio, Diaz, Paloma, and Aedo, Ignacio. 2010. Framing the design space for novel crisis-related mashups: The eStoryS example. In: *Proceedings of 7th International Conference on Information Systems for Crisis Response and Management (ISCRAM)*. Seattle, Washington, USA: ISCRAM.

Benevenuto, Fabrıcio, Magno, Gabriel, Rodrigues, Tiago, and Almeida, Virgılio. 2010. Detecting spammers on Twitter. Pages 75–83 of: *Proceedings of 7th Annual Collaboration, Electronic Messaging, Anti-Abuse and Spam Conference CEAS*, vol. 6. Redmond, Washington, USA: CEAS Conference.

Bengtsson, Linus, Lu, Xin, Thorson, Anna, Garfield, Richard, and Von Schreeb, Johan. 2011. Improved response to disasters and outbreaks by tracking population movements with mobile phone network data: A post-earthquake geospatial study in Haiti. *PLoS Medicine*, **8**(8), e1001083.

Benkler, Yochai. 2006. *The wealth of networks: How social production transforms markets and freedom*. Yale University Press.

Berlingerio, Michele, Francesco, Calabrese, Giusy, Di Lorenzo, Xiaowen, Dong, Yiannis, Gkoufas, and Mavroeidis, Dimitrios. 2013. Safercity: A system for detecting and analyzing incidents from social media. Pages 1077–1080 of: *Proceedings of 13th International Conference on Data Mining Workshops ICDMW*. Dallas, Texas, USA: IEEE.

Bernstein, Michael S., Suh, Bongwon, Hong, Lichan, Chen, Jilin, Kairam, Sanjay, and Chi, Ed H. 2010. Eddi: Interactive topic-based browsing of social status streams. Pages 303–312 of: *Proceedings of 23nd Annual ACM Symposium on User Interface Software and Technology*. New York, USA: ACM.

Bhamidi, Shankar, Steele, J. Michael, and Zaman, Tauhid. 2015. Twitter event networks and the superstar model. *The Annals of Applied Probability*, **25**(5), 2462–2502.

Bhatt, Shreyansh P., Purohit, Hemant, Hampton, Andrew, Shalin, Valerie, Sheth, Amit, and Flach, John. 2014. Assisting coordination during crisis: A domain ontology based approach to infer resource needs from tweets. Pages 297–298 of: *Proceedings of ACM Web Science Conference*. Bloomington, Indiana, USA: ACM.

Bird, Steven, Klein, Ewan, and Loper, Edward. 2009. *Natural language processing with Python analyzing text with the natural language toolkit*. O'Reilly Media.

Blanford, Justine I., Bernhardt, Jase, Savelyev, Alexander, Wong-Parodi, Gabrielle, Carleton, Andrew M., Titley, David W., and MacEachren, Alan M. 2014. Tweeting and tornadoes. In: *Proceedings of 11th International Conference on Information Systems for Crisis Response and Management (ISCRAM)*. University Park, Pennsylvania, USA: ISCRAM.

Blei, David M., Ng, Andrew Y., and Jordan, Michael I. 2003. Latent Dirichlet Allocation. *The Journal of Machine Learning Research*, **3**, 993–1022.

Boldi, Paolo, and Vigna, Sebastiano. 2014. Axioms for centrality. *Internet Mathematics*, **10**(3-4), 222–262.

Bollen, Johan, Mao, Huina, and Zeng, Xiaojun. 2011. Twitter mood predicts the stock market. *Journal of Computational Science*, **2**(1), 1–8.

Bollobás, Béla, and Riordan, Oliver M. 2003. Mathematical results on scale-free random graphs. Pages 1–34 of: *Handbook of Graphs and Networks: from the Genome to the Internet*. Weinheim: Wiley-VCH, Germany.

Bonanno, George A., Brewin, Chris R., Kaniasty, Krzysztof, and La Greca, Annette M. 2010. Weighing the costs of disaster consequences, risks, and resilience in individuals, families, and communities. *Psychological Science in the Public Interest*, **11**(1), 1–49.

Bosch, Harald, Thom, Dennis, Heimerl, Florian, Puttmann, Edwin, Koch, Steffen, Kruger, Robert, Worner, Michael, and Ertl, Thomas. 2013. Scatterblogs2: Real-time monitoring of microblog messages through user-guided filtering. *Visualization and Computer Graphics, IEEE Transactions on*, **19**(12), 2022–2031.

Bossu, Rémy, Mazet-Roux, Gilles, Douet, Vincent, Rives, Sergio, Marin, Sylvie, and Aupetit, Michael. 2008. Internet users as seismic sensors for improved earthquake response. *Eos, Transactions American Geophysical Union*, **89**(25), 225–226.

Bowser, Anne, and Tsai, Janice Y. 2015. Supporting ethical Web research: A new research ethics review. Pages 151–161 of: *Proceedings of 24th International Conference on World Wide Web*. Florence, Italy: ACM, for IW3C2.

boyd, danah, and Crawford, Kate. 2012. Critical questions for Big Data: Provocations for a cultural, technological, and scholarly phenomenon. *Information, Communication & Society*, **15**(5), 662–679.

Brants, Thorsten, Chen, Francine, and Farahat, Ayman. 2003 (July). A system for new event detection. Pages 330–337 of: *Proceedings of 26th International Conference on Research and Development in Information Retrieval (SIGIR)*. ACM, Toronto, Canada.

Brennan, Sean, Sadilek, Adam, and Kautz, Henry. 2013. Towards understanding global spread of disease from everyday interpersonal interactions. Pages 2783–2789 of: *Proceedings of 23rd International Joint Conference on Artificial Intelligence IJCAI*. Beijing, China: AAAI Press.

Bressler, George H., Jennex, Murray E., and Frost, Eric G. 2012. Exercise24: Using social media for crisis response. *The World Financial Review*, Mar., 77–80.

Bricout, John C., and Baker, Paul MA. 2010. Leveraging online social networks for people with disabilities in emergency communications and recovery. *International Journal of Emergency Management*, **7**(1), 59–74.

Brill, Eric. 2000. Part-of-speech tagging. Chap. 17, pages 403–414 of: *Handbook of Natural Language Processing*. CRC Press.

Brown, John Seely, and Duguid, Paul. 2002. *The social life of information*. Harvard Business Press.

Bruns, Axel. 2014. Crisis communication. *The Media and Communications in Australia*, 351–355.

Bruns, Axel, Burgess, Jean E, Crawford, Kate, and Shaw, Frances. 2012. *#qldfloods and @qpsmedia: Crisis communication on Twitter in the 2011 south east Queensland floods*. Tech. rept. ARC Centre, Queensland University of Technology.

Burns, Alex, and Eltham, Ben. 2009. Twitter free Iran: An evaluation of Twitter's role in public diplomacy and information operations in Iran's 2009 election crisis. In: *Record of the Communications Policy and Research Forum*. Network Insight Institute. ISBN 978-0-9804344-4-6.

Burton, Scott H., Tanner, Kesler W., Giraud-Carrier, Christophe G., West, Joshua H., and Barnes, Michael D. 2012. "Right time, right place" health communication on Twitter: Value and accuracy of location information. *Journal of Medical Internet Research*, **14**(6), e156.

Butler, Declan. 2013. Crowdsourcing goes mainstream in typhoon response. *Nature (News)*, Nov.

Calhoun, Craig. 2004. A world of emergencies: Fear, intervention, and the limits of cosmopolitan order. *Canadian Review of Sociology/Revue Canadienne de Sociologie*, **41**(4), 373–395.

Cameron, Mark A., Power, Robert, Robinson, Bella, and Yin, Jie. 2012. Emergency situation awareness from Twitter for crisis management. Pages 695–698 of: *Social Web for Disaster Management (SWDM), Companion: Proceedings of 21st International Conference on World Wide Web Conference (WWW)*. Lyon, France: ACM.

Canini, Kevin Robert, Suh, Bongwon, and Pirolli, Peter L. 2011. Finding credible information sources in social networks based on content and social structure. Pages 1–8 of: *Proceedings of IEEE 3rd International Conference on Privacy, Security, Risk and Trust PASSAT*. Boston, Massachusetts, USA: IEEE.

Capelo, Luis, Chang, Natalie, and Verity, Andrej. 2012 (Aug.). *Guidance for collaborating with volunteer and technical communities*. Tech. rept. Digital Humanitarian Network.

Caragea, Cornelia, McNeese, Nathan, Jaiswal, Anuj, Traylor, Greg, Kim, H., Mitra, Prasenjit, Wu, Dinghao, Tapia, A., Giles, Lee, Jansen, Bernard J., et al. 2011. Classifying text messages for the Haiti earthquake. In: *Proceedings of 8th International Conference on Information Systems for Crisis Response and Management (ISCRAM)*. Lisbon, Portugal: ISCRAM.

Caragea, Cornelia, Squicciarini, Anna, Stehle, Sam, Neppalli, Kishore, and Tapia, Andrea H. 2014. Mapping moods: Geo-mapped sentiment analysis during Hurricane Sandy. In: *Proceedings of 11th International Conference on Information Systems for Crisis Response and Management (ISCRAM)*. University Park, Pennsylvania, USA: ISCRAM.

Carpenter, Hutch. 2011. Motivating the crowd to participate in your innovation initiative. Chap. 9 of: Sloane, Paul (ed), *A Guide to Open Innovation and Crowdsourcing: Advice from Leading Experts*. Kogan Page.

Carton, Samuel, Park, Souneil, Zeffer, Nicole, Adar, Eytan, Mei, Qiaozhu, and Resnick, Paul. 2015. Audience analysis for competing memes in social media. In: *Proceedings of 9th International AAAI Conference on Web and Social Media*. Oxford, UK: AAAI Press.

Carvin, Andy. 2013. *Distant witness*. City University of New York CUNY Journalism Press.

Castells, Manuel. 2001. *The internet galaxy: Reflections on the internet, business, and society*. Oxford University Press.

Castillo, Carlos, Mendoza, Marcelo, and Poblete, Barbara. 2011. Information credibility on Twitter. Pages 675–684 of: *Proceedings of 20th International Conference on World Wide Web Conference (WWW)*. Hyderabad, India: ACM.

Castillo, Carlos, Mendoza, Marcelo, and Poblete, Barbara. 2013. Predicting information credibility in time-sensitive social media. *Internet Research*, **23**(5), 560–588.

Cha, Meeyoung, Haddadi, Hamed, Benevenuto, Fabricio, and Gummadi, P Krishna. 2010 (May). Measuring user influence in Twitter: The million follower fallacy. Page 30 of: *Proceedings of 4th International AAAI Conference on Weblogs and Social Media (ICWSM)*, vol. 10.

Cha, Meeyoung, Benevenuto, Fabrício, Haddadi, Hamed, and Gummadi, Krishna. 2012. The world of connections and information flow in Twitter. *Systems, Man and Cybernetics, Part A: Systems and Humans, IEEE Transactions on*, **42**(4), 991–998.

Chakrabarti, Deepayan, and Faloutsos, Christos. 2012. Graph mining: Laws, tools, and case studies. *Synthesis Lectures on Data Mining and Knowledge Discovery*, **7**(1), 1–207.

Chakrabarti, Soumen, Van den Berg, Martin, and Dom, Byron. 1999. Focused crawling: A new approach to topic-specific Web resource discovery. *Computer Networks*, **31**(11), 1623–1640.

Chang, Chia Hui, Kayed, Mohammed, Girgis, Moheb R., and Shaalan, Khaled F. 2006. A survey of Web information extraction systems. *Knowledge and Data Engineering, IEEE Transactions on*, **18**(10), 1411–1428.

Charikar, Moses S. 2002. Similarity estimation techniques from rounding algorithms. Pages 380–388 of: *Proceedings of 34th Annual ACM Symposium on Theory of Computing*. Montreal, Quebec, Canada: ACM.

Charlton, Kym. 2012. *Disaster management and social media-a case study*. Tech. rept. Media and Public Affairs Branch, Queensland Police Service.

Charlwood, J., Dennis, A., Gissing, A., Quick, L., and Varma, S. 2012. Use of social media during flood events. In: *Proceedings of Floodplain Management Association Meeting*.

Chen, Jiaoyan, Chen, Huajun, Zheng, Guozhou, Pan, Jeff Z, Wu, Honghan, and Zhang, Ningyu. 2014. Big smog meets Web science: Smog disaster analysis based on social media and device data on the Web. Pages 505–510 of: *Web Science Track, Companion: Proceedings of the 23rd International Conference on World Wide Web (WWW)*. Seoul, Korea: ACM, for IW3C2.

Chen, Ling, and Roy, Abhishek. 2009. Event detection from Flickr data through wavelet-based spatial analysis. Pages 523–532 of: *Proceedings of 18th ACM Conference on Information and Knowledge Management (CIKM)*. Hong Kong, China: ACM.

Chen, Rongjuan, and Sakamoto, Yasuaki. 2013. Perspective matters: Sharing of crisis information in social media. Pages 2033–2041 of: *Proceedings of 46th Annual Hawaii International Conference on System Sciences (HICSS)*. Maui, Hawaii, USA: IEEE.

Chen, Rongjuan, and Sakamoto, Yasuaki. 2014. Feelings and perspective matter: Sharing of crisis information in social media. Pages 1958–1967 of: *Proceedings of 47th Annual Hawaii International Conference on System Sciences (HICSS)*. Waikoloa, Hawaii, USA: IEEE.

Chen, Wei, Lakshmanan, Laks V. S., and Castillo, Carlos. 2013. Information and influence propagation in social networks. *Synthesis Lectures on Data Management*, **5**, 1–177. Morgan and Claypool Publishers.

Cheng, Justin, Adamic, Lada, Dow, P. Alex, Kleinberg, Jon Michael, and Leskovec, Jure. 2014. Can cascades be predicted? Pages 925–936 of: *Proceedings of 23rd International Conference on World Wide Web*. Seoul, Korea: IW3C2.

Cheng, Tao, and Wicks, Thomas. 2014. Event detection using Twitter: A spatio-temporal approach. *PLoS ONE*, **9**(6), e97807.

Cheng, Zhiyuan, Caverlee, James, and Lee, Kyumin. 2010. You are where you tweet: A content-based approach to geo-locating Twitter users. Pages 759–768 of: *Proceedings of Conference on Information and Knowledge Management (CIKM)*. Toronto, ON, Canada: ACM.

Choi, Hyunyoung, and Varian, Hal. 2012. Predicting the present with Google trends. *Economic Record*, **88**, 2–9.

Choi, Seonhwa, and Bae, Byunggul. 2015. The real-time monitoring system of social Big Data for disaster management. Pages 809–815 of: *Computer Science and Its Applications*. Springer.

De Choudhury, Munmun, Diakopoulos, Nicholas, and Naaman, Mor. 2012. Unfolding the event landscape on Twitter: Classification and exploration of user categories. Pages 241–244 of: *Proceedings of ACM Conference on Computer Supported Cooperative Work (CSCW)*. Seattle, Washington, USA: ACM.

Chowdhury, Soudip Roy, Imran, Muhammad, Asghar, Muhammad Rizwan, Amer-Yahia, Sihem, and Castillo, Carlos. 2013. Tweet4act: Using incident-specific profiles for classifying crisis-related messages. In: *Proceedings of 10th International Conference on Information Systems for Crisis Response and Management (ISCRAM)*. Baden Baden, Germany: ISCRAM.

Cinnamon, Jonathan, and Schuurman, Nadine. 2013. Confronting the data-divide in a time of spatial turns and volunteered geographic information. *GeoJournal*, **78**(4), 657–674.

Ciot, Morgane, Sonderegger, Morgan, and Ruths, Derek. 2013 (Oct.). Gender inference of Twitter users in non-English contexts. Pages 1136–1145 of: *Proceedings of Conference on Empirical Methods in Natural Language Processing (EMNLP)*.

Clark, Tim, Keßler, Carsten, and Purohit, Hemant. 2015. Feasibility of information interoperability in the humanitarian domain. In: *Proceedings on AAAI Spring Symposia Series*. AAAI Press.

Clary, E. Gil, and Snyder, Mark. 1999. The motivations to volunteer theoretical and practical considerations. *Current Directions in Psychological Science*, **8**(5), 156–159.

Cobb, Camille, McCarthy, Ted, Perkins, Annuska, Bharadwaj, Ankitha, Comis, Jared, Do, Brian, and Starbird, Kate. 2014. Designing for the deluge: Understanding and supporting the distributed, collaborative work of crisis volunteers. Pages 888–899 of: *Proceedings of 17th ACM Conference on Computer-Supported Cooperative Work and Social Computing (CSCW)*. Baltimore, Maryland, USA: ACM.

Coleman, David J., Georgiadou, Yola, Labonte, Jeff, et al. 2009. Volunteered geographic information: The nature and motivation of produsers. *International Journal of Spatial Data Infrastructures Research*, **4**(1), 332–358.

Committee on Public Response to Alerts and Warnings Using Social Media. 2013. *Public response to alerts and warnings using social media: Report of a workshop on current knowledge and research gaps.* Tech. rept. National Academies Press.

Comunello, Francesca, Mulargia, Simone, Polidoro, Piero, Casarotti, Emanuele, and Lauciani, Valentino. 2015. No misunderstandings during earthquakes: Elaborating and testing a standardized tweet structure for automatic earthquake detection information. In: *Proceedings of 12th International Conference on Information Systems for Crisis Response and Management (ISCRAM).* Kristiansand, Norway: ISCRAM.

Corley, Courtney D., Dowling, Chase, Rose, Stuart J., and McKenzie, Taylor. 2013. Social sensor analytics: Measuring phenomenology at scale. Pages 61–66 of: *Proceedings of IEEE International Conference on Intelligence and Security Informatics ISI.* Seattle, Washington, USA: IEEE.

COVOST. 2014 (Apr.). *Colorado virtual operations support team handbook.* Tech. rept. COVOST.

Crane, Riley, and Sornette, Didier. 2008. Robust dynamic classes revealed by measuring the response function of a social system. *PNAS,* **105**(41), 15649–15653.

Crawford, Kate, and Finn, Megan. 2014. The limits of crisis data: Analytical and ethical challenges of using social and mobile data to understand disasters. *GeoJournal,* 1–12.

Crowe, Adam. 2012. *Disasters 2.0: The application of social media systems for modern emergency management.* 1st edn. CRC Press.

Crutcher, Michael, and Zook, Matthew. 2009. Placemarks and waterlines: Racialized cyberscapes in post-Katrina Google Earth. *Geoforum,* **40**(4), 523–534.

Dai, Wenyuan, Xue, Gui-Rong, Yang, Qiang, and Yu, Yong. 2007. Transferring naive bayes classifiers for text classification. Pages 540–545 of: *Proceedings of 22nd AAAI Conference on Artificial Intelligence,* vol. 22. Vancouver, Canada: AAAI Press.

Dailey, Dharma, and Starbird, Kate. 2014. Visible skepticism: Community vetting after Hurricane Irene. In: *Proceedings of 11th International Conference on Information Systems for Crisis Response and Management (ISCRAM).* University Park, Pennsylvania, USA: ISCRAM.

Dashti, Shideh, Palen, Leysia, Heris, Mehdi P., Anderson, Kenneth M., and Anderson, Scott. 2014. Supporting disaster reconnaissance with social media data: A design-oriented case study of the 2013 Colorado Floods. In: *Proceedings of 11th International Conference on Information Systems for Crisis Response and Management (ISCRAM).* University Park, Pennsylvania, USA: ISCRAM.

Denef, Sebastian, Bayerl, Petra S., and Kaptein, Nico A. 2013. Social media and the police: Tweeting practices of British police forces during the August 2011 riots. Pages 3471–3480 of: *Proceedings of ACM Conference on Human Factors in Computing Systems (SIGCHI).* Paris, France: ACM.

Derczynski, Leon, Maynard, Diana, Rizzo, Giuseppe, van Erp, Marieke, Gorrell, Genevieve, Troncy, Raphaël, Petrak, Johann, and Bontcheva, Kalina. 2015. Analysis of named entity recognition and linking for tweets. *Information Processing & Management,* **51**(2), 32–49.

Diakopoulos, Nicholas, De Choudhury, Munmun, and Naaman, Mor. 2012. Finding and assessing social media information sources in the context of journalism.

Pages 2451–2460 of: *Proceedings of Conference on Human Factors in Computing Systems (SIGCHI)*. Austin, Texas, USA: ACM.

Diaz, Fernando. 2014. Experimentation standards for crisis informatics. *SIGIR Forum*, **48**(2), 22–30.

Diaz, Fernando, Gamon, Michael, Hofman, Jake, Kiciman, Emre, and Rothschild, David. 2016 (Jan). Online and social media data as an imperfect continuous panel survey. *PLoS ONE*.

Díaz, Paloma, Aedo, Ignacio, and Herranz, Sergio. 2014. Citizen participation and social technologies: Exploring the perspective of emergency organizations. Pages 85–97 of: Hanachi, Chihab, Bénaben, Frédérick, and Charoy, François (eds), *Information Systems for Crisis Response and Management in Mediterranean Countries*. Lecture Notes in Business Information Processing, vol. 196. Springer International Publishing.

Dong, Xin, Gabrilovich, Evgeniy, Heitz, Geremy, Horn, Wilko, Lao, Ni, Murphy, Kevin, Strohmann, Thomas, Sun, Shaohua, and Zhang, Wei. 2014. Knowledge vault: A Web-scale approach to probabilistic knowledge fusion. Pages 601–610 of: *Proceedings of 20th ACM SIGKDD International Conference on Knowledge Discovery and Data Mining*. New York, USA: ACM.

Dong, Xin L., Gabrilovich, Evgeniy, Murphy, Kevin, Dang, Van, Horn, Wilko, Lugaresi, Camillo, Sun, Shaohua, and Zhang, Wei. 2015. Knowledge-based trust: Estimating the trustworthiness of Web sources. Pages 938–949 of: *Proceedings of 41st International Conference on Very Larga Data Bases VLDB*. Kohala, Hawaii, USA: PVLDB.

Dou, Wenwen, Wang, Xiaoyu, Skau, Drew, Ribarsky, William, and Zhou, Michelle X. 2012. Leadline: Interactive visual analysis of text data through event identification and exploration. Pages 93–102 of: *Proceedings of IEEE Conference on Visual Analytics Science and Technology VAST*. Seattle, Washington, USA: IEEE.

Dunant, Jean-Henry. 1862. *A memory of Solferino*. Geneva, Switzerland: International Committee of the Red Cross (1986).

Dynes, Russell R. 1970. *Organized behavior in disaster*. Heath Lexington Books.

Dynes, Russell R. 1994. Community emergency planning: False assumptions and inappropriate analogies. *International Journal of Mass Emergencies and Disasters*, **12**(2), 141–158.

Earle, Paul, Guy, Michelle, Buckmaster, Richard, Ostrum, Chris, Horvath, Scott, and Vaughan, Amy. 2010. OMG earthquake! Can Twitter improve earthquake response? *Seismological Research Letters*, **81**(2), 246–251.

Earle, Paul S., Bowden, Daniel C., and Guy, Michelle. 2011. Twitter earthquake detection: Earthquake monitoring in a social world. *Annals of Geophysics*, **54**(6), 708–715.

Easley, David, and Kleinberg, Jon. 2010. *Networks, crowds, and markets*. Cambridge: Cambridge University Press.

Elwood, Sarah. 2008. Volunteered geographic information: Future research directions motivated by critical, participatory, and feminist GIS. *GeoJournal*, **72**(3-4), 173–183.

Endsley, Mica R. 1995. Toward a theory of situation awareness in dynamic systems. *Human Factors: The Journal of the Human Factors and Ergonomics Society*, **37**(1), 32–64.

Eppler, Martin J. 2006. *Managing information quality: Increasing the value of information in knowledge-intensive products and processes*. Springer Science & Business Media.

Ettredge, Michael, Gerdes, John, and Karuga, Gilbert. 2005. Using Web-based search data to predict macroeconomic statistics. *Communications of ACM*, **48**(11), 87–92.

European Parliament and Council. 1995. Directive 95/46/EC of the European Parliament and of the Council of 24 October 1995 on the protection of individuals with regard to the processing of personal data and on the free movement of such data. *Official Journal of the European Union*, **L 281**, 0031–0050.

Evnine, Ariel, Gros, Andreas, and Hofleitner, Aude. 2014 (Aug.). *On Facebook when the Earth shakes...* Tech. rept. Facebook Data Science.

Farnham, Shelly, Pedersen, E., and Kirkpatrick, Robert. 2006. Observation of Katrina/Rita groove deployment: Addressing social and communication challenges of ephemeral groups. Pages 39–49 of: *Proceedings of 3rd International Conference on Information Systems for Crisis Response and Management (ISCRAM)*. Newark, New Jersey, USA: ISCRAM.

Fawcett, Tom. 2004. ROC graphs: Notes and practical considerations for researchers. *Machine Learning*, **31**, 1–38.

Feldman, Ronen. 2013. Techniques and applications for sentiment analysis. *Communications of the ACM*, **56**(4), 82–89.

Felicio, SPAS., Silva, VSR., Dargains, AR., Souza, PRA., Sampaio, F., Carvalho, PVR., Gomes, JO., and Borges, MRS. 2014. Stop disasters game experiment with elementary school students in Rio de Janeiro: Building safety culture. In: *Proceedings of 11th International Conference on Information Systems for Crisis Response and Management (ISCRAM)*. University Park, Pennsylvania, USA: ISCRAM.

Fischer, Henry W. 1998. *Response to disaster: Fact versus fiction and its perpetuation: the sociology of disaster*. University Press of America.

Fogg, BJ., and Tseng, Hsiang. 1999 (May). The elements of computer credibility. Pages 80–87 of: *Proceedings of Conference on Human Factors in Computing Systems (CHI)*. ACM, Pittsburgh, Pennsylvania, USA.

Fraustino, Julia D., Liu, Brooke, and Jin, Yan. 2012 (Apr.). *Social media use during disasters: A review of the knowledge base and gaps (final report, START)*. Tech. rept. Human Factors/Behavioral Sciences Division, Science and Technology Directorate, U.S. Department of Homeland Security, College Park, Maryland, USA.

Frey, Brendan J., and Dueck, Delbert. 2007. Clustering by passing messages between data points. *Science*, **315**(5814), 972–976.

Friberg, Therese, Prödel, Stephan, and Koch, Rainer. 2010. Analysis of information quality criteria in a crisis situation as a characteristic of complex situations. Page 14 of: *Proceedings of 15th International Conference on Information Quality*, vol. 12. Little Rock, Arkansas, USA: MIT Information Quality (MITIQ) Program.

Friberg, Therese, Prödel, Stephan, and Koch, Rainer. 2011. Information quality criteria and their importance for experts in crisis situations. Pages 145–149 of: *Proceedings of 8th International Conference on Information Systems for Crisis Response and Management (ISCRAM)*. Lisbon, Portugal: ISCRAM.

Fritz, Charles E., and Mathewson, John H. 1957. *Convergence behavior in disasters: A problem in social control: a special report prepared for the committee on disaster studies*. National Academy of Sciences National Research Council.

Fu, King-wa, White, James, Chan, Yuen-ying, Zhou, Ling, Zhang, Qiang, and Lu, Qibin. 2010. Enabling the disabled: Media use and communication needs of people with disabilities during and after the Sichuan earthquake in China. *International Journal of Emergency Management (IJEM)*, **7**(1), 75–87.

Gansberg, Martin. 1964. Thirty-seven who saw murder didn't call the police. *New York Times*, Online.

Gao, Huiji, Barbier, Geoffrey, and Goolsby, Rebecca. 2011. Harnessing the crowd-sourcing power of social media for disaster relief. *IEEE Intelligent Systems*, **26**(3), 10–14.

Gao, Liang, Song, Chaoming, Gao, Ziyou, Barabási, Albert-László, Bagrow, James P, and Wang, Dashun. 2014. Quantifying information flow during emergencies. *Scientific Reports*, **4**(Feb.).

Gao, Wei, and Sebastiani, Fabrizio. 2015 (Aug.). Tweet sentiment: From classification to quantification. In: *Conference on Advances in Social Networks Analysis and Mining (ASONAM)*.

Gardner, Robert Owen. 2013. The emergent organization: Improvisation and order in Gulf Coast disaster relief. *Symbolic Interaction*, **36**(3), 237–260.

Gardner-Chloros, Penelope. 2009. *Code-switching*. Cambridge University Press.

Gayo-Avello, Daniel. 2011. Don't turn social media into another "Literary Digest" poll. *Communications of ACM*, **54**(10), 121–128.

Gayo-Avello, Daniel. 2012. No, you cannot predict elections with Twitter. *Internet Computing, IEEE*, **16**(6), 91–94.

Gefen, David. 2002. Reflections on the dimensions of trust and trustworthiness among online consumers. *ACM Sigmis Database*, **33**(3), 38–53.

Geiger, David, Rosemann, Michael, and Fielt, Erwin. 2011. Crowdsourcing information systems: A systems theory perspective. In: *Proceedings of 22nd Australasian Conference on Information Systems (ACIS)*. Sydney, Australia: Association for Information Systems (AIS).

Gelernter, Judith, and Mushegian, Nikolai. 2011. Geo-parsing messages from microtext. *Transactions in GIS*, **15**(6), 753–773.

Gleed, Gregory. 2011. Local perspectives of the Haiti earthquake response. *Humanitarian Exchange Magazine*, **1**(52), 42–44.

Goel, Sharad, Hofman, Jake M., Lahaie, Sébastien, Pennock, David M., and Watts, Duncan J. 2010. Predicting consumer behavior with Web search. *Proceedings of the National Academy of Sciences*, **107**(41), 17486–17490.

Goel, Sharad, Watts, Duncan J., and Goldstein, Daniel G. 2012. The structure of online diffusion networks. Pages 623–638 of: *Proceedings of 13th ACM Conference on Electronic Commerce*. Valencia, Spain: ACM.

Gomide, Janaína, Veloso, Adriano, Meira Jr., Wagner, Almeida, Virgílio, Benevenuto, Fabrício, Ferraz, Fernanda, and Teixeira, Mauro. 2011. Dengue surveillance based on a computational model of spatio-temporal locality of Twitter. In: *Proceedings of 3rd International Web Science Conference*. Koblenz, Germany: ACM.

González-Bailón, Sandra, Borge-Holthoefer, Javier, Rivero, Alejandro, and Moreno, Yamir. 2011. The dynamics of protest recruitment through an online network. *Scientific Reports*, **1**, P.7.

González-Bailón, Sandra, Borge-Holthoefer, Javier, and Moreno, Yamir. 2013. Broadcasters and hidden influentials in online protest diffusion. *American Behavioral Scientist*, 0002764213479371.

van Gorp, Annemijn F. 2014. Integration of volunteer and technical communities into the humanitarian aid sector: Barriers to collaboration. In: *Proceedings of 11th International Conference on Information Systems for Crisis Response and Management (ISCRAM)*. University Park, Pennsylvania, USA: ISCRAM.

Graham, Mark, Hale, Scott A., and Gaffney, Devin. 2014. Where in the world are you? Geolocation and language identification in Twitter. *The Professional Geographer*, **66**(4), 568–578.

Graham, Shawn, Milligan, Ian, and Weingart, Scott. 2015. *Exploring big historical data: The historian's macroscope*. Imperial College Press.

Gruhl, Daniel, Nagarajan, Meena, Pieper, Jan, Robson, Christine, and Sheth, Amit. 2009. Context and domain knowledge enhanced entity spotting in informal text. Pages 260–276 of: Bernstein, Abraham, Karger, DavidR., Heath, Tom, Feigenbaum, Lee, Maynard, Diana, Motta, Enrico, and Thirunarayan, Krishnaprasad (eds), *The Semantic Web–ISWC 2009*. Lecture Notes in Computer Science, vol. 5823. Springer Berlin Heidelberg.

Guo, Qi, Diaz, Fernando, and Yom-Tov, Elad. 2013a. Updating users about time critical events. Pages 483–494 of: *Advances in Information Retrieval*. Lecture Notes in Computer Science. Springer Berlin Heidelberg.

Guo, Qi, Diaz, Fernando, and Yom-Tov, Elad. 2013b. Updating users about time critical events. Pages 483–494 of: *Advances in Information Retrieval*. Springer.

Gupta, Aditi, and Kumaraguru, Ponnurangam. 2012. Credibility ranking of tweets during high impact events. In: *Proceedings of 1st Workshop on Privacy and Security in Online Social Media PSOSM, at WWW 2012*. Lyon, France: ACM.

Gupta, Aditi, Lamba, Hemank, Kumaraguru, Ponnurangam, and Joshi, Anupam. 2013. Faking Sandy: Characterizing and identifying fake images on Twitter during Hurricane Sandy. Pages 729–736 of: *Privacy and Security in Online Social Media (PSOSM), Companion: Proceedings of 22nd International Conference on World Wide Web Conference (WWW)*. Rio de Janeiro, Brazil: ACM, for IW3C2.

Gupta, Aditi, Kumaraguru, Ponnurangam, Castillo, Carlos, and Meier, Patrick. 2014. Tweetcred: Real-time credibility assessment of content on Twitter. Pages 228–243 of: *Proceedings of 1st Workshop on Privacy and Security in Online Social Media SocInfo*. Barcelona, Spain: Springer.

Guy, Michelle, Earle, Paul, Ostrum, Chris, Gruchalla, Kenny, and Horvath, Scott. 2010. Integration and dissemination of citizen reported and seismically derived earthquake information via social network technologies. Pages 42–53 of: *Advances in Intelligent Data Analysis IX*. Springer.

Guyon, Isabelle, and Elisseeff, André. 2003. Special issue on variable and feature selection. *Journal of Machine Learning Research*, **3**(Mar.), 1157–1461.

Haklay, Mordechai, and Weber, Patrick. 2008. OpenStreetMap: User-generated street maps. *Pervasive Computing, IEEE*, **7**(4), 12–18.

Harnesk, Dan, and Hartikainen, Heidi. 2011. Multi-layers of information security in emergency response. *International Journal of Information Systems for Crisis Response and Management (IJISCRAM)*, **32**(2), 1–17.

Harvard Humanitarian Initiative. 2011. *Disaster relief 2.0 report: The future of information sharing in humanitarian emergencies*. Washington, D.C. and Berkshire, U.K.: UN Foundation.

Hecht, Brent, Hong, Lichan, Suh, Bongwon, and Chi, Ed H. 2011. Tweets from Justin Bieber's heart: The dynamics of the location field in user profiles. Pages 237–246 of: *Proceedings of Conference on Human Factors in Computing Systems (SIGCHI)*. Vancouver, Canada: ACM.

Hecht, Brent J., and Gergle, Darren. 2010. On the localness of user-generated content. Pages 229–232 of: *Proceedings of 2010 ACM Conference on Computer Supported Cooperative Work*. Savannah, Georgia, USA: ACM.

Henderson, Keith, Gallagher, Brian, Eliassi-Rad, Tina, Tong, Hanghang, Basu, Sugato, Akoglu, Leman, Koutra, Danai, Faloutsos, Christos, and Li, Lei. 2012. Rolx: Structural role extraction and mining in large graphs. Pages 1231–1239 of: *Proceedings of 18th ACM International Conference on Knowledge Discovery and Data Mining (SIGKDD)*. Beijing, China: ACM.

Herfort, Benjamin, de Albuquerque, João Porto, Schelhorn, Svend-Jonas, and Zipf, Alexander. 2014. Does the spatiotemporal distribution of tweets match the spatiotemporal distribution of flood phenomena? A study about the river Elbe flood in June 2013. In: *Proceedings of 11th International Conference on Information Systems for Crisis Response and Management (ISCRAM)*. University Park, Pennsylvania, USA: ISCRAM.

Hermida, Alfred. 2014. *Tell everyone: Why we share and why it matters*. Doubleday Canada.

Herold, Rebecca. 2006. Addressing privacy issues during disaster recovery. *Information Systems Security*, **14**(6), 16–22.

Hichens, Evelyn. 2011. *The many faces of crowdsourcing in humanitarian disasters*. M.Phil. thesis, School of Geography, Earth and Environmental Sciences.

Hiltz, Starr R., Kushma, Jane, and Plotnick, Linda. 2014. Use of social media by u.s. public sector emergency managers: Barriers and wish lists. In: *Proceedings of 11th International Conference on Information Systems for Crisis Response and Management (ISCRAM)*. University Park, Pennsylvania, USA: ISCRAM.

Hiltz, Starr Roxanne, Diaz, Paloma, and Mark, Gloria. 2011. Introduction: Social media and collaborative systems for crisis management. *ACM Transactions on Computer-Human Interaction (TOCHI)*, **18**(4), Article 18, 6 pages.

Hofmann, Thomas. 1999 (Aug.). Probabilistic latent semantic indexing. Pages 50–57 of: *Proceedings of 22nd International Conference on Research and Development in Information Retrieval (SIGIR)*. ACM, Berkeley, California, USA.

Hokudai Earthquake Project. 2011. *General consumer survey*. Press release.

Hristidis, Vagelis, Chen, Shu-Ching, Li, Tao, Luis, Steven, and Deng, Yi. 2010. Survey of data management and analysis in disaster situations. *Journal of Systems and Software*, **83**(10), 1701–1714.

Hua, Ting, Chen, Feng, Zhao, Liang, Lu, Chang-Tien, and Ramakrishnan, Naren. 2013 (Aug.). STED: Semi-supervised targeted-interest event detection in Twitter. Pages 1466–1469 of: *Proceedings of 19th ACM International Conference on Knowledge Discovery and Data Mining SIGKDD*. ACM, Chicago, Illinois, USA.

Hughes, Amanda L. 2014. Participatory design for the social media needs of emergency public information officers. In: *Proceedings of 11th International Conference on Information Systems for Crisis Response and Management (ISCRAM)*. University Park, Pennsylvania, USA: ISCRAM.

Hughes, Amanda L., St. Denis, Lise Ann, Palen, Leysia, and Anderson, Kenneth. 2014a. Online public communications by police and fire services during the 2012

Hurricane Sandy. Pages 1505–1514 of: *Proceedings of ACM Conference on Human Factors in Computing Systems (SIGCHI)*. Toronto, Canada: ACM.

Hughes, Amanda L., Peterson, Steve, and Palen, Leysia. 2014b. Social media in emergency management. Chap. 11, pages 349–392 of: Trainor, J. E., and Subbio, T. (eds), *Issues in Disaster Science and Management: a Critical Dialogue between Scientists and Emergency Managers*. FEMA in Higher Education Program.

Hughes, LA., Palen, L., Sutton, J., Liu, BS., and Vieweg, S. 2008. Site-seeing in disasters: An examination of on-line social convergency. In: *Proceedings of 5th International Conference on Information Systems for Crisis Response and Management (ISCRAM)*, vol. 4. Washington, DC, USA: ISCRAM.

Hui, Cindy, Tyshchuk, Yulia, Wallace, William A., Magdon-Ismail, Malik, and Goldberg, Mark. 2012. Information cascades in social media in response to a crisis: A preliminary model and a case study. Pages 653–656 of: *Proceedings of 21st International Conference on World Wide Web*. Lyon, France: ACM.

Hutchins, Edwin. 1995. *Cognition in the wild*. MIT Press.

ICRC. 2013. Managing sensitive protection information. Chap. 6, pages 77–102 of: *Professional Standards for Protection Work*. International Committee of the Red Cross.

Ienco, Dino, Bonchi, Francesco, and Castillo, Carlos. 2010. The meme ranking problem: Maximizing microblogging virality. Pages 328–335 of: *Data Mining Workshops (ICDMW), 2010 IEEE International Conference on*. IEEE.

Ikawa, Yohei, Enoki, Miki, and Tatsubori, Michiaki. 2012. Location inference using microblog messages. Pages 687–690 of: *Proceedings of 21st International Conference on World Wide Web Conference (WWW)*. Lyon, France: ACM.

Ikawa, Yohei, Vukovic, Maja, Rogstadius, Jakob, and Murakami, Akiko. 2013. Location-based insights from the social Web. In: *Proceedings of 2nd International Workshop on Social Web for Disaster Management (SWDM) at WWW 2013*. Rio de Janeiro, Brazil: IW3C2.

Imran, Muhammad, Lykourentzou, Ioanna, Naudet, Yannick, and Castillo, Carlos. 2013a. Engineering crowdsourced stream processing systems. *arXiv preprint arXiv:1310.5463*, 32 pages.

Imran, Muhammad, Elbassuoni, Shady Mamoon, Castillo, Carlos, Diaz, Fernando, and Meier, Patrick. 2013b. Extracting information nuggets from disaster-related messages in social media. In: *Proceedings of 10th International Conference on Information Systems for Crisis Response and Management (ISCRAM)*. Baden Baden, Germany: ISCRAM.

Imran, Muhammad, Elbassuoni, Shady, Castillo, Carlos, Diaz, Fernando, and Meier, Patrick. 2013c. Practical extraction of disaster-relevant information from social media. Pages 1021–1024 of: *Social Web for Disaster Management (SWDM), Companion: Proceedings of 22nd International Conference on World Wide Web Conference (WWW)*. Rio de Janeiro, Brazil: ACM.

Imran, Muhammad, Castillo, Carlos, Lucas, Ji, Meier, Patrick, and Vieweg, Sarah. 2014a. AIDR: Artificial Intelligence for Disaster Response. Pages 159–162 of: *Social Web for Disaster Management (SWDM), Companion: Proceedings of 23rd International Conference on World Wide Web (WWW)*. Seoul, Korea: ACM, for IW3C2.

Imran, Muhammad, Castillo, Carlos, Lucas, Ji, Patrick, M, and Rogstadius, Jakob. 2014b. Coordinating human and machine intelligence to classify microblog communications in crises. In: *Proceedings of 11th International Conference on Information Systems for Crisis Response and Management (ISCRAM)*. University Park, Pennsylvania, USA: ISCRAM.

Imran, Muhammad, Castillo, Carlos, Diaz, Fernando, and Vieweg, Sarah. 2015. Processing social media messages in mass emergency: A survey. *ACM Computing Surveys*, **47**(4), 67:1–67:38.

Ingersoll, Grant S., Morton, Thomas S., and Farris, Andrew L. 2013. *Taming text: How to find, organize, and manipulate it*. 1st edn. Manning Publications.

Intagorn, Suradej, and Lerman, Kristina. 2013. Mining geospatial knowledge on the social Web. *Using Social and Information Technologies for Disaster and Crisis Management*, 98–112.

Ito, Jun, Song, Jing, Toda, Hiroyuki, Koike, Yoshimasa, and Oyama, Satoshi. 2015. Assessment of tweet credibility with LDA features. Pages 953–958 of: *Proceedings of 24th International Conference on World Wide Web Companion*. Florence, Italy: ACM, for IW3C2.

Iyengar, Akshaya, Finin, Tim, and Joshi, Anupam. 2011. Content-based prediction of temporal boundaries for events in Twitter. Pages 186–191 of: *Proceedings of IEEE 3rd International Conference on Privacy, Security, Risk and Trust PASSAT*. Boston, Massachusetts, USA: IEEE.

Jadhav, Ashutosh, Purohit, Hemant, Kapanipathi, Pavan, Ananthram, Pramod, Ranabahu, Ajith, Nguyen, Vinh, Mendes, Pablo N., Smith, Alan Gary, and Sheth, Amit. 2010. *Twitris 2.0: Semantically empowered system for understanding perceptions from social data*. Tech. rept. Kno.e.sis Publications, Wright State University.

Jennex, Murray E. 2012. Social media–truly viable for crisis response. In: *Proceedings of 9th International Conference on Information Systems for Crisis Response and Management (ISCRAM)*. Vancouver, Canada: ISCRAM.

Joachims, Thorsten. 2002. *Learning to classify text using support vector machines: Methods, theory and algorithms*. Kluwer Academic Publishers.

Joseph, Kenneth, Landwehr, Peter M., and Carley, Kathleen M. 2014. An approach to selecting keywords to track on Twitter during a disaster. In: *Proceedings of 11th International Conference on Information Systems for Crisis Response and Management (ISCRAM)*. University Park, Pennsylvania, USA: ISCRAM.

Jurafsky, Daniel, and Martin, James H. 2008. *Speech and language processing, 2nd edition*. 2nd edn. Prentice Hall.

Jurgens, David, Finethy, Tyler, McCorriston, James, Xu, Yi Tian, and Ruths, Derek. 2015 (May). Geolocation prediction in Twitter using social networks: A critical analysis and review of current practice. In: *Proceedings of 9th International AAAI Conference on Web and Social Media (ICWSM)*.

Karandikar, Anand. 2010. *Clustering short status messages: A topic model based approach*. M.Phil. thesis, University of Maryland.

Katz, Leo. 1953. A new status index derived from sociometric analysis. *Psychometrika*, **18**(1), 39–43.

Kedzie, Chris, McKeown, Kathleen, and Diaz, Fernando. 2015 (July). Predicting salient updates for disaster summarization. In: *Proceedings of 53rd Annual Meeting of the Association for Computational Linguistics (ACL)*.

Keegan, Brian, Gergle, Darren, and Contractor, Noshir. 2013. Hot off the wiki: Structures and dynamics of Wikipedia's coverage of breaking news events. *American Behavioral Scientist*, 0002764212469367.

Kenett, Dror Y., Morstatter, Fred, Stanley, H. Eugene, and Liu, Huan. 2014. Discovering social events through online attention. *PLoS ONE*, **9**(7), e102001.

Kenter, Tom, Balog, Krisztian, and de Rijke, Maarten. 2015. Evaluating document filtering systems over time. *Information Processing & Management*, 791–808.

Khurdiya, Arpit, Dey, Lipika, Mahajan, Diwakar, and Verma, Ishan. 2012. Extraction and compilation of events and sub-events from Twitter. Pages 504–508 of: *Proceedings of IEEE/WIC/ACM International Conferences on Web Intelligence and Intelligent Agent Technology WI-IAT*. Macau, China: IEEE Computer Society.

Killian, Lewis M. 2002. Methods for disaster research: Unique or not? Pages 49–93 of: Stallings, Robert A. (ed), *Methods of Disaster Research*. Philadelphia, USA: Xlibris.

Kireyev, Kirill, Palen, Leysia, and Anderson, K. 2009. Applications of topics models to analysis of disaster-related Twitter data. In: *NIPS Workshop on Applications for Topic Models: Text and beyond*, vol. 1.

Kogan, Marina, Palen, Leysia, and Anderson, Kenneth M. 2015. Think local, retweet global: Retweeting by the geographically-vulnerable during Hurricane Sandy. Pages 981–993 of: *Proceedings of 18th ACM Conference on Computer Supported Cooperative Work and Social Computing (CSCW)*. San Francisco, California, USA: ACM.

Koutra, Danai, Bennett, Paul, and Horvitz, Eric. 2015. Events and controversies: Influences of a shocking news event on information seeking. In: *Proceedings of 24th International Conference on World Wide Web Conference (WWW)*. Florence, Italy: ACM, for IW3C2.

Kumar, Shamanth, Barbier, Geoffrey, Abbasi, Mohammad Ali, and Liu, Huan. 2011 (July). TweetTracker: An analysis tool for humanitarian and disaster relief. In: *Proceedings of 5th International AAAI Conference on Weblogs and Social Media (ICWSM)*.

Kumar, Shamanth, Morstatter, Fred, and Liu, Huan. 2013a. *Twitter data analytics*. 2014 edn. SpringerBriefs in Computer Science. Springer.

Kumar, Shamanth, Morstatter, Fred, Zafarani, Reza, and Liu, Huan. 2013b. Whom should I follow? Identifying relevant users during crises. Pages 139–147 of: *Proceedings of 24th ACM Conference on Hypertext and Social Media Hypertext*. Paris, France: ACM.

Kumaran, Girdhar, Allan, James, and McCallum, Andrew. 2004. *Classification models for new event detection*. Tech. rept. University of Massachusetts Amherst.

Kurkinen, K., Hakkinen, M., Sullivan, H., and Lauttamus, Markku. 2010. Optimizing mobile social media interfaces for rapid internal communication by emergency services. In: *Proceedings of 7th International Conference on Information Systems for Crisis Response and Management (ISCRAM)*. Seattle, Washington, USA: ISCRAM.

Kwak, Haewoon, and An, Jisun. 2014a. A first look at global news coverage of disasters by using the GDELT dataset. Pages 300–308 of: *Social Informatics*. Springer.

Kwak, Haewoon, and An, Jisun. 2014b (Oct.). Understanding news geography and major determinants of global news coverage of disasters. In: *Computational Journalism Symposium*.

Kwak, Haewoon, Lee, Changhyun, Park, Hosung, and Moon, Sue. 2010. What is Twitter, a social network or a news media? Pages 591–600 of: *Proceedings of 19th International Conference on World Wide Web*. Raleigh, North Carolina, USA: ACM.

Lafferty, John D., McCallum, Andrew, and Pereira, Fernando C. N. 2001. Conditional random fields: Probabilistic models for segmenting and labeling sequence data. Pages 282–289 of: *Proceedings of 18th International Conference on Machine Learning*. ICML '01. San Francisco, California, USA: Morgan Kaufmann Publishers Inc.

LaLone, Nick, Tapia, Andrea H., Case, Nathan A., MacDonald, E. A., Hall, M., and Heavner, Matt. 2015 (May). Hybrid community participation in crowdsourced early warning systems. In: *Proceedings of 12th International Conference on Information Systems for Crisis Response and Management (ISCRAM)*.

Laney, Doug. 2001. 3D data management: Controlling data volume, velocity and variety. *META Group Research Note*, **6**, 70.

Lanquillon, Carsten, and Renz, Ingrid. 1999. Adaptive information filtering: Detecting changes in text streams. Pages 538–544 of: *Proceedings of 8th International Conference on Information and Knowledge Management (CIKM)*. Kansas City, Missouri, USA: ACM.

Latonero, Mark, and Shklovski, Irina. 2011. Emergency management, Twitter, and social media evangelism. *International Journal of Information Systems for Crisis Response and Management*, **3**(4), 67–86.

Law, Edith, and Ahn, Luis. 2011. Human computation. *Synthesis Lectures on Artificial Intelligence and Machine Learning*, **5**(3), 121 pages.

Lazer, David, Kennedy, Ryan, King, Gary, and Vespignani, Alessandro. 2014. The parable of Google flu: Traps in big data analysis. *Science*, **343**, 1203–1205.

Le, Anh, Lin, Yu-Ru, and Pelechrinis, Konstantinos. 2014. Information network mining: A case for emergency scenarios. Pages 23–28 of: *KDD-LESI 2014: Proceedings of 1st KDD Workshop on Learning about Emergencies from Social Information at KDD'14*. New York, USA: ACM.

Leavitt, Alex, and Clark, Joshua A. 2014. Upvoting hurricane Sandy: Event-based news production processes on a social news site. Pages 1495–1504 of: *Proceedings of Conference on Human Factors in Computing Systems (SIGCHI)*. Toronto, Canada: ACM.

Lee, Pei, Lakshmanan, Laks VS., and Milios, Evangelos E. 2013. Event evolution tracking from streaming social posts. *arXiv preprint arXiv:1311.5978*, 13 pages.

Leetaru, Kalev, and Schrodt, Philip A. 2014. *GDELT: Global Database of Events, Language, and Tone*. Online Website.

Leskovec, Jure, Kleinberg, Jon, and Faloutsos, Christos. 2005 (Aug.). Graphs over time: Densification laws, shrinking diameters and possible explanations. Pages 177–187 of: *Proceedings of 11th ACM SIGKDD International Conference on Knowledge Discovery in Data Mining*. ACM, Chicago, Illinois, USA.

Lewandowsky, Stephan, Stritzke, Werner GK., Freund, Alexandra M., Oberauer, Klaus, and Krueger, Joachim I. 2013. Misinformation, disinformation, and violent conflict:

From Iraq and the "war on terror" to future threats to peace. *American Psychologist*, **68**(7), 487–501.

Lewis, William D., Munro, Robert, and Vogel, Stephan. 2011. Crisis MT: Developing a cookbook for MT in crisis situations. Pages 501–511 of: *Proceedings of 6th Workshop on Statistical Machine Translation*. Association for Computational Linguistics.

Li, Hongmin, Guevara, Nicolais, Herndon, Nic, Caragea, Doina, Neppalli, Kishore, Caragea, Cornelia, Squicciarini, Anna, and Tapia, Andrea H. 2015. Twitter mining for disaster response: A domain adaptation approach. In: *Proceedings of 12th International Conference on Information Systems for Crisis Response and Management (ISCRAM)*. Kristiansand, Norway: ISCRAM.

Li, Huaye, Sakamoto, Yasuaki, Chen, Rongjuan, and Tanaka, Yuko. 2014. The psychology behind people's decision to forward disaster-related tweets. *Howe School Research Paper*, **36**(July), 15 pages.

Li, Rui, Lei, Kin Hou, Khadiwala, Ravi, and Chang, KC-C. 2012 (Apr.). Tedas: A Twitter-based event detection and analysis system. Pages 1273–1276 of: *Proceedings of 28th International Conference on Data Engineering ICDE*. IEEE, Washington DC, USA.

Lindsay, Bruce R. 2011 (Sept.). *Social media and disasters: Current uses, future options, and policy considerations*. Tech. rept. Congressional Research Service.

Lingad, John, Karimi, Sarvnaz, and Yin, Jie. 2013. Location extraction from disaster-related microblogs. Pages 1017–1020 of: *Social Web for Disaster Management (SWDM), Companion: Proceedings of 22nd International Conference on World Wide Web Conference (WWW)*. Rio de Janeiro, Brazil: IW3C2. ACM.

Link, Daniel, Horita, Flávio E. A., de Albuquerque, João P., Hellingrath, Bernd, and Ghasemivandhonaryar, Shabdiz. 2015. A method for extracting task-related information from social media based on structured domain knowledge. In: *Americas Conference on Information Systems*.

Liu, Bing. 2010. Sentiment analysis and subjectivity. Chap. 26, pages 627–666 of: Indurkhya, Nitin, and Damerau, Fred J. (eds), *Handbook of Natural Language Processing*, second edn. Chapman and Hall/CRC.

Liu, Bing. 2012. *Sentiment analysis and opinion mining*. Synthesis Lectures on Human Language Technologies. Morgan & Claypool.

Liu, Bing. 2015. *Sentiment analysis: Mining opinions, sentiments, and emotions*. Cambridge University Press.

Liu, S., and Palen, Leysia. 2009. Spatiotemporal mashups: A survey of current tools to inform next generation crisis support. In: *Proceedings of 6th International Conference on Information Systems for Crisis Response and Management (ISCRAM)*, vol. 9. Gothenburg, Sweden: ISCRAM.

Liu, Shuangyan, Shaw, Duncan, and Brewster, Christopher. 2013. Ontologies for crisis management: A review of state of the art in ontology design and usability. In: *Proceedings of 10th International Conference on Information Systems for Crisis Response and Management (ISCRAM)*. Baden Baden, Germany: ISCRAM.

Liu, Sophia B. 2014. Crisis crowdsourcing framework: Designing strategic configurations of crowdsourcing for the emergency management domain. *Computer Supported Cooperative Work (CSCW)*, **23**(4-6), 389–443.

Liu, Sophia B., Palen, Leysia, Sutton, Jeannette, Hughes, Amanda L., and Vieweg, Sarah. 2008. In search of the bigger picture: The emergent role of on-line photo sharing in times of disaster. In: *Proceedings of 5th International Conference on Information Systems for Crisis Response and Management (ISCRAM)*. Washington, DC, USA: ISCRAM.

Liu, Ying, Zhang, Dengsheng, Lu, Guojun, and Ma, Wei-Ying. 2007. A survey of content-based image retrieval with high-level semantics. *Pattern Recognition*, **40**(1), 262–282.

Lohmann, Steffen, Ziegler, Jürgen, and Tetzlaff, Lena. 2009. Comparison of tag cloud layouts: Task-related performance and visual exploration. Pages 392–404 of: *Human-Computer Interaction–INTERACT 2009*. Springer.

De Longueville, Bertrand, Smith, Robin S., and Luraschi, Gianluca. 2009. OMG, from here, I can see the flames! A use case of mining location based social networks to acquire spatio-temporal data on forest fires. Pages 73–80 of: *Proceedings of International Workshop on Location Based Social Networks LBSN*. Washington DC, USA: ACM.

Lu, Hung-Yi Y., Case, Donald O., Lustria, Mia Liza L., Kwon, Nahyun, Andrews, James E., Cavendish, Sarah E., and Floyd, Brenikki R. 2007. Predictors of online information seeking by international students when disaster strikes their countries. *Cyberpsychology & behavior: the impact of the Internet, multimedia and virtual reality on behavior and society*, **10**(5), 709–712.

Lu, Yafeng, Hu, Xia, Wang, Feng, Kumar, Shamanth, Liu, Huan, and Maciejewski, Ross. 2015. Visualizing social media sentiment in disaster scenarios. Pages 1211–1215 of: *Proceedings of 24th International Conference on World Wide Web Companion*. Florence, Italy: ACM, for IW3C2.

Ludwig, Thomas, Siebigteroth, Tim, and Pipek, Volkmar. 2015a. CrowdMonitor: Monitoring physical and digital activities of citizens during emergencies. Pages 421–428 of: *Proceedings of Conference on Human Factors in Computing Systems (SIGCHI)*. Seoul, Korea: ACM.

Ludwig, Thomas, Reuter, Christian, and Pipek, Volkmar. 2015b. Social haystack: Dynamic quality assessment of citizen-generated content during emergencies. *ACM Transactions on Computer-Human Interaction (TOCHI)*, **22**(4), Article 17.

MacEachren, Alan M., Jaiswal, Anuj, Robinson, Anthony C., Pezanowski, Scott, Savelyev, Alexander, Mitra, Prasenjit, Zhang, Xiao, and Blanford, Justine. 2011. Senseplace2: Geotwitter analytics support for situational awareness. Pages 181–190 of: *Proceedings of IEEE Conference on Visual Analytics Science and Technology VAST*. Providence, Richmond, USA: IEEE.

Malik, Momin M, Lamba, Hemank, Nakos, Constantine, and Pfeffer, Jürgen. 2015 (May). Population bias in geotagged tweets. In: *Proceedings of 9th International AAAI Conference on Web and Social Media (ICWSM)*.

Malone, Thomas W, Laubacher, Robert, and Dellarocas, Chrysanthos. 2010. The collective intelligence genome. *IEEE Engineering Management Review*, **38**(3), 38–52.

Mao, Andrew, Mason, Winter A., Suri, Siddharth, and Watts, Duncan J. 2014. An experimental study of collective self–organization in crisis mapping. In: *Conference on Digital Experimentation (CODE@MIT)*. Cambridge, Massachussetts, USA: MIT.

Marcus, Adam, Bernstein, Michael S., Badar, Osama, Karger, David R., Madden, Samuel, and Miller, Robert C. 2011. Twitinfo: Aggregating and visualizing microblogs for event exploration. Pages 227–236 of: *Proceedings of Conference on Human Factors in Computing Systems (SIGCHI)*. Vancouver, Canada: ACM.

Marwick, Alice, and boyd, danah. 2011. To see and be seen: Celebrity practice on Twitter. *Convergence: The International Journal of Research into New Media Technologies*, **17**(2), 139–158.

Marwick, Alice E. 2013. *Status update: Celebrity, publicity, and branding in the social media age*. Yale University Press.

Mason, Winter, and Watts, Duncan J. 2010. Financial incentives and the performance of crowds. *ACM SigKDD Explorations Newsletter*, **11**(2), 100–108.

Mathioudakis, Michael, and Koudas, Nick. 2010. TwitterMonitor: Trend detection over the Twitter stream. Pages 1155–1158 of: *Proceedings of International Conference on Management of Data (SIGMOD)*. Indianapolis, USA: ACM.

Matykiewicz, Pawel, and Pestian, John. 2012. Effect of small sample size on text categorization with support vector machines. Pages 193–201 of: *Proceedings of 2012 Workshop on Biomedical Natural Language Processing*. Montreal, Canada: Association for Computational Linguistics.

McClendon, Susan, and Robinson, Anthony C. 2013. Leveraging geospatially-oriented social media communications in disaster response. *International Journal of Information Systems for Crisis Response and Management (IJISCRAM)*, **5**(1), 22–40.

McCosker, Anthony. 2013. De-framing disaster: Affective encounters with raw and autonomous media. *Continuum*, **27**(3), 382–396.

McCreadie, Richard, Macdonald, Craig, and Ounis, Iadh. 2014. Incremental update summarization: Adaptive sentence selection based on prevalence and novelty. Pages 301–310 of: *Proceedings of 23rd ACM International Conference on Conference on Information and Knowledge Management*. Shanghai, China: ACM.

McCreadie, Richard, Macdonald, Craig, and Ounis, Iadh. 2015a. Crowdsourced rumour identification during emergencies. Pages 965–970 of: *Companion Proceedings of Crowdsourced Rumour Identification During Emergencies RDSM at WWW 2015*. Florence, Italy: ACM, for IW3C2.

McCreadie, Richard, Kappler, Karolin, Kardara, Magdalini, Kaltenbrunner, Andreas, Macdonald, Craig, Soldatos, John, and Ounis, Iadh. 2015b. SUPER: Towards the use of social sensors for security assessments and proactive management of emergencies. In: *Proceedings of Social Web for Disaster Management (SWDM) at WWW 2015*. Florence, Italy: ACM.

McKnight, D. Harrison, and Chervany, Norman L. 2001. Trust and distrust definitions: One bite at a time. Pages 27–54 of: *Trust in Cyber-societies*. Springer.

McMinn, Andrew J., Moshfeghi, Yashar, and Jose, Joemon M. 2013. Building a large-scale corpus for evaluating event detection on Twitter. Pages 409–418 of: *Proceedings of Conference on Information and Knowledge Management (CIKM)*. San Francisco, California, USA: ACM.

Meesters, Kenny, and van de Walle, Bartel. 2013. Disaster in my backyard: A serious game introduction to disaster information management. In: *Proceedings of 10th International Conference on Information Systems for Crisis Response and Management (ISCRAM)*. Baden Baden, Germany: ISCRAM.

Mei, Shike, Li, Han, Fan, Jing, Zhu, Xiaojin, and Dyer, Charles R. 2014. Inferring air pollution by sniffing social media. Pages 534–539 of: *Advances in Social Networks Analysis and Mining (ASONAM), IEEE/ACM International Conference on*. IEEE.

Meier, Patrick. 2015. *Digital humanitarians*. CRC Press.

Mejova, Yelena, Weber, Ingmar, and Macy, Michael (eds). 2015. *Twitter: A digital socioscope*. Cambridge University Press.

Meladianos, Polykarpos, Nikolentzos, Giannis, Rousseau, François, Stavrakas, Yannis, and Vazirgiannis, Michalis. 2015 (May). Degeneracy-based real-time sub-event detection in Twitter stream. In: *Proceedings of 9th International AAAI Conference on Web and Social Media (ICWSM)*.

Melville, Prem, Gryc, Wojciech, and Lawrence, Richard D. 2009. Sentiment analysis of blogs by combining lexical knowledge with text classification. Pages 1275–1284 of: *Proceedings of 15th ACM International Conference on Knowledge Discovery and Data Mining (SIGKDD)*. Paris, France: ACM.

Melville, Prem, Chenthamarakshan, Vijil, Lawrence, Richard D., Powell, James, Mugisha, Moses, Sapra, Sharad, Anandan, Rajesh, and Assefa, Solomon. 2013. Amplifying the voice of youth in Africa via text analytics. Pages 1204–1212 of: *Proceedings of 19th ACM International Conference on Knowledge Discovery and Data Mining (SIGKDD)*. Chicago, Illinois, USA: ACM.

Mendoza, Marcelo, Poblete, Barbara, and Castillo, Carlos. 2010. Twitter under crisis: Can we trust what we RT? Pages 71–79 of: *Proceedings of 1st Workshop on Social Media Analytics SOMA*. Washington DC, USA: ACM.

Merrick, D., and Duffy, Tom. 2013. Utilizing community volunteered information to enhance disaster situational awareness. In: *Proceedings of 10th International Conference on Information Systems for Crisis Response and Management (ISCRAM)*. Baden Baden, Germany: ISCRAM.

Metaxas, Panagiotis, and Mustafaraj, Eni. 2013. The rise and the fall of a citizen reporter. Pages 248–257 of: *Proceedings of 5th Annual ACM Web Science Conference WebSci*. Paris, France: ACM.

Meyer, Brett, Bryan, Kevin, Santos, Yamara, and Kim, Beomjin. 2011. TwitterReporter: Breaking news detection and visualization through the geo-tagged Twitter network. Pages 84–89 of: *Proceedings of 26th International Conference on Computers and Their Applications (CATA)*.

Middleton, Stuart E., Middleton, Lee, and Modafferi, Stefano. 2014. Real-time crisis mapping of natural disasters using social media. *Intelligent Systems, IEEE*, 9–17.

Mileti, Dennis. 1999. *Disasters by design: A reassessment of natural hazards in the United States*. Natural Hazards and Disasters: Reducing Loss and Building Sustainability in a Hazardous World. Joseph Henry Press.

Mislove, Alan, Marcon, Massimiliano, Gummadi, Krishna P., Druschel, Peter, and Bhattacharjee, Bobby. 2007. Measurement and analysis of online social networks. Pages 29–42 of: *Proceedings of 7th ACM SIGCOMM Conference on Internet Measurement*. San Diego, California, USA: ACM.

Mitchell, Jeffrey T., Thomas, Deborah SK., Hill, Arleen A., and Cutter, Susan L. 2000. Catastrophe in reel life versus real life: Perpetuating disaster myth through Hollywood films. *International Journal of Mass Emergencies and Disasters*, **18**(3), 383–402.

Mitra, Tanushree, and Gilbert, Eric. 2015. CREDBANK: A large-scale social media corpus with associated credibility annotations. In: *Proceedings of 9th International AAAI Conference on Web and Social Media*.

Mittelstadt, Sebastian, Wang, Xiaoyu, Eaglin, Todd, Thom, Dennis, Keim, Daniel, Tolone, William, and Ribarsky, William. 2015. An integrated in-situ approach to impacts from natural disasters on critical infrastructures. Pages 1118–1127 of: *Proceedings of 48th Annual Hawaii International Conference on System Sciences (HICSS)*. Kauai, Hawaii, USA: IEEE.

Moreno, Jacob Levy. 1934. *Who shall survive? A new approach to the problem of human interrelations*. Monographic series num. 58. Washington DC: Nervous and Mental Disease Publishing Co.

Morrow, Nathan, Mock, Nancy, Papendieck, Adam, and Kocmich, Nicholas. 2011 (Apr.). *Independent evaluation of the Ushahidi Haiti Project*. Tech. rept. Development Information Systems International.

Morstatter, Fred, Pfeffer, Jürgen, and Liu, Huan. 2014. When is it biased?: Assessing the representativeness of Twitter's streaming API. Pages 555–556 of: *Web Science Track, Companion: Proceedings of 23rd International Conference on World Wide Web (WWW)*. Seoul, Korea: ACM.

Murthy, Dhiraj, and Longwell, Scott A. 2013. Twitter and disasters. *Information, Communication, and Society*, **16**(6), 837–855.

Musaev, Aibek, Wang, De, and Pu, Calton. 2014. LITMUS: Landslide detection by integrating multiple sources. In: *Proceedings of 11th International Conference on Information Systems for Crisis Response and Management (ISCRAM)*. University Park, Pennsylvania, USA: ISCRAM.

Nagar, Seema, Seth, Aaditeshwar, and Joshi, Anupam. 2012. Characterization of social media response to natural disasters. Pages 671–674 of: *Social Web for Disaster Management (SWDM), Companion: Proceedings of 21st International Conference on World Wide Web Conference (WWW)*. Lyon, France: ACM.

Nagarajan, Meena, Sheth, Amit, and Velmurugan, Selvam. 2011. Citizen sensor data mining, social media analytics and development centric Web applications. Pages 289–290 of: *Proceedings of 20th International Conference on World Wide Web Conference (WWW)*. Hyderabad, India: ACM.

Nagy, Ahmed, and Stamberger, Jeannie. 2012. Crowd sentiment detection during disasters and crises. In: *Proceedings of 9th International Conference on Information Systems for Crisis Response and Management (ISCRAM)*. Vancouver, Canada: ISCRAM.

Nelson, Christie, and Pottenger, William M. 2013. Optimization of emergency response using higher order learning and clustering of 911 text messages. Pages 486–491 of: *Technologies for Homeland Security (HST), 2013 IEEE International Conference on*. IEEE.

Nenkova, Ani, and McKeown, Kathleen. 2011. *Automatic summarization*. Vol. 5. Now Publishers.

Neubig, Graham, Matsubayashi, Yuichiroh, Hagiwara, Masato, and Murakami, Koji. 2011. Safety information mining-what can NLP do in a disaster. Pages 965–973 of: *Proceedings of 5th International Joint Conference on Natural Language Processing (IJCNLP)*, vol. 11. Chiang Mai, Thailand: ACL.

Nguyen, Minh-Tien, Kitamoto, Asanobu, and Nguyen, Tri-Thanh. 2015. TSum4act: A framework for retrieving and summarizing actionable tweets during a disaster for reaction. Pages 64–75 of: *Advances in Knowledge Discovery and Data Mining*. Springer.

Oh, Onook, Agrawal, Manish, and Rao, H. Raghav. 2011. Information control and terrorism: Tracking the Mumbai terrorist attack through Twitter. *Information Systems Frontiers*, **13**(1), 33–43.

Okolloh, Ory. 2009. Ushahidi, or 'testimony': Web 2.0 tools for crowdsourcing crisis information. *Participatory Learning and Action*, **59**(1), 65–70.

Olafsson, Gisli. 2012. Call for open humanitarian information. Pages 100–105 of: Pipek, Volkmar, Landgren, Jonas, and Palen, Leysia (eds), *Proceedings of ACM Conference on Computer Supported Cooperative Work (CSCW)*. International Reports on Socio Informatics, vol. 9. Seattle, Washington, USA: ACM.

Olteanu, Alexandra, Castillo, Carlos, Diaz, Fernando, and Vieweg, Sarah. 2014 (June). CrisisLex: A lexicon for collecting and filtering microblogged communications in crises. In: *Proceedings of 8th International AAAI Conference on Weblogs and Social Media (ICWSM)*.

Olteanu, Alexandra, Vieweg, Sarah, and Castillo, Carlos. 2015. What to expect when the unexpected happens: Social media communications across crises. Pages 994–1009 of: *Proceedings of Conference on Computer-Supported Cooperative Work (CSCW)*. Vancouver, Canada: ACM.

Onorati, Teresa, Malizia, Alessio, Díaz, Paloma, and Aedo, Ignacio. 2013. Interaction design principles for Web emergency management information systems. Page 326 of: *Using Social and Information Technologies for Disaster and Crisis Management*. IGI Global.

ORI Market Research. 2012. *Social media election survey report*. Press release.

Owoputi, Olutobi, O'Connor, Brendan, Dyer, Chris, Gimpel, Kevin, Schneider, Nathan, and Smith, Noah A. 2013 (June). Improved part-of-speech tagging for online conversational text with word clusters. Pages 380–390 of: *Proceedings of Conference of the North American Chapter of the Association for Computational Linguistics: Human Language Technologies NAACL-HLT*.

Oxendine, Christopher E., Schnebele, Emily, Cervone, Guido, and Waters, Nigel. 2014. Fusing non-authoritative data to improve situational awareness in emergencies. In: *Proceedings of 11th International Conference on Information Systems for Crisis Response and Management (ISCRAM)*. University Park, Pennsylvania, USA: ISCRAM.

Ozturk, Pinar, Li, Huaye, and Sakamoto, Yasuaki. 2015. Combating rumor spread on social media: The effectiveness of refutation and warning. Pages 2406–2414 of: *Proceedings of 48th Annual Hawaii International Conference on System Sciences HICSS*. Kauai, Hawaii, USA: IEEE.

Page, Lawrence, Brin, Sergey, Motwani, Rajeev, and Winograd, Terry. 1998 (Jan.). *The PageRank citation ranking: Bringing order to the Web*. Tech. rept. Stanford InfoLab, Stanford University.

Palen, Leysia, and Liu, Sophia B. 2007. Citizen communications in crisis: Anticipating a future of ICT-supported public participation. Pages 727–736 of: *Proceedings of Conference on Human Factors in Computing Systems (SIGCHI)*. San Jose, California, USA: ACM.

Palen, Leysia, Hiltz, Starr Roxanne, and Liu, Sophia B. 2007. Online forums supporting grassroots participation in emergency preparedness and response. *Communications of the ACM*, **50**(3), 54–58.

Palen, Leysia, Vieweg, Sarah, Liu, Sophia B., and Hughes, Amanda Lee. 2009. Crisis in a networked world features of computer-mediated communication in the April 16, 2007, Virginia Tech event. *Social Science Computer Review*, **27**(4), 467–480.

Palen, Leysia, Anderson, Kenneth M., Mark, Gloria, Martin, James, Sicker, Douglas, Palmer, Martha, and Grunwald, Dirk. 2010. A vision for technology-mediated support for public participation and assistance in mass emergencies and disasters. In: *Proceedings of 2010 ACM-BCS Visions of Computer Science Conference*. Edinburgh, Scotland, UK: ACM, for British Computer Society.

Palen, Leysia 2014 (Dec.). *Frontiers of crisis informatics*. Computer Science Colloquia, University of Colorado, Boulder.

Palen, Leysia, Soden, Robert, Anderson, T. Jennings, and Barrenechea, Mario. 2015. Success and scale in a data-producing organization: The socio-technical evolution of OpenStreetMap in response to humanitarian events. Pages 4113–4122 of: *Proceedings of 33rd Annual ACM Conference on Human Factors in Computing Systems*. Seoul, Korea: ACM.

Pang, Bo, and Lee, Lillian. 2008. *Opinion mining and sentiment analysis*. Foundations and Trends in Information Retrieval, Vol. 2. Now Publishers.

Parsons, Sophie, Atkinson, Peter M., Simperl, Elena, and Weal, Mark. 2015. Thematically analysing social network content during disasters through the lens of the disaster management lifecycle. In: *Proceedings of Social Web for Disaster Management (SWDM) at WWW 2015*. Florence, Italy: ACM.

Perng, Sung-Yueh, Büscher, Monika, Wood, Lisa, Halvorsrud, Ragnhild, Stiso, Michael, Ramirez, Leonardo, and Al-Akkad, Amro. 2013. Peripheral response: Microblogging during the 22/7/2011 Norway attacks. *International Journal of Information Systems for Crisis Response and Management*, **5**(1), 41–57.

Perry, Ronald W. 2006. What is a disaster? New answers to old questions. Chap. 1 of: Rodriguez, Havidan, Quarantelli, Enrico L., and Dynes, Russell (eds), *Handbook of Disaster Research*. Springer.

Petak, William J. 1985. Emergency management: A challenge for public administration. *Public Administration Review*, 3–7.

Petrović, Saša, Osborne, Miles, and Lavrenko, Victor. 2010. Streaming first story detection with application to Twitter. Pages 181–189 of: *Proceedings of 48th Annual Meeting of the Association for Computational Linguistics (ACL)*.

Phan, Tuan Q., and Airoldi, Edoardo M. 2015. A natural experiment of social network formation and dynamics. *Proceedings of the National Academy of Sciences*, **112**(21), 6595–6600.

Phuvipadawat, Swit, and Murata, Tsuyoshi. 2010. Breaking news detection and tracking in Twitter. Pages 120–123 of: *Proceedings of IEEE/WIC/ACM International Conferences on Web Intelligence and Intelligent Agent Technology WI-IAT*, vol. 3. Toronto, Canada: IEEE.

Pickard, Galen, Pan, Wei, Rahwan, Iyad, Cebrian, Manuel, Crane, Riley, Madan, Anmol, and Pentland, Alex. 2011. Time-critical social mobilization. *Science*, **334**(6055), 509–512.

Plotnick, Linda, Hiltz, Starr Roxanne, Kushma, Jane A., and Tapia, Andrea. 2015. Red tape: Attitudes and issues related to use of social media by U.S. county-level emergency managers. In: *Proceedings of 12th International Conference on Information Systems for Crisis Response and Management (ISCRAM)*. Kristiansand, Norway: ISCRAM.

Plutchik, Robert. 1991. *The emotions*. University Press of America.

Pohl, Daniela, Bouchachia, Abdelhamid, and Hellwagner, Hermann. 2012. Automatic identification of crisis-related sub-events using clustering. Pages 333–338 of: *Proceedings of 11th International Conference on Machine Learning and Applications (ICMLA)*, vol. 2. Boca Raton, Florida, USA: IEEE.

Popoola, Abdulfatai, Krasnoshtan, Dmytro, Toth, Attila-Peter, Naroditskiy, Victor, Castillo, Carlos, Meier, Patrick, and Rahwan, Iyad. 2013. Information verification during natural disasters. Pages 1029–1032 of: *Social Web for Disaster Management (SWDM), Companion: Proceedings of 22nd International Conference on World Wide Web Conference (WWW)*. Rio de Janeiro, Brazil: ACM, for IW3C2.

Porter, Martin F. 1980. An algorithm for suffix stripping. *Program: Electronic Library and Information Systems*, **14**(3), 130–137.

Potts, Liza. 2013. *Social media in disaster response: How experience architects can build for participation*. 1st edn. ATTW Series in Technical and Professional Communication. Routledge.

Power, Robert, Robinson, Bella, and Ratcliffe, David. 2013. Finding fires with Twitter. Pages 80–89 of: *Proceedings of the Australasian Language Technology Association (ALTA) Workshop*.

Power, Robert, Robinson, Bella, Colton, John, and Cameron, Mark. 2014. Emergency situation awareness: Twitter case studies. Pages 218–231 of: Hanachi, Chihab, Bénaben, Frédérick, and Charoy, François (eds), *Information Systems for Crisis Response and Management in Mediterranean Countries*. Lecture Notes in Business Information Processing, vol. 196. Springer International Publishing.

Preece, Jennifer, and Shneiderman, Ben. 2009. The reader-to-leader framework: Motivating technology-mediated social participation. *AIS Transactions on Human-Computer Interaction*, **1**(1), 13–32.

Prelog, Andrew J. 2010. *Social change and disaster annotated bibliography*. Ph.D. thesis, Department of Economics, Colorado State University.

Prutsalis, Mark, Bitner, David, Bodduluri, Praneeth, Boon, Francis, de Silva, Chamindra, Konig, Dominic, and Treadgold, Gavin. 2010. The Sahana Software Foundation response to the 2010 Haiti earthquake: A new standard for free and open source disaster data management systems. In: *Proceedings of 7th International Conference on Information Systems for Crisis Response and Management (ISCRAM)*. Seattle, Washington, USA: ISCRAM.

Purohit, Hemant, and Sheth, Amit. 2013. Twitris v3: From citizen sensing to analysis, coordination and action. Pages 746–747 of: *Proceedings of 7th International AAAI Conference on Weblogs and Social Media (ICWSM)*. Boston, Massachusetts, USA: AAAI Press.

Purohit, Hemant, Hampton, Andrew, Shalin, Valerie L., Sheth, Amit P., Flach, John, and Bhatt, Shreyansh. 2013. What kind of conversation is Twitter? Mining psycholinguistic cues for emergency coordination. *Computers in Human Behavior*, **29**(6), 2438–2447.

Purohit, Hemant, Castillo, Carlos, Diaz, Fernando, Sheth, Amit, and Meier, Patrick. 2014a. Emergency-relief coordination on social media: Automatically matching resource requests and offers. *First Monday Online Journal*, **19**(1).

Purohit, Hemant, Hampton, Andrew, Bhatt, Shreyansh, Shalin, Valerie L., Sheth, Amit P., and Flach, John M. 2014b. Identifying seekers and suppliers in social media communities to support crisis coordination. *Computer Supported Cooperative Work (CSCW)*, **23**(4-6), 513–545.

Purohit, Hemant, Ruan, Yiye, Fuhry, David, Parthasarathy, Srinivasan, and Sheth, Amit. 2014c. On understanding divergence of online social group discussion. In: *Proceedings of 8th International AAAI Conference on Weblogs and Social Media*. Ann Arbor, Michigan, USA: AAAI Press.

Purohit, Hemant, Bhatt, Shreyansh, Hampton, Andrew, Shalin, Valerie L., Sheth, Amit P., and Flach, John. 2014d. With whom to coordinate, why and how in ad-hoc social media communications during crisis response. In: *Proceedings of 11th International Conference on Information Systems for Crisis Response and Management (ISCRAM)*. University Park, Pennsylvania, USA: ISCRAM.

Qu, Yan, Huang, Chen, Zhang, Pengyi, and Zhang, Jun. 2011. Microblogging after a major disaster in China: A case study of the 2010 Yushu earthquake. Pages 25–34 of: *Proceedings of Conference on Computer-Supported Cooperative Work (CSCW)*. Hangzhou, China: ACM.

Quarantelli, Enrico L. 2002. The Disaster Research Center (DRC) field studies of organized behavior in disasters. Pages 94–116 of: Stallings, Robert A. (ed), *Methods of Disaster Research*. Philadelphia, USA: Xlibris.

Quinn, Alexander J., Bederson, Benjamin B., Yeh, Tom, and Lin, Jimmy. 2011. CrowdFlow: Integrating machine learning with mechanical turk for speed-cost-quality flexibility. In: *CHI 2011 Workshop on Crowdsourcing and Human Computation*.

Ramakrishnan, Naren, Butler, Patrick, Muthiah, Sathappan, Self, Nathan, Khandpur, Rupinder, Saraf, Parang, Wang, Wei, Cadena, Jose, Vullikanti, Anil, Korkmaz, Gizem, Kuhlman, Chris, Marathe, Achla, Zhao, Liang, Hua, Ting, Chen, Feng, Lu, Chang Tien, Huang, Bert, Srinivasan, Aravind, Trinh, Khoa, Getoor, Lise, Katz, Graham, Doyle, Andy, Ackermann, Chris, Zavorin, Ilya, Ford, Jim, Summers, Kristen, Fayed, Youssef, Arredondo, Jaime, Gupta, Dipak, and Mares, David. 2014. "Beating the news" with EMBERS: Forecasting civil unrest using open source indicators. Pages 1799–1808 of: *Proceedings of 19th ACM International Conference on Knowledge Discovery and Data Mining (SIGKDD)*. New York, USA: ACM.

Ramakrishnan, Raghu, and Gehrke, Johannes. 2002. *Database management systems*. 3rd edn. McGraw-Hill Higher Education.

Ratkiewicz, Jacob, Conover, Michael, Meiss, Mark, Gonçalves, Bruno, Patil, Snehal, Flammini, Alessandro, and Menczer, Filippo. 2011. Truthy: Mapping the spread of astroturf in microblog streams. Pages 249–252 of: *Proceedings of 20th International Conference Companion on World Wide Web*. Hyderabad, India: ACM.

Rees, Gavin. 2014. Tips for coping with traumatic imagery. Chap. 9.2 of: Silverman, Craig (ed), *Verification Handbook*. European Journalism Centre.

Resnick, Paul, Carton, Samuel, Park, Souneil, Shen, Yuncheng, and Zeffer, Nicole. 2014. Rumorlens: A system for analyzing the impact of rumors and corrections in social media. In: *Proceedings of Computational Journalism Conference*. New York, USA: Brown Institute for Media Innovation, Columbia University.

Reuter, Christian, and Scholl, Simon. 2014. Technical limitations for designing applications for social media. Page 131 of: *Mensch and Computer 2014–Workshopband*. Walter de Gruyter GmbH & Co KG.

Reuter, Christian, Marx, Alexandra, and Pipek, Volkmar. 2011. Social software as an infrastructure for crisis management–a case study about current practice and potential usage. In: *Proceedings of 8th International Conference on Information Systems for Crisis Response and Management (ISCRAM)*. Lisbon, Portugal: ISCRAM.

Reuter, Christian, Marx, Alexandra, and Pipek, Volkmar. 2012. Crisis management 2.0: Towards a systematization of social software use in crisis situations. *International Journal of Information Systems for Crisis Response and Management (IJISCRAM)*, 4(1), 1–16.

Reuter, Christian, Heger, Oliver, and Pipek, Volkmar. 2013. Combining real and virtual volunteers through social media. In: *Proceedings of 10th International Conference on Information Systems for Crisis Response and Management (ISCRAM)*. Baden Baden, Germany: ISCRAM.

Reuter, Christian, Ludwig, Thomas, Ritzkatis, Michael, and Pipek, Volkmar. 2015a. Social-QAS: Tailorable quality assessment service for social media content. Pages 156–170 of: *End-User Development*. Springer.

Reuter, Christian, Ludwig, Thomas, Kaufhold, Marc-André, and Pipek, Volkmar. 2015b. XHELP: Design of a cross-platform social-media application to support volunteer moderators in disasters. Pages 4093–4102 of: *Proceedings of the Conference on Human Factors in Computing Systems (SIGCHI)*. Seoul, Korea: ACM Press.

Ribeiro Jr., Sílvio S., Davis Jr., Clodoveu A., Oliveira, Diogo Rennó R, Meira Jr., Wagner, Gonçalves, Tatiana S., and Pappa, Gisele L. 2012. Traffic observatory: A system to detect and locate traffic events and conditions using Twitter. Pages 5–11 of: *Proceedings of 5th ACM SIGSPATIAL International Workshop on Location-Based Social Networks*. Redondo Beach, California, USA: ACM.

Ritter, A., Cherry, C., and Dolan, B. 2010. Unsupervised modeling of Twitter conversations. *Human Language Technologies: The 2010 Annual Conference of the North American Chapter of the Association for Computational Linguistics*, 172–180.

Robinson, A., Savelyev, Alexander, Pezanowski, Scott, and MacEachren, Alan M. 2013a. Understanding the utility of geospatial information in social media. Pages 918–922 of: *Proceedings of 10th International Conference on Information Systems for Crisis Response and Management (ISCRAM)*. Baden Baden, Germany: ISCRAM.

Robinson, Bella, Power, Robert, and Cameron, Mark. 2013b. A sensitive Twitter earthquake detector. Pages 999–1002 of: *Social Web for Disaster Management (SWDM), Companion: Proceedings of 22nd International Conference on World Wide Web Conference (WWW)*. Rio de Janeiro, Brazil: ACM, for IW3C2.

Robinson, Bella, Power, Robert, and Cameron, Mark. 2015. Disaster monitoring. Chap. 6 of: Mejova, Yelena, Weber, Ingmar, and Macy, Michael (eds), *Twitter: a Digital Socioscope*. Cambridge University Press.

Robinson, L., and Wall, I. 2012. *Still left in the dark? How people in emergencies use communication to survive – and how humanitarian agencies can help*. Tech. rept. 6. BBC Media Action, London, U.K.

Robson, Edward S. 2012 (Nov.). *Calling for "backup"–indemnification for digital volunteers*. Commons Lab Blog. Blogpost.

Roche, Stephane, Propeck-Zimmermann, Eliane, and Mericskay, Boris. 2013. Geoweb and crisis management: Issues and perspectives of volunteered geographic information. *GeoJournal*, **78**(1), 21–40.

Rodriguez, Havidan, Quarantelli, Enrico L., and Dynes, Russell (eds). 2006. *Handbook of disaster research*. 1st edn. Handbooks of Sociology and Social Research. Springer.

Rodriguez, Manuel Gomez, and Leskovec, Jure. 2014. Visualizing information networks: The 2011 Fukushima earthquake. *AI Matters*, **1**(1), 23–24.

Rogstadius, Jakob, Vukovic, Maja, Teixeira, Claudio, Kostakos, Vassilis, Karapanos, Evangelos, and Laredo, Jim Alain. 2013. CrisisTracker: Crowdsourced social media curation for disaster awareness. *IBM Journal of Research and Development*, **57**(5), 4–1.

Rosa, Kevin Dela, and Ellen, Jeffrey. 2009. Text classification methodologies applied to micro-text in military chat. Pages 710–714 of: *Proceedings of 8th International Conference on Machine Learning and Applications (ICMLA)*. Miami, Florida, USA: IEEE.

Roy, Senjuti Basu, Lykourentzou, Ioanna, Thirumuruganathan, Saravanan, Amer-Yahia, Sihem, and Das, Gautam. 2015. Task assignment optimization in knowledge-intensive crowdsourcing. *The VLDB Journal*, 1–25.

Ruan, Yiye, and Parthasarathy, Srinivasan. 2014. Simultaneous detection of communities and roles from large networks. Pages 203–214 of: *Proceedings of 2nd ACM Conference on Online Social Networks*. Dublin, Ireland: ACM.

Rudra, Koustav, Ghosh, Subham, Ganguly, Niloy, Goyal, Pawan, and Ghosh, Saptarshi. 2015 (Oct.). Extracting situational information from microblogs during disaster events: A classification-summarization approach. In: *Proceedings of Conference on Information and Knowledge Management (CIKM)*.

Russell, Matthew A. 2014. *Mining the social Web*. O'Reilly.

Ruths, Derek, and Pfeffer, Jürgen. 2014. Social media for large studies of behavior. *Science*, **346**(6213), 1063–1064.

Sakai, Tatsuhiro, and Tamura, Keiichi. 2015. Real-time analysis application for identifying bursty local areas related to emergency topics. *SpringerPlus*, **4**(1), 1–17.

Sakaki, Takeshi, Okazaki, Makoto, and Matsuo, Yutaka. 2010. Earthquake shakes Twitter users: Real-time event detection by social sensors. Pages 851–860 of: *Proceedings of 19th International Conference on World Wide Web Conference (WWW)*. Raleigh, North Carolina, USA: ACM.

Sakaki, Takeshi, Okazaki, Masahide, and Matsuo, Yoshikazu. 2013. Tweet analysis for real-time event detection and earthquake reporting system development. *Knowledge and Data Engineering, IEEE Transactions on*, **25**(4), 919–931.

Saleem, Haji M., Xu, Yishi, and Ruths, Derek. 2014. Novel situational information in mass emergencies: What does Twitter provide? *Procedia Engineering*, **78**, 155–164.

Salfinger, Andrea, Girtelschmid, Sylva, Pröll, Birgit, Retschitzegger, Werner, and Schwinger, Wieland. 2015a. Crowd-sensing meets situation awareness–a research roadmap for crisis management. Pages 153–162 of: *Proceedings of 48th Annual*

Hawaii International Conference on System Sciences (HICSS). Kauai, Hawaii, USA: IEEE.

Salfinger, Andrea, Retschitzegger, Werner, Schwinger, Wieland, and Pröll, Birgit. 2015b. CrowdSA–towards adaptive and situation-driven crowd-sensing for disaster situation awareness. Pages 14–20 of: *Cognitive Methods in Situation Awareness and Decision Support (CogSIMA), 2015 IEEE International Inter-Disciplinary Conference on.* IEEE.

Salton, G., Wong, A., and Yang, C. S. 1975. A vector space model for automatic indexing. *Communications of ACM*, **18**(11), 613–620.

Sarcevic, Aleksandra, Palen, Leysia, White, Joanne, Starbird, Kate, Bagdouri, Mossaab, and Anderson, Kenneth. 2012. Beacons of hope in decentralized coordination: Learning from on-the-ground medical twitterers during the 2010 Haiti earthquake. Pages 47–56 of: *Proceedings of ACM Conference on Computer Supported Cooperative Work (CSCW).* Seattle, Washington, USA: ACM.

Sayyadi, Hassan, Hurst, Matthew, and Maykov, Alexey. 2009. Event detection and tracking in social streams. Pages 311–314 of: *Proceedings of 3rd International AAAI Conference on Weblogs and Social Media (ICWSM).* San Jose, California, USA: AAAI Press.

Schram, Aaron, and Anderson, Kenneth M. 2012. MySQL to NoSQL: Data modeling challenges in supporting scalability. Pages 191–202 of: *Proceedings of 3rd Annual Conference on Systems, Programming, and Applications: Software for Humanity.* Tucson, Arizona, USA: ACM.

Schuler, Doug. 1994. Social computing. *Communications of ACM*, **37**(1), 28–29.

Schulz, Axel, Ristoski, Petar, and Paulheim, Heiko. 2013. I see a car crash: Real-time detection of small scale incidents in microblogs. Pages 22–33 of: *The Semantic Web: ESWC 2013 Satellite Events.* Springer.

Sebastiani, Fabrizio. 2002. Machine learning in automated text categorization. *ACM computing surveys (CSUR)*, **34**(1), 1–47.

Sebastiani, Fabrizio. 2014. Text quantification. Pages 819–822 of: de Rijke, Maarten, Kenter, Tom, de Vries, Arjen P., Zhai, Cheng Xiang, de Jong, Franciska, Radinsky, Kira, and Hofmann, Katja (eds), *Advances in Information Retrieval.* Lecture Notes in Computer Science, vol. 8416. Springer International Publishing.

Sellam, Thibault, and Alonso, Omar. 2015. Raimond: Quantitative data extraction from Twitter to describe events. Pages 251–268 of: Cimiano, Philipp, Frasincar, Flavius, Houben, Geert-Jan, and Schwabe, Daniel (eds), *Engineering the Web in the Big Data Era.* Lecture Notes in Computer Science, vol. 9114. Springer International Publishing.

Sha, Yongzhong, Yan, Jinsong, and Cai, Guoray. 2014. Detecting public sentiment over PM 2.5 pollution hazards through analysis of Chinese microblog. In: *Proceedings of 11th International Conference on Information Systems for Crisis Response and Management (ISCRAM).* University Park, Pennsylvania, USA: ISCRAM.

Shaw, Frances, Burgess, Jean, Crawford, Kate, and Bruns, Axel. 2013. Sharing news, making sense, saying thanks: Patterns of talk on Twitter during the Queensland floods. *Australian Journal of Communication.*

Sherchan, Wanita, Nepal, Surya, and Paris, Cecile. 2013. A survey of trust in social networks. *ACM Computing Surveys*, **45**(4), 47:1–47:33.

Sheth, Amit. 2009. Citizen sensing, social signals, and enriching human experience. *IEEE Internet Computing*, **1**(4), 87–92.

Sheth, Amit, Purohit, Hermant, Jadhav, Ashutosh, Kapanipathi, Pavan, and Chen, Lu. 2010. *Understanding events through analysis of social media*. Tech. rept. Wright State University, Ohio Center of Excellence in Knowledge-Enabled Computing (Kno.e.sis).

Sheth, Amit, Jadhav, Ashutosh, Kapanipathi, Pavan, Lu, Chen, Purohit, Hemant, Smith, Gary A., and Wang, Wenbo. 2014. Twitris: A system for collective social intelligence. In: Alhajj, Reda (ed), *Encyclopedia of Social Network Analysis and Mining*. Springer.

Shibutani, Tamotsu. 1966. *Improvised news: A sociological study of rumor*. Ardent Media.

Silverman, Craig (ed). 2014. *Verification handbook*. European Journalism Centre.

Simon, Tomer, Goldberg, Avishay, Aharonson-Daniel, Limor, Leykin, Dmitry, and Adini, Bruria. 2014. Twitter in the cross fire–the use of social media in the Westgate Mall terror attack in Kenya. *PloS one*, **9**(8), e104136.

Smith, Luke, Liang, Qiuhua, James, Phil, and Lin, Wen. 2015. Assessing the utility of social media as a data source for flood risk management using a real-time modelling framework. *Journal of Flood Risk Management*, Jan.

Solove, Daniel J. 2013. *Nothing to hide: The false tradeoff between privacy and security*. Yale University Press.

Sorensen, John H. 2000. Hazard warning systems: Review of 20 years of progress. *Natural Hazards Review*, **1**(2), 119–125.

Spiro, E, Irvine, C, DuBois, C, and Butts, C. 2012. Waiting for a retweet: Modeling waiting times in information propagation. In: *2012 NIPS Workshop of Social Networks and Social Media Conference*.

Sreenivasan, Nirupama Dharmavaram, Lee, Chei Sian, and Goh, Dion Hoe-Lian. 2011. Tweet me home: Exploring information use on Twitter in crisis situations. Pages 120–129 of: *Online Communities and Social Computing*, vol. 6778. Springer-Verlag Berlin Heidelberg. ISBN 978-3-642-21796-8.

St. Denis, Lise Ann, Hughes, Amanda L., and Palen, Leysia. 2012. Trial by fire: The deployment of trusted digital volunteers in the 2011 Shadow Lake fire. In: *Proceedings of 9th International Conference on Information Systems for Crisis Response and Management (ISCRAM)*. Vancouver, Canada: ISCRAM.

St. Denis, Lise Ann, Palen, Leysia, and Anderson, Kenneth M. 2014. Mastering social media: An analysis of Jefferson county's communications during the 2013 Colorado Floods. In: *Proceedings of 11th International Conference on Information Systems for Crisis Response and Management (ISCRAM)*. University Park, Pennsylvania, USA: ISCRAM.

Stahl, Bernd Carsten. 2006. On the difference or equality of information, misinformation, and disinformation: A critical research perspective. *Informing Science: International Journal of an Emerging Transdiscipline*, **9**, 83–96.

Stallings, Robert A., and Quarantelli, Enrico L. 1985. Emergent citizen groups and emergency management. *Public Administration Review*, **45**, 93–100.

Stamatatos, Efstathios. 2009. A survey of modern authorship attribution methods. *Journal of the American Society for information Science and Technology*, **60**(3), 538–556.

Starbird, Kate. 2012a. *Crowdwork, crisis and convergence: How the connected crowd organizes information during mass disruption events.* Ph.D. thesis, University of Colorado.

Starbird, Kate. 2012b. Digital volunteerism: Examining connected crowd work during mass disruption events. Pages 116–123 of: Pipek, Volkmar, Landgren, Jonas, and Palen, Leysia (eds), *Proceedings of ACM Conference on Computer Supported Cooperative Work (CSCW).* International Reports on Socio Informatics, vol. 9. Seattle, Washington, USA: ACM.

Starbird, Kate. 2013. Delivering patients to Sacré Coeur: Collective intelligence in digital volunteer communities. Pages 801–810 of: *Proceedings of ACM Conference on Human Factors in Computing Systems (SIGCHI).* Paris, France: ACM.

Starbird, Kate, and Palen, Leysia. 2010. Pass it on? Retweeting in mass emergency. In: *Proceedings of 7th International Conference on Information Systems for Crisis Response and Management (ISCRAM).* Seattle, Washington, USA: ISCRAM.

Starbird, Kate, and Palen, Leysia. 2011. Voluntweeters: Self-organizing by digital volunteers in times of crisis. Pages 1071–1080 of: *Proceedings of Conference on Human Factors in Computing Systems (SIGCHI).* Vancouver, Canada: ACM.

Starbird, Kate, and Stamberger, Jeannie. 2010. Tweak the tweet: Leveraging microblogging proliferation with a prescriptive syntax to support citizen reporting. In: *Proceedings of 7th International Conference on Information Systems for Crisis Response and Management (ISCRAM).* Seattle, Washington, USA: ISCRAM.

Starbird, Kate, Palen, Leysia, Hughes, Amanda L, and Vieweg, Sarah. 2010. Chatter on the red: What hazards threat reveals about the social life of microblogged information. Pages 241–250 of: *Proceedings of ACM Conference on Computer-Supported Cooperative Work (CSCW).* Savannah, Georgia, USA: ACM.

Starbird, Kate, Muzny, Grace, and Palen, Leysia. 2012. Learning from the crowd: Collaborative filtering techniques for identifying on-the-ground twitterers during mass disruptions. In: *Proceedings of 9th International Conference on Information Systems for Crisis Response and Management (ISCRAM).* Vancouver, Canada: ISCRAM.

Strötgen, Jannik, and Gertz, Michael. 2013. Multilingual and cross-domain temporal tagging. *Language Resources and Evaluation,* **47**(2), 269–298.

Suh, Bongwon, Convertino, Gregorio, Chi, Ed H., and Pirolli, Peter. 2009. The singularity is not near: Slowing growth of Wikipedia. Page Article 8 of: *Proceedings of 5th International Symposium on Wikis and Open Collaboration.* Orlando, Florida, USA: ACM.

Sultanik, Evan A., and Fink, Clayton. 2012. Rapid geotagging and disambiguation of social media text via an indexed gazetteer. In: *Proceedings of 9th International Conference on Information Systems for Crisis Response and Management (ISCRAM),* vol. 190. Vancouver, Canada: ISCRAM.

Sutherlin, Gwyneth. 2013. A voice in the crowd: Broader implications for crowdsourcing translation during crisis. *Journal of Information Science,* **39**(3), 397–409.

Sutton, Jeannette, Spiro, Emma S., Johnson, Britta, Fitzhugh, Sean, Gibson, Ben, and Butts, Carter T. 2013. Warning tweets: Serial transmission of messages during the warning phase of a disaster event. *Information, Communication & Society,* **17**(6), 765–787.

Sutton, Jeannette N. 2010. Twittering Tennessee: Distributed networks and collaboration following a technological disaster. In: *Proceedings of 7th International Conference on Information Systems for Crisis Response and Management (ISCRAM)*. Seattle, Washington, USA: ISCRAM.

Sutton, Jeannette N., Spiro, Emma S., Johnson, Britta, Fitzhugh, Sean M., Greczek, Mathew, and Butts, Carter T. 2012. Connected communications: Network structures of official communications in a technological disaster. In: *Proceedings of 9th International Systems for Crisis Response and Management Conference*. Vancouver, Canada: ISCRAM.

Tang, Jie, Sun, Jimeng, Wang, Chi, and Yang, Zi. 2009. Social influence analysis in large-scale networks. Pages 807–816 of: *Proceedings of 15th ACM International Conference on Knowledge Discovery and Data Mining (SIGKDD)*. Paris, France: ACM.

Tapia, Andrea H., and Moore, Kathleen. 2014. Good enough is good enough: Overcoming disaster response organizations' slow social media data adoption. *Computer Supported Cooperative Work (CSCW)*, **23**(4-6), 483–512.

Tapia, Andrea H., Moore, Kathleen A., and Johnson, Nicolas. 2013. Beyond the trustworthy tweet: A deeper understanding of microblogged data use by disaster response and humanitarian relief organizations. Pages 770–778 of: *Proceedings of 10th International Conference on Information Systems for Crisis Response and Management (ISCRAM)*. Baden Baden, Germany: ISCRAM.

Taylor, Mel, Wells, Garrett, Howell, Gwyneth, and Raphael, Beverley. 2012. The role of social media as psychological first aid as a support to community resilience building. *Australian Journal of Emergency Management, The*, **27**(1), 20–26.

Temnikova, Irina, Vieweg, Sarah, and Castillo, Carlos. 2015. The case for readability of crisis communications in social media. In: *Proceedings of Social Web for Disaster Management (SWDM) at WWW 2015*. Florence, Italy: ACM.

Terpstra, Teun, de Vries, A., Stronkman, R., and Paradies, GL. 2012. Towards a realtime Twitter analysis during crises for operational crisis management. In: *Proceedings of 9th International Conference on Information Systems for Crisis Response and Management (ISCRAM)*. Vancouver, Canada: ISCRAM.

Thom, Dennis, Krüger, Robert, Bechstedt, Ulrike, Platz, Axel, Zisgen, Julia, Volland, Bernd, and Ertl, Thomas. 2015. Can Twitter really save your life? a case study of visual social media analytics for situation awareness. In: *IEEE Pacific Visualization Symposium (PacificVis)*.

Thomson, Robert, Ito, Naoya, Suda, Hinako, Lin, Fangyu, Liu, Yafei, Hayasaka, Ryo, Isochi, Ryuzo, and Wang, Zian. 2012. Trusting tweets: The Fukushima disaster and information source credibility on Twitter. Page 10 of: *Proceedings of 9th International Conference on Information Systems for Crisis Response and Management (ISCRAM)*. Vancouver, Canada: ISCRAM.

Tinati, Ramine, Carr, Leslie, Hall, Wendy, and Bentwood, Jonny. 2012. Identifying communicator roles in Twitter. Pages 1161–1168 of: *Proceedings of 21st International Conference Companion on World Wide Web*. Rio de Janeiro, Brazil: ACM.

Toffler, Alvin. 1990. *Future shock*. Bantam.

Traverso, Stefania, Cerutti, Valentina, Stock, Kristin, and Jackson, Mike. 2014. EDIT: A methodology for the treatment of non-authoritative data in the reconstruction of disaster scenarios. Pages 32–45 of: *Information Systems for Crisis Response and Management in Mediterranean Countries*. Springer.

Truelove, Marie, Vasardani, Maria, and Winter, Stephan. 2014. Towards credibility of micro-blogs: characterising witness accounts. *GeoJournal*, 1–21.

Tucker, S., Lanfranchi, V., Ireson, N., Sosa, A., Burel, G., and Ciravegna, F. 2012. "Straight to the information I need": Assessing collational interfaces for emergency response. In: *Proceedings of 9th International Conference on Information Systems for Crisis Response and Management (ISCRAM)*. Vancouver, Canada: ISCRAM.

Tufekci, Zeynep. 2014 (June). Big questions for social media Big Data: Representativeness, validity and other methodological pitfalls. In: *Proceedings of 8th International AAAI Conference on Weblogs and Social Media (ICWSM)*.

Tufekci, Zeynep. 2014. Engineering the public: Big Data, surveillance and computational politics. *First Monday Online Journal*, **19**(7).

Tufte, Edward R. 2001. *The visual display of quantitative information*. 2nd edn. Graphics.

Tumasjan, A., Sprenger, T. O., Sandner, P. G., and Welpe, I. M. 2010. Predicting elections with Twitter: What 140 characters reveal about political sentiment. Pages 178–185 of: *Proceedings of 4th International AAAI Conference on Weblogs and Social Media*. Washington DC, USA: AAAI Press.

Turoff, Murray, Chumer, Michael, de Walle, Bartel Van, and Yao, Xiang. 2004. The design of a Dynamic Emergency Response Management Information System (DERMIS). *Journal of Information Technology Theory and Application (JITTA)*, **5**(4), Article 3.

Tyshchuk, Yulia, Hui, Cindy, Grabowski, Martha, and Wallace, William. 2012. Social media and warning response impacts in extreme events: Results from a naturally occurring experiment. Pages 818–827 of: *System Science (HICSS), 2012 45th Hawaii International Conference on*. IEEE.

Uddin, Muhammad Moeen, Imran, Muhammad, and Sajjad, Hassan. 2014. Understanding types of users on Twitter. In: *Proceedings of 7th IEEE International Conference on Social Computing and Networking (SocialCom)*. Sydney, Australia: IEEE.

U.K. Ministry of Defence. 2014. *Understanding and intelligence support to joint operations*. 3rd edn. Joint Doctrine Publication (JDP). Development, Concepts and Doctrine Centre (DCDC), Ministry of Defence, UK.

UN OCHA. 2012. *Humanitarianism in the network age*. UN OCHA Policy and Studies Series. UN Office for the Coordination of Humanitarian Affairs.

UN OCHA. 2014a. *Humanitarianism in the age of cyber-warfare*. OCHA Policy and Studies Series. UN OCHA Policy Development and Studies Branch.

UN OCHA. 2014b (Dec.). *World humanitarian data and trends*. Tech. rept. United Nations Office for the Coordination of Humanitarian Affairs.

Varga, István, Sano, Motoki, Torisawa, Kentaro, Hashimoto, Chikara, Ohtake, Kiyonori, Kawai, Takao, Oh, Jong-Hoon, and De Saeger, Stijn. 2013. Aid is out there: Looking for help from tweets during a large scale disaster. Pages 1619–1629 of: *Proceedings of 51th Annual Meeting of the Association for Computational Linguistics (ACL)*. Sofia, Bulgaria: ACL.

Verma, Sudha, Vieweg, Sarah, Corvey, William J., Palen, Leysia, Martin, James H., Palmer, Martha, Schram, Aaron, and Anderson, Kenneth Mark. 2011 (July). Natural language processing to the rescue? Extracting "situational awareness" tweets during mass emergency. In: *Proceedings of 5th International AAAI Conference on Weblogs and Social Media (ICWSM)*.

Vickery, Graham, and Wunsch-Vincent, Sacha. 2007. *Participative Web and user-created content: Web 2.0 wikis and social networking*. Organization for Economic Cooperation and Development (OECD).

Vieweg, Sarah. 2012. *Situational awareness in mass emergency: A behavioral and linguistic analysis of microblogged communications*. Ph.D. thesis, University of Colorado, Boulder.

Vieweg, Sarah, and Hodges, Adam. 2014. Rethinking context: Leveraging human and machine computation in disaster response. *Computer*, **47**(4), 22–27.

Vieweg, Sarah, Hughes, Amanda L, Starbird, Kate, and Palen, Leysia. 2010. Microblogging during two natural hazards events: What Twitter may contribute to situational awareness. Pages 1079–1088 of: *Proceedings of Conference on Human Factors in Computing Systems (SIGCHI)*. Atlanta, Georgia, USA: ACM.

Vieweg, Sarah, Castillo, Carlos, and Imran, Muhammad. 2014. Integrating social media communications into the rapid assessment of sudden onset disasters. Pages 444–461 of: *Proceedings of International Conference on Social Informatics SocInfo*. Barcelona, Spain: Springer.

Vigen, Tyler. 2015. *Spurious correlations*. Hachette Books.

Virtual Social Media Working Group and DHS First Responders Group. 2014 (June). *Using social media for enhanced situational awareness and decision support*. Tech. rept. U.S. Department of Homeland Security. Report by the Virtual Social Media Working Group and DHS First Responders Group.

De Waal, Alex. 1987. On the perception of poverty and famines. *International Journal of Moral and Social Studies*, **2**, 251–262.

De Waal, Alex. 1997. *Famine crimes: Politics and the disaster relief industry in Africa*. Indiana University Press.

Wagner, Johanna Grombach. 2005. An IHL/ICRC perspective on "humanitarian space". *Humanitarian Exchange Magazine*, **32**(Dec.), 24–26.

Waldman, Annie P., Verity, Andrej, and Roberts, Shadrock. 2013 (July). *Guidance for collaborating with formal humanitarian organizations*. Tech. rept. Digital Humanitarian Network.

Walsh, Lynda. 2006. *Sins against science: The scientific media hoaxes of Poe, Twain, and others*. SUNY Press.

Wang, Richard Y., and Strong, Diane M. 1996. Beyond accuracy: What data quality means to data consumers. *Journal of Management Information Systems*, 5–33.

Wang, Xinyue, Tokarchuk, Laurissa, Cuadrado, Félix, and Poslad, Stefan. 2013. Exploiting hashtags for adaptive microblog crawling. Pages 311–315 of: *Proceedings of IEEE/ACM International Conference on Advances in Social Networks Analysis and Mining (ASONAM)*. Ontario, Canada: ACM.

Watts, Duncan J. 2004. The "new" science of networks. *Annual Review of Sociology*, 243–270.

Watts, Duncan J., Peretti, Jonah, and Frumin, Michael. 2007. *Viral marketing for the real world*. Harvard Business School Pub.

Wei, Xing, and Croft, W Bruce. 2006. LDA-based document models for ad-hoc retrieval. Pages 178–185 of: *Proceedings of 29th International Conference on Research and Development in Information Retrieval (SIGIR)*. Seattle, Washington, USA: ACM.

Weng, Jianshu, and Lee, Bu-Sung. 2011. Event detection in Twitter. Pages 401–408 of: *Proceedings of 5th International AAAI Conference on Weblogs and Social Media (ICWSM)*. Barcelona, Spain: AAAI Press.

Whipkey, Katie, and Verity, Andrej. 2015 (Sept.). *Guidance for incorporating Big Data into humanitarian operations*. Tech. rept. Digital Humanitarian Network.

White, Connie M. 2011. *Social media, crisis communication, and emergency management: Leveraging Web 2.0 technologies*. 1st edn. CRC Press.

White, James D., and Fu, King-Wa. 2012. Who do you trust? Comparing people-centered communications in disaster situations in the United States and China. *Journal of Comparative Policy Analysis: Research and Practice*, **14**(2), 126–142.

White, Joanne I., and Palen, Leysia. 2015. Expertise in the wired wild west. Pages 662–675 of: *Proceedings of 18th ACM Conference on Computer Supported Cooperative Work and Social Computing*. Vancouver, Canada: ACM.

White, Joanne I., Palen, Leysia, and Anderson, Kenneth M. 2014. Digital mobilization in disaster response: The work and self-organization of on-line pet advocates in response to Hurricane Sandy. Pages 866–876 of: *Proceedings of 17th ACM Conference on Computer Supported Cooperative Work and Social Computing*. Baltimore, Maryland, USA: ACM.

Whiting, Anita, and Williams, David. 2013. Why people use social media: A uses and gratifications approach. *Qualitative Market Research: An International Journal*, **16**(4), 362–369.

Whittaker, Zack. 2012. Internet usage rocketed on the East Coast during Sandy: Report. *ZDNet Online*, Oct.

Wilensky, Hiroko. 2014. Twitter as a navigator for stranded commuters during the Great East Japan earthquake. In: *Proceedings of 11th International Conference on Information Systems for Crisis Response and Management (ISCRAM)*. University Park, Pennsylvania, USA: ISCRAM.

Wu, Shao-Yu, Wang, Ming-Hung, and Chen, Kuan-Ta. 2011. Privacy crisis due to crisis response on the Web. Pages 197–205 of: *Proceedings on 10th IEEE International Conference on Trust, Security and Privacy in Computing and Communications (TrustCom)*. Changsha, China: IEEE.

Wukich, Clayton, and Mergel, Ines A. 2014. Closing the citizen-government communication gap: Content, audience, and network analysis of government tweets. *Social Science Research Network Working Paper Series*, Aug., 35 pages.

Yang, Christopher C., Shi, Xiaodong, and Wei, Chih-Ping. 2009. Discovering event evolution graphs from news corpora. *IEEE Transactions on Systems, Man and Cybernetics*, 850–863.

Yin, Jie, Lampert, Andrew, Cameron, Mark, Robinson, Bella, and Power, Robert. 2012. Using social media to enhance emergency situation awareness. *IEEE Intelligent Systems*, **27**(6), 52–59.

Young, William Chad, Blumenstock, Joshua E., Fox, Emily B., and McCormick, Tyler H. 2014. Detecting and classifying anomalous behavior in spatiotemporal network data. Pages 29–33 of: *KDD-LESI 2014: Proceedings of 1st KDD Workshop on Learning about Emergencies from Social Information at KDD'14*. New York, USA: ACM.

Zafarani, Reza, Abbasi, Mohammad A., and Liu, Huan. 2014. *Social media mining: An introduction*. Cambridge University Press.

Zagheni, Emilio, and Weber, Ingmar. 2015. Demographic research with non-representative internet data. *International Journal of Manpower*, **36**(1), 13–25.

Zaki, Mohammed J., and Meira, Wagner. 2014. *Data mining and analysis: Fundamental concepts and algorithms*. Cambridge University Press.

Zhang, Haibo, and Comfort, Louise. 2014 (Nov.). The rapid emergence of communication networks following the april 20, 2013 Ya'an earthquake in Lushan county, China. In: *APPAM Fall Research Conference*.

Zhou, Yiping, Nie, Lan, Rouhani-Kalleh, Omid, Vasile, Flavian, and Gaffney, Scott. 2010. Resolving surface forms to Wikipedia topics. Pages 1335–1343 of: *Proceedings of 23rd International Conference on Computational Linguistics COLING*. Beijing, China: Association for Computational Linguistics.

Zielinski, Andrea, Bügel, Ulrich, Middleton, L, Middleton, SE, Tokarchuk, L, Watson, K, and Chaves, F. 2012. Multilingual analysis of Twitter news in support of mass emergency events. Page 8085 of: *EGU General Assembly Conference Abstracts*, vol. 14.

Zielinski, Andrea, Middleton, S., Tokarchuk, L., and Wang, Xinyue. 2013. Social media text mining and network analysis for decision support in natural crisis management. Pages 840–845 of: *Proceedings of 10th International Conference on Information Systems for Crisis Response and Management (ISCRAM)*. Baden Baden, Germany: ISCRAM.

Zook, Matthew, Graham, Mark, Shelton, Taylor, and Gorman, Sean. 2010. Volunteered geographic information and crowdsourcing disaster relief: A case study of the Haitian earthquake. *World Medical & Health Policy*, **2**(2), 7–33.

Index

Terms and Acronyms

API Application Programming Interface, a series of protocols that connect applications. In the crisis data context, typically a protocol for software to interact with an online social networking site   22

AUC Area Under the Curve: the area under the Receiver Operating Characteristic curve, a standard evaluation metric for automatic classification   63

choropleth map A map in which predefined regions are colored according to a certain variable   140

crisis An unstable situation that may or may not lead to a disaster   4

dasymmetric map A variant of a choropleth map where additional information is used to create an improved subdivision of regions   141

digital volunteering The practice of performing volunteer work using digital technologies, almost always through Internet-connected devices   97

disaster A disruption of routine and of social structure, norms, and/or values   3

disinformation False information that is intentionally spread   115

emoji An inlined image or ideogram included in a message to express an idea or convey an emotion   30

emoticon A sequence of characters used to convey an emotion through a stylized drawing, e.g., ":-)" to represent a smile   30

geocoding A process by which an item is associated with machine-readable location information, based on inferences done from its content   44

GPS Global Positioning System, a satellite-based navigation system, accessible from many smartphones, that provides location information anywhere on Earth   44

hashtag A convention for user-defined topics found in many social media platforms, where a word preceded by the "#" sign (known as the hash, pound, or number symbol) is understood as a topic marker   25

HCI Human-Computer Interaction, the area of computer science that designs and studies the way in which people interact with computing technologies   150

ICRC International Committee of the Red Cross, an humanitarian organization that is the oldest and most recognized organization within the Red Cross movement   154

IDF Inverse Document Frequency, an heuristic for weighting terms that gives more importance to terms that occur in fewer documents/messages   30

IRB Institutional Review Board, a committee within an organization tasked with reviews of ethics of activities done within the organization   158

isarithmic map Also known as a contour map, represents a continuous variable through curves having a constant value   141

LDA   Latent Dirichlet Allocation, a topic modeling method that describes a process by which words in documents are generated, based on a distribution of topics for each document   64

LSH   Locality-Sensitive Hashing, a dimensionality reduction method that maps items using hash functions, in such a way that similar items are mapped to similar hash values.   66

microtext   Text that is brief, semistructured, and is often characterized by unstructured or informal grammar and language   14

misinformation   False information that is unintentionally spread   115

multidocument text summarization   A series of methods to generate a brief summary of the information contained in a set of documents   85

NGO   Nongovernmental Organization, a nonprofit organization that is not part of a government (e.g., the Red Cross is a large NGO)   55

NLP   Natural Language Processing, the area of computer science that studies methods to process human language   35

NoSQL   "Not only SQL," database software that is not based on a relational data model   31

OCHA   The United Nations Office for the Coordination of Humanitarian Affairs, an organization within the United Nations in charge of the response to large disasters and humanitarian crises   155

ontology   An explicit description of concepts within a domain and relationships among them   47

POS tagging   Part Of Speech tagging, a process by which each word in a text is annotated with the class to which it belongs   40

precision   A measure of specificity in automatic classification: the probability that an item that a system has classified as belonging to a class, actually belongs to that class   62

RDBMS   Relational Database Management Systems, database software based on a relational data model   31

recall   A measure of sensitivity in automatic classification: the probability that an item that actually belongs to a class is classified automatically as belonging to that class   62

ROC   Receiver Operating Characteristic: a representation of the performance of a classifier under different thresholds expressed in terms of false positive rate (on the X axis) and true positive rate (on the Y axis)   63

situational awareness   A state of knowing the variables of a situation or environment, including perceiving, understanding, and being able to make predictions about these variables in the near future   1

social media   A variety of social software platforms in which people can create, share, and exchange user-generated content   5

social software   Computer systems and applications that serve as an intermediary or a focus for social relationships   5

SVM   Support Vector Machines, a supervised machine learning method for binary classification, which can be extended to multiclass classification   60

TDT   Topic Detection and Tracking, various techniques for tracking how events develop and unfold over time in a timestamped document collection   83

TPS   Tweets per second, a measure used to compare peaks of activity in Twitter across different events   20

UGC   User-Generated Content, content published online in a publicly accessible manner or to a group of people, containing a certain amount of creative work, and created outside of professional routines and practices   5

VOST   Virtual Operations Support Team, an established group of digital volunteers helping during an emergency, usually in collaboration with a formal organization   100

VTCs   Volunteer and Technical Communities, volunteer groups that provide technology support, or support through technology, to humanitarian organizations   101

word n-gram   A sequence of exactly n words appearing contiguously on a text   30